REGIONAL GROWTH AND UNEMPLOYMENT IN THE UNITED KINGDOM

Regional Growth and Unemployment in the United Kingdom

R. J. DIXON
Lecturer in Economics
University of Papua New Guinea

and

A. P. THIRLWALL
Reader in Economics
University of Kent at Canterbury

M

First published 1975 by
THE MACMILLAN PRESS LTD.
London and Basingstoke
Associated companies in New York
Dublin Melbourne Johannesburg and Madras

SBN 333 15561 0

Printed in Great Britain by
Redwood Burn Limited, Trowbridge & Esher

Contents

Preface

The purpose of the book is to use economic analysis to gain insight into the growth and unemployment experience of the regions of the United Kingdom during the post-war years. The research relies heavily on Census of Production data for 1958, 1963 and 1968 (provisional), and on data provided by the Department of Employment. We are grateful to the Department of Trade and Industry and to the Department of Employment for their generous co-operation, particularly in making available much unpublished data.

It is important to stress from the outset that the work as a whole should be regarded as a study in regional, rather than spatial, economics. Economic analysis is applied to regions as economies and no attempt is made to use the spatial techniques of theoretical geography. We trust that those regional economists who disparage studies of the economics of regions because 'space' is left out will none the less find the study interesting. As an attempt to apply economic theory to the analysis of regional phenomena, the work indicates how the data should be interpreted in the light of the variety of economic models applied, *given the assumptions of the models.* The nature of the assumptions is particularly important to bear in mind in considering the chapters on growth which use production functions. On the empirical side, the book stresses throughout the close interrelationship between the industrial structure of regions, the pressure of regional demand and the rate of regional growth.

As a guide to the book it may be helpful for the reader to turn first to chapter 11 which contains a summary and conclusions.

The study has its origins in two Ph.D. theses: one submitted by Thirlwall to the University of Leeds in 1967; the other submitted by Dixon to the University of Kent in 1973, for which Professor A. J. Brown was supervisor and examiner, respectively. We are indebted to Professor Brown for his constructive criticism and encouragement in both capacities. Our approach to regional economic analysis has been considerably influenced by him. The final manuscript was read with unusual thoroughness by our colleague Mr Ian Gordon. We are deeply grateful to him for taking so much time in helping us to eradicate mistakes and to clarify exposition. With foresight we would have enlisted him as co-author! As far as the division of work between the present authors is concerned, most of the research on Census of Production data was done by Dixon, while most of the research on unemployment was done by Thirlwall. The writing, however, has been a joint responsibility.

Finally, we must thank the editors of the *Scottish Journal of Political Economy*, the *Manchester School of Economic and Social Studies*, the *Oxford Economic Papers*, and the *Oxford Bulletin of Economics and Statistics* for allowing us to replicate ideas and results already published by us in their journals, and last, but not least, we extend a special thank you to our typist, Miss Marilyn Spice, who coped expertly with successive drafts of the book.

R.J.D.
A.P.T.

1 Introduction

The purpose of this book is to analyse regional differences in the structure of manufacturing production; in the level and growth of manufacturing output per head, and in the percentage level of unemployment in the United Kingdom economy over the post-war period. The analyses of structure and growth are based, in the main, on the regional tables of the 1963 and 1968 (provisional) Census of Production Reports,[1] and the analysis of unemployment is based on data supplied by the Department of Employment (formerly the Department of Employment and Productivity and, before that, the Ministry of Labour) covering employees in all occupations.

Because the work for this book has stretched over a long period, and the administrator's propensity to alter regional boundaries has been extremely high, the regions taken for analysis are not always the same. In particular, the sections of the book on structure and growth take the new Standard Regions as the regional units, while most of the sections on unemployment take the old Standard Regions. The ten new Standard Regions are as follows: South East (SE); East Anglia (EA); South West (SW); East Midlands (EM); West Midlands (WM); Yorkshire and Humberside (YH); North West (NW); North (N); Wales (W); and Scotland (S). The ten old Standard Regions were: London and South East (LSE); East and South (ES); South West (SW); Midlands (M); North Midlands (NM); East and West Ridings (EWR); North West (NW); North (N); Scotland (S); Wales (W). The new standard regions of the South East and East Anglia are broadly equivalent in area to

[1] Board of Trade, *Report on the Census of Production 1963*, (London; HMSO, 1970), part 133, and 'Area Analyses of the Provisional Results of the Census of Production for 1968', *Board of Trade Journal*, vol. 199, 1970, pp. 488–96.

the old Standard Regions of London and South East and East and South. Sometimes in the book the two southern regions are aggregated and called, the South East (SE). Similarly, the new Standard Regions of East Midlands, West Midlands and Yorkshire and Humberside cover the same geographic area as the old Standard Regions of the Midlands, North Midlands, and East and West Ridings. Sometimes, the three Midlands regions are aggregated and called the Midlands (M). The boundaries of the other regions have remained virtually unchanged over time.

The time period of the analysis also varies from one section of the book to another, and sometimes the data are not very recent. It should be stressed, however, that the book is intended to be analytic rather than descriptive, with emphasis on techniques of analysis, and on the broad policy conclusions that emerge from the analysis which are not likely to require modification by the addition of more data—notwithstanding regional policy which is designed to alter the pattern of interregional variations in the variables in which we are interested. The dominant theme throughout all the chapters is the variety of regional experience, irrespective of the time period considered, and the stability of the interregional differences which have persisted despite regional policy.

It should also be stressed from the outset that in using the Census of Production data, the insights gained into the functioning of regional economies have only been obtained at certain costs. These costs have to do with the restrictive assumptions used at various stages of the analysis necessitated by data deficiencies, especially the absence of capital and price data for the regions. An essential part of any study of regional phenomena at the present time must be concerned with the development of methods of analysis which attempt to overcome data limitations. These methods may cover a wide range, varying from a simple reformulation of the problem at hand, or the judicious use of assumptions, to the generation of additional (surrogate) data. In our case, without the liberal use of restrictive assumptions, the application of conventional economic models would appear, when confronted with the limited data, to be very incomplete and unable to bear the heavy burden placed upon them. Whenever necessary, we attempt to deal explicitly with 'crucial assumptions' even at the risk of repetition.

THE VARIETY OF REGIONAL EXPERIENCE

The main indices of regional experience in which we are interested are: the level of productivity in manufacturing industry; the growth of productivity and employment in manufacturing, and the total level of unemployment. Regional policy has been concerned mainly with the existence and persistence of interregional variations in the percentage level of unemployment. As we shall see, however, there are quite wide disparities in other broad indices of economic welfare which frequently correlate with unemployment rate differences. For example, high unemployment, a low rate of growth of job opportunities and low *per capita* income frequently go

TABLE 1.1 Output per worker and average earnings in the manufacturing sector of United Kingdom Regions (£s) 1963

Region	*Net output per worker**	*Average earnings†*
SE	1495	770
EA	1345	675
SW	1390	725
EM	1240	665
WM	1305	741
YH	1245	670
NW	1310	695
N	1425	725
W	1540	775
S	1350	680
NI	1035	556
UK	1362	718

* Net output in each region divided by total employment.
† Total wages and salaries divided by total employment.

Source: Board of Trade, *Report on the Census of Production 1963* (London; HMSO, 1970), part 133, p. 6f.

together. As a preliminary to examining the sources of these differences in the chapters to follow, let us briefly summarise the differences that appear to exist.

The level of productivity or output per worker in manufacturing industry will be an important determinant of regional income per head. The level of output per worker and average earnings per worker in manufacturing industry in 1963 are shown in table 1.1. The growth of productivity and the growth of employment are shown in table 1.2. The unemployment experience is shown in table 1.3. The tables speak for themselves, but at least three important facts need to be stressed. Firstly, if regional variety, and the regional 'problem', are defined in terms of differences in the percentage level of unemployment in different parts of the country, a clear divide

TABLE 1.2 The growth of labour productivity and employment in manufacturing industry

Region	*Average annual growth of net output per worker 1958–68**	*Average annual rate of growth of employment 1958–68*
SE	7.1	0.6
EA	8.0	3.4
SW	6.8	1.4
EM	9.4	1.3
WM	6.8	0.8
YH	6.1	−0.1
NW	7.5	−0.9
N	6.0	−0.1
W	5.9	1.6
S	7.0	−0.2
NI	9.4	−0.1
UK	7.1	0.3

* At current prices. Regional price indices are not available. The average annual rate of growth of wholesale prices of all manufactured goods in the country as a whole was 2.2 per cent p.a. over the period.

Sources: Report of the Census of Production 1963, op. cit., and *British Labour Statistics: Historical Abstract 1886–1968*, Department of Employment and Productivity, 1971.

TABLE 1.3 The percentage level of unemployment

Region	1951	1952	1953	1954	1955	1956	1957	1958	1959	1960	1961	1962	1963	1964	1965	1966	1967	1968	1969	1970	1971	1972	Av.
SE / EA	0.9	1.3	1.2	1.0	0.7	0.8	1.1	1.4	1.3	1.0	1.0	1.3	1.6	1.0	1.0	1.1	1.7	1.6	1.6	1.7	2.1	2.2	1.3
SW	1.2	1.5	1.6	1.4	1.1	1.3	1.8	2.2	2.1	1.7	1.4	1.7	2.1	1.5	1.6	1.8	2.5	2.5	2.7	2.8	3.4	3.5	2.0
WM	0.4	0.9	1.1	0.6	0.5	1.1	1.3	1.6	1.5	1.0	1.4	1.8	2.0	0.9	0.9	1.3	2.5	2.2	2.1	2.4	3.9	3.6	1.6
EM																							
YH / NW	0.7	1.5	1.0	0.8	0.6	0.7	0.9	1.8	1.7	1.1	1.0	1.5	1.9	1.1	1.0	1.2	2.0	2.3					
	1.2	3.7	2.1	1.5	1.4	1.3	1.6	2.7	2.8	1.9	1.6	2.5	3.1	2.1	1.6	1.5	2.5	2.5	2.4	2.7	3.9	4.7	2.4
N	2.2	2.6	2.4	2.3	1.8	1.5	1.7	2.4	3.3	2.9	2.5	3.7	5.0	3.3	2.6	2.6	4.0	4.7	4.8	4.7	5.7	6.4	3.4
W	2.7	2.8	2.9	2.4	1.8	2.0	2.6	3.8	3.8	2.7	2.6	3.1	3.6	2.6	2.6	2.9	4.1	4.0	4.0	3.9	4.7	5.2	3.4
S	2.5	3.3	3.0	2.8	2.4	2.4	2.6	3.8	4.4	3.6	3.1	3.8	4.8	3.6	3.0	2.9	3.9	3.8	3.6	4.2	5.8	6.4	3.6
NI	6.1	10.3	8.1	7.0	6.8	6.4	7.3	9.3	7.8	6.7	7.5	7.5	7.9	6.6	6.1	6.1	7.7	7.2					7.9
UK	1.3	2.2	1.8	1.5	1.2	1.3	1.6	2.2	2.3	1.7	1.6	2.1	2.6	1.7	1.5	1.6	2.5	2.5	2.5	2.6	3.4	3.8	2.1

Source: Department of Employment, *British Labour Statistics: Historical Abstracts.*

is apparent between regions in the northern half of the country which have experienced persistently high rates of unemployment and regions in the southern half of the country which have experienced persistently low rates of unemployment compared to the national average. Moreover, there has been very little change in the ranking of regions, at least over the last twenty years. Secondly, it is apparent that the regions with higher than average unemployment have experienced lower than average employment growth rates. What is cause and what is effect is not certain. It could be that high unemployment discourages demand, or that unemployment itself is the outcome of the growth of demand for labour falling short of the rate of growth of natural labour supply, with net emigration acting as a stabilising influence preventing unemployment from rising continuously. What is clear from table 1.2 is that it cannot be said that the low rate of growth of employment in high unemployment regions is due to higher than average rates of labour productivity growth in manufacturing industry. If anything, the average rate of growth of labour productivity in the northern half of the country has been slightly less than in the south so that for any given rate of growth of output, the rate of growth of employment should, if anything, have been slightly higher in the north than in the south. The problem is not therefore on the supply side (assuming population growth to be the same in each region), but must lie on the demand side in one form or another. It could be a general deficiency of demand for goods from these regions or some structural problem of high unemployment in one or two sectors. This is something that will be examined carefully later.

Thirdly, it should be stressed that average earnings in manufacturing industry as an index of depression are not closely associated with levels of regional unemployment, as can be seen from table 1.1. Average earnings in manufacturing in Wales and in the North region, for example, exceed the national average, while earnings in East Anglia fall below the national average. Earnings in manufacturing, however, only constitute approximately 35 per cent of gross regional product. There are also earnings in the agriculture and service sectors to consider. The figures of gross domestic product at factor cost for 1961 given by Woodward[2] show four of the old Standard Regions with *per capita* incomes higher than the national average, London and South East, East and South, Midland and North Midland – all regions with unemployment below the national average. Thus, low average *per capita* income seems to be associated with high unemployment and high *per capita* income with low unemployment. The two important indices of welfare tend to be closely associated.

TECHNIQUES OF ANALYSIS

In considering regional performance, and the variety of regional experience in general, two particular frameworks or techniques of analysis will be employed: first, models (in particular the neoclassical model) of economic growth, and secondly, mathematical techniques related to the analysis of variance. We need to say at the outset the *use* to be made of these techniques and their relationship to the themes of 'regional growth' and 'regional variety'. With regard to the application of models of economic growth, there are two fundamental considerations which have shaped the approach adopted. The first is the belief that not only is a growth viewpoint *desirable* but also *necessary* (as Domar long ago observed).[3] The benefits to be gained from adopting a growth-orientated approach derive from the perspective afforded into the functional relationships between key economic variables, and the differing policy conclusions yielded compared to those derived from a static analysis.[4] This consideration is doubly important because much of the discussion about regional inequality and regional policy in the United Kingdom, while basically concerned with regional economic growth, has largely taken place outside the context of research which embodies growth models.

[2] V. H. Woodward, *Regional Social Accounts for the United Kingdom 1961 and 1964*, NIESR, Regional Papers I (Cambridge University Press, 1970).

[3] E. Domar, 'Capital Expansion, Rate of Growth, and Employment', *Econometrica*, Apr 1946, p. 147.

[4] An excellent demonstration of this view is provided in J. R. Sargent, *Out of Stagnation*, Fabian Tract No. 343, 1963.

The second consideration (and an important one in terms of the techniques to be used) is that, paradoxically, many models of economic growth may be used to great effect in the study of differences between regions at a point in time. This is in addition to the study of the movements in key economic variables within a given region over time. We are able to employ this 'cross-sectional' approach because in many growth models (as distinct from dynamic models) 'time' neither shapes the analysis nor determines the mathematical technique to be employed. Indeed 'time' often appears only in the form of subscripts which are added almost as an afterthought. Moreover the application of the neoclassical model to compare different economies (states) at the same point in time does not open itself to many of the criticisms of the neoclassical model which are directed at its use to study processes through time.[5] It is surprising that previous research in regional economics has overlooked the potential of the theory of economic growth to analyse regional differences at a point in time. The realisation and application of this insight is an important aspect of the present work.

To analyse the variety of regional experience, which Brown has described as the *raison d'être* of regional economics,[6] we require appropriate techniques of analysis. A common procedure for analysing interregional differences is to decompose the total difference between the performance of a region and all other regions (the nation) into two components or factors – one measuring the contribution of structural differences between the region and the nation; the other measuring the contribution of factors specific to the region (supposedly independent of structure). The method of calculating the contribution of each of the factors is fairly straightforward. First, the difference term of the factors must be defined. This is the difference between the observed value of the factor in the region and the weighted mean of all observed values of the factor. Secondly, the weighting term must be decided on. This,

[5] On this point see J. R. Hicks, *Capital and Growth* (Clarendon Press, 1965), p. 294.

[6] A. J. Brown, 'Surveys of Applied Economics: Regional Economics with Special Reference to the United Kingdom', *Economic Journal*, Dec 1969.

when multiplied by the difference term, gives the total contribution of that factor to the total difference. The problem is to decide on the weights to apply which, in general, may be regional or national weights or the mean of the two. Later in the book these procedures will be applied specifically to an analysis of regional employment growth rate differentials and to answer the question of why unemployment in some regions is more cyclically sensitive than in others. It will be helpful here, however, to lay out the general methodology for later reference.

STANDARDISATION PROCEDURES FOR THE ANALYSIS OF INTERREGIONAL DIFFERENCES

If R is the value of a variable in a region, let

$$R = \sum_i p_{ir} r_i,$$

where r_i is the value of the variable in industries in the region and p_{ir} is a set of industry weights in the region which sum to unity. Similarly, if N is the national value of the same variable let

$$N = \sum_i p_{in} n_i$$

where n_i is the value of the variable in industries in the nation and p_{in} is a set of industry weights in the nation which sum to unity. It is clear that R may differ from N because $p_{ir} \neq p_{in}$ and/or $r_i \neq n_i$. Inequalities between p_{ir} and p_{in} relate to structural differences between the region and the nation, and divergencies between r_i and n_i relate to 'within' industry (or regional specific) differences. The effects of these two inequalities on the difference between R and N can be measured by standardisation procedures which apply different weighting schemes to the difference terms. The effect of differences between the industrial structure of a region and the nation is defined by the difference term $(p_{ir} - p_{in})$ for all i; and the effect of regional specific differences is defined by the difference term $(r_i - n_i)$ for all i. However, the estimated contribution of these two differences to the total difference between the value of the variable in the region and the nation will depend on the weighting system employed. There are five main possibilities:

$$R-N = \sum_i r_i(p_{ir}-p_{in}) + \sum_i p_{in}(r_i-n_i) \tag{1.1}$$

$$R-N = \sum_i n_i(p_{ir}-p_{in}) + \sum_i p_{ir}(r_i-n_i) \tag{1.2}$$

$$R-N = \sum_i r_i(p_{ir}-p_{in}) + \sum_i p_{ir}(r_i-n_i) + \sum_i (p_{ir}-p_{in})(n_i-r_i) \tag{1.3}$$

$$R-N = \sum_i n_i(p_{ir}-p_{in}) + \sum_i p_{in}(r_i-n_i) + \sum_i (p_{in}-p_{ir})(n_i-r_i) \tag{1.4}$$

$$R-N = \sum_i \tfrac{1}{2}(r_i+n_i)(p_{ir}-p_{in}) + \sum_i \tfrac{1}{2}(p_{ir}+p_{in})(r_i-n_i) \tag{1.5}$$

What weighting scheme should be adopted is completely arbitrary. It must depend on the nature and purpose of the study (and on the data available). The first two schemes above use a mixed weighting system, applying a regional weight to one of the difference terms and a national weight to the other difference term. These particular schemes have the property that the two difference components exhaust the total difference, and no allowance is made for possible interaction effects between the two difference terms. Once the contribution of one of the differences to the total difference is calculated the other is obtained automatically as a residual (which will include interaction effects if any exist). In some contexts this may be a weakness of using mixed weighting systems, if interaction effects are thought to be strong. For example, if the industrial structure of regions is thought to be a primary determinant of the growth performance of individual industries within the region, it can be argued that the influence of industrial structure on regional growth will be distorted unless the interaction between structure and growth is considered separately and interaction effects are attributed to structure. Schemes (1.3) and (1.4) contain interaction terms between 'structural' and 'regional specific' differences. They arise from applying exclusively regional or national weights to the two difference terms. Comparing (1.1) with (1.3) and (1.2) with (1.4) it is easily seen that if there is positive interaction between structure and growth, the influence of structural differences on the total difference between *R* and *N* will be exaggerated in the former case and underestimated in the latter case unless the interaction term is added to the 'pure' contribution of structure. The interaction term may also be interesting in its own right. In the context of employment and output growth, the sign of the interaction term will indicate tendencies for the regional industrial structure to diverge from, or converge on, the national structure. This, in turn, may be indirect evidence of the existence or otherwise of comparative advantage.[7] If there is no interest in the interaction term, the easiest way to overcome the problem of choice of the weighting system to employ is to apply the mean of national and regional weights, thus allocating the interaction term equally between the two components of the total difference. This is equivalent to taking the mean of base period and current period weights in index number problems of a more familiar form.

It should be stressed that no causation is implied by the approach. It is purely a classificatory device, the main purpose of which is to give information of the extent to which attention should be focused on the structure of a region as opposed to the performance of its individual industries compared with the performance of the same industries elsewhere.

Analysis of variance and the 'evaluation of inner products'

Another technique which may be used to measure and assess interregional differences is analysis of variance. This technique, which is very useful in the context of regression analysis, may be used to summarise information contained within a data matrix. In particular, it provides a method which enables an assessment of the importance (and significance) of industrial,

[7] See N. Cunningham, 'A Note on the Proper Distribution of Industry', *Oxford Economic Papers*, Mar 1969.

vis-à-vis regional, sources of variation. An advantage of the method is that it is amenable to statistical tests of significance since it evaluates deviations from the arithmetic mean. For many purposes, however, a weighted mean (e.g. a national average) is a more meaningful benchmark than the arithmetic mean, particularly in regional studies. A technique is therefore required that will decompose and evaluate the sources of variation in a series of regional deviations from a weighted mean. To avoid confusion with analysis of variance, the decomposition of deviations from the weighted mean will be referred to as an 'evaluation of inner products'; the variance of a series being a specific type of inner product.[8] The mathematics of the technique bears many similarities to variance analysis, especially as it is applied in regression models.[9] Suppose that the difference between the value of a variable in the region and in the nation is $R-N$, and that the difference is the sum of two component differences, (r_1-n_1) and (r_2-n_2), where r and n refer to regional and national values respectively. To evaluate the contribution of each component to the interregional variation, we square both sides and sum over all regions to yield:

$$\begin{aligned}\sum_r (R-N)^2 &= \sum_r [(r_1-n_1)+(r_2-n_2)]^2\\ &= \sum_r (r_1-n_1)^2 + \sum_r (r_2-n_2)^2\\ &\qquad + \sum_r 2[(r_1-n_1)(r_2-n_2)]\end{aligned}$$

The components of the total sum of squares can now be evaluated in terms of their proportional importance in 'explaining' the total sum of squared deviations from the weighted mean (N). The term $\sum_r 2(r_1-n_1)(r_2-n_2)$ is an interaction term similar to the interaction term found in analysis of variance. Since in using this approach, however, we are not

[8] H. Scheffé, *The Analysis of Variance* (John Wiley, 1959), p. 375.
[9] J. Johnston, *Econometric Methods* (McGraw-Hill, 1963).

concerned with deviations from the arithmetic mean, the statistical tests of significance normally associated with the analysis of variance are inapplicable. We hope to demonstrate that the technique is a useful addition to the tool-kit of regional economists interested in evaluating the relative importance of sources of interregional variation.

THE INDUSTRIAL STRUCTURE OF THE REGIONS

A number of studies have demonstrated the importance of the industrial structure of regions as a determinant of regional performance. The use of standardisation procedures described earlier has revealed that the industrial structure of regions is an important determinant of comparative regional performance with respect to a number of 'welfare' indices. It will be seen later that industrial structure is an important determinant (although not the most important determinant) of interregional unemployment rate differences. In addition it has been demonstrated that the industrial composition of regions is a major determinant of female activity rates.[10] These are themselves an important source of variation in total activity rates between regions,[11] which in turn are responsible for a sizeable proportion of differences in the level of GDP *per capita* between regions. In a similar vein, studies using analysis of variance, based on data classified by industry and region, show that inter-industry differences account for a significantly large proportion of variations in such variables as: productivity and average earnings,[12] female activity rates,[13] and unemployment rates.[14]

In order to understand interregional variations over a wide range of indices, it seems important to us to make some attempt to explain the industrial structure of regions and

[10] A. J. Brown, op. cit., p. 771.

[11] J. Bowers, *The Anatomy of Regional Activity Rates*, NIESR, Regional Papers 1 (Cambridge University Press, 1970).

[12] V. H. Woodward, op. cit., p. 89.

[13] J. Bowers, op. cit., p. 33.

[14] A. P. Thirlwall, *Regional Unemployment and Public Policy in Great Britain 1948 to 1964*, unpublished Ph.D. thesis, 1967; cited in A. J. Brown, op. cit., p. 769.

changes in this structure over time. This is the subject of the opening chapters. A second reason for attempting to study the industrial composition of regions relates to our interest in the criteria of economic efficiency. To the extent that patterns of regional specialisation are unrelated to alternative measures of regional comparative advantage, it may be possible to conclude that there exists a welfare loss to the region arising from the misallocation of resources. Similarly, if it can be demonstrated that industries do not tend to locate in regions which possess an absolute advantage in that activity, it may be that there is a resultant welfare loss to the nation as a whole.

2 Regional Specialisation and the Location of Manufacturing Industries in the United Kingdom: 1958 and 1963

This chapter is concerned with an examination of regional specialisation and the location of industry. It is divided into two parts: one dealing with the *level* (or degree) of specialisation and localisation, the other dealing with *patterns* of specialisation and localisation. The first part discusses briefly measures of the level of regional specialisation and the localisation of industry, and describes these measures for the manufacturing industries and regions of the United Kingdom in the years 1958 and 1963. The second part attempts to explain the patterns of specialisation and location with the aid of hypotheses derived from the theory of international trade.

Interregional differences in the level and patterns of industrial structure are of interest for two main reasons. Firstly, because a number of studies, as we saw in chapter 1, reveal that differences in industrial structure are an important source of interregional differences with respect to a number of important economic phenomena. If one of the tasks of regional economics is to explain regional variations, 'composition differences' need to be understood. The second reason for interest in industrial structure concerns the relationship that might be expected to exist between patterns of regional specialisation and comparative, or absolute, costs. If regions can gain from specialisation and trade, it is interesting to see whether any relationship exists between relative costs and specialisation patterns. Such a study should also provide evidence of the scope for increasing output per employee from interregional resource shifts.

THE LEVEL OF REGIONAL SPECIALISATION AND INDUSTRIAL LOCALISATION

The conventional measure of the degree to which the industrial composition of employment of one region differs from that of all other regions taken together is the Coefficient of Regional Specialisation (CRS).[1] Using the national composition of employment as a benchmark, the coefficient measures the extent to which the proportional distribution of industrial employment in one region differs from the corresponding distribution in all regions taken together. Thus:

$$CRS_r = \tfrac{1}{2}\sum_i \left| \frac{L_{ir}}{L_r} - \frac{L_i}{L} \right| \tag{2.1}$$

where

L_{ir} is employment in industry i in region r

L_r is total employment in region r

L_i is employment in all regions in industry i

and

L is total employment in all regions.

The coefficient varies in value between 0 and 1: zero if the industrial distribution of manufacturing employment in a region is identical to that of the nation; unity if the region has no employment in common with the nation. The proportions of each region's manufacturing workforce employed in different industries in the years 1958 and 1963 are presented in tables 2.A2 and 2.A3 of the appendix to the chapter. Data on the proportion of national manufacturing employment in each industrial order are presented in table 2.A7. Regional values of the Coefficient of Regional Specialisation for the years 1958 and 1963 are given in table 2.1. Northern Ireland, Wales and East Anglia appear to be the most specialised regions, and Scotland, the South East and North West the least specialised. It is also apparent that there has

[1] On alternative measures and their inter-relatedness, see W. Isard (*et alia*), *Methods of Regional Analysis* (M.I.T. Press, 1960); and A. P. Thirlwall and C. P. Harris, 'Measuring the Localisation of Industry', *Manchester School*, Jan 1967.

TABLE 2.1 Coefficients of regional specialisation in manufacturing industry

Region	*1958*	*1963*
N	0.279	0.237
YH	0.217	0.183
EM	0.218	0.162
EA	0.287	0.238
SE	0.155	0.184
SW	0.233	0.214
WM	0.280	0.294
NW	0.178	0.110
W	0.295	0.276
S	0.168	0.128
NI	0.343	0.314

Source: Calculated from data in tables 2.A2, 2.A3 and 2.A7 of the appendix.

been a tendency in most regions for specialisation to decline over time.[2]

There tends to be a negative association between the degree of regional specialisation and the size of regions as measured by the proportion of national manufacturing employment concentrated in each region.[3] A rank correlation between the Coefficients of Regional Specialisation (ranked from highest to lowest), and the percentage distribution of manufacturing employment (also ranked from highest to lowest) gives a coefficient of -0.760 for 1958 and -0.553 for 1963, both of which are statistically significant at the 95 per cent confidence level.[4]

A similar coefficient to the CRS may be calculated for each

[2] This tendency has also been noted in A. P. Thirlwall, 'Weighting Systems and Regional Analysis: A Reply to Mr Cunningham', *Oxford Economic Papers*, Mar 1969.

[3] This is also found in the case of national economies where small countries tend to be highly specialised in one or two commodities.

[4] In part the negative association may be due to a statistical illusion in that more 'weight' is given to the larger regions in the calculation of national percentages. We should therefore expect *a priori* the larger regions to evidence less specialisation compared with the nation.

TABLE 2.2 Coefficients of industry localisation 1958 and 1963

Industry	*1958*	*1963*
III	0.102	0.112
IV	0.192	0.184
V	0.367	0.362
VI	0.092	0.085
VII	0.351	0.329
VIII	0.216	0.177
IX	0.271	0.250
X	0.414	0.416
XI	0.100	0.099
XII	0.146	0.145
XIII	0.129	0.116
XIV	0.174	0.161
XV	0.244	0.230
XVI	0.167	0.140

Source: Calculated from data in tables 2.A4, 2.A5 and 2.A6.

manufacturing industry, measuring the extent to which the percentage distribution of employment in a particular industry between regions differs from that of manufacturing as a whole. This is termed the Coefficient of Localisation (CL) and is measured by:[5]

$$\mathrm{CL}_i = \tfrac{1}{2}\sum_r \left| \frac{L_{ir}}{L_i} - \frac{L_r}{L} \right| \qquad (2.2)$$

The data for calculating CL for each industry in 1958 and 1963 are given in tables 2.A4, 2.A5 and 2.A6 of the appendix to the chapter. The values of CL for each manufacturing order are given in table 2.2.[6] Textiles (X), metal manufacture (V), and shipbuilding and marine engineering (VII) appear to be the most localised industries; while engineering and electrical goods (VI); food, drink and tobacco (III), and leather, leather goods and fur (XI) appear to be the least localised.

[5] W. Isard (*et alia*), op. cit., pp. 249–54; A. P. Thirlwall and C. P. Harris, op. cit., p. 55.

[6] See table 2.A1 of the appendix for the names of the industries to which the Order numbers refer.

There is no evidence that the degree of localisation is related to the size of the industry in question, but it has been claimed that there are theoretical grounds for expecting an association between the average plant size in an industry and the degree of localisation. In Lösch's theory of location,[7] industries differ in the extent to which increasing returns prevail. These differences, in turn, explain differences in plant size and the different sizes of market area and thus the spatial distribution of industry. To test this hypothesis, data on average plant size in industry[8] obtained from the Census of Production Reports was related to the CL for each industry; and the rank correlation coefficient calculated. The rank correlation coefficients for 1958 and 1963 are both positive but not significantly different from zero at the 95 per cent confidence level.

CHANGES IN THE DEGREE OF SPECIALISATION AND LOCALISATION

To examine changes in regional specialisation and industrial localisation over time, two measures of change suggest themselves. One measure of change is simply to calculate the difference in the CRS between two periods. An alternative is to compute the Coefficient of Regional Redistribution (CRR)[9] defined as

$$\mathrm{CRR}_r = \tfrac{1}{2}\sum_i \left| \left(\frac{L_{ir}}{L_r}\right)_t - \left(\frac{L_{ir}}{L_r}\right)_{t-1} \right| \qquad (2.3)$$

The coefficient ranges between zero (no change in the distribution of regional employment over the period) and unity (complete reallocation of resources). What transpires from both measures is that there was a general tendency in most regions over the limited period 1958–63 for the industrial

[7] A. Lösch, *The Economics of Location* (John Wiley and Sons, 1967). For a good discussion of Lösch's model see S. Valavanis, 'Lösch on Location', *American Economic Review*, Sep 1955.

[8] Measured by the mean number of employees per establishment. Florence has argued, however, that the arithmetic mean is a misleading measure of average plant size. See P. S. Florence, *Post-War Investment, Location and the Size of Plant* (Cambridge, 1962), pp. 28–31.

[9] W. Isard (*et alia*), op. cit., p. 275.

structure to converge towards the national industrial structure. Only the South East and West Midlands regions increased their degree of specialisation relative to the nation. Redistribution was greatest in East Anglia and the North West, and least in the West Midlands and the South East. It seems that other regions in the country were altering their industrial structure over the period such as to duplicate the structure of the South East and West Midlands. This is partly a reflection of the decline of heavily localised industries in some regions and partly a reflection of the way government policy affects the movement of industry. Since policy has always operated to divert the expansion of firms from the South East and Midlands to the 'peripheral' regions, it acts in effect to transfer the industrial structure of the centre to the periphery. There is, in fact, a close association between the Coefficient of Regional Redistribution and measures of industrial movement between regions over the period. The rank correlation coefficient between CRR_r and the proportion of total moves going to each region over the period 1960 to 1966 is +0.555, and between CRR_r and the 'propensity to attract moving firms', +0.562.[10] Both coefficients are significantly different from zero at the 95 per cent confidence level.

We might expect relatively rapid employment growth in a region to provide the potential for resource reallocation, and for resource reallocation to be reflected in relatively high levels of productivity growth. It turns out, however, that there is no association between the extent of redistribution and the growth of employment or productivity. The rank correlation coefficients between CRR and employment growth on the one hand and productivity growth on the other are both insignificantly different from zero.[11]

Measures of locational change may also be computed for each industry. Either the change in the localisation coefficient can be taken or the Coefficient of Industrial Redistribution (CIR) computed, defined as:[12]

[10] Details of the computations and sources of the data on movement can be found in chapter 3.

[11] These relationships will be explored further, however, in chapter 6.

[12] W. Isard (*et alia*), op. cit., p. 254.

$$\text{CIR}_i = \tfrac{1}{2}\sum_r \left| \left(\frac{L_{ir}}{L_i}\right)_t - \left(\frac{L_{ir}}{L_i}\right)_{t-1} \right| \qquad (2.4)$$

It transpires that most industries, with the exception of food, drink and tobacco (III), and textiles (X), have tended to become more dispersed over the limited period 1958 to 1963 – a tendency found over a longer time period by Thirlwall and Harris.[13] Locational change has been greatest in shipbuilding and marine engineering (VII) and textiles (X). As with the CRR, there is no association between the Coefficient of Industrial Redistribution and the growth of the labour force or labour productivity.

Patterns of regional specialisation and trade in the United Kingdom: a test of some hypotheses

Little attention has been devoted by regional economists to the empirical study of the basis of regional specialisation and industrial location. Major exceptions are the works of Nicholson for the United Kingdom, based on the 1948 Census of Production,[14] and of Moroney and Walker which considers the ability of the Heckscher-Ohlin theorem to account for the observed pattern of specialisation in the southern States of the USA.[15] The purpose here is twofold. Firstly we shall be interested in explaining the patterns of regional specialisation and trade in the United Kingdom, using the Heckscher-Ohlin theorem and other hypotheses of the basis of regional specialisation – in particular, hypotheses derived from the classical theory of international trade. Secondly, we shall be interested in assessing the efficiency of resource allocation within and between regions. For this purpose the particular determinants of allocative and locational decisions are im-

[13] Op. cit., p. 60.

[14] R. J. Nicholson, 'The Regional Location of Industry: An Empirical Study based on the Regional Tables of the 1948 Census of Production', *Economic Journal*, Sep 1956. But see also comments on the paper by A. J. Brown, 'Surveys of Applied Economics . . .', op. cit., pp. 775–7.

[15] J. R. Moroney and J. M. Walker, 'A Regional Test of the Heckscher-Ohlin Hypothesis', *Journal of Political Economy*, Dec 1966.

material; we are simply interested in the outcome of these forces as reflected in the prevailing pattern of specialisation, and their relationship with certain efficiency criteria, such as labour productivity. To the extent that prices both reflect opportunity costs and are correctly perceived (and this leads, in turn, to 'correct' resource reallocation), the two interests merge into one. At the outset, the analysis will proceed on this basis, although it may become necessary later to question the assumptions that prices reflect opportunity costs and are correctly perceived.

From the observed pattern of regional specialisation, it is also possible, given certain assumptions, to make inferences about regional trading patterns. Assuming that differences in the composition of demand do not offset the ordering of regional advantages as determined by supply conditions, the industrial composition of regional trade may be considered to be arrayed in the same order as the industrial composition of regional specialisation in production.

The major assumption on which the analysis is based is that the pattern of resource allocation, and the quantity composition of trade, are determined by differences in relative prices.[16] It is the determinants of relative price differences which alternative theories of the basis of trade seek to explain.[17] In order to derive appropriate measures of regional advantage it is also necessary to make assumptions about whether specialisation and trade are determined by comparative or absolute advantage. That is, assumptions must be made about the mobility (or specificity) of resources. Initially it will be assumed that regions specialise according to comparative advantage; that is, it is assumed that resources are regional specific. Later the possibility is considered that the observed pattern of specialisation reflects differences in absolute regional advantage. If none of the hypotheses as to

[16] For an interesting discussion of the relationship between specialisation, trade and industrial location, see W. Isard, *Location and Space Economy* (M.I.T. Press, 1956).

[17] For a detailed discussion of the methodology of empirical studies of patterns of trade, see J. Bhagwati, 'The Pure Theory of International Trade: A Survey', *Economic Journal*, Mar 1964.

the basis of relative price differences appears to account successfully for the observed patterns of regional specialisation it may be necessary at the end to question the validity of the assumptions that underly the analysis. Let us first begin, however, by discussing the measurement of the *pattern* of regional specialisation which theory seeks to explain.

MEASURING THE PATTERN OF REGIONAL SPECIALISATION

The *pattern* of specialisation within each region is measured by the Employment Location Quotient (ELQ).[18] For each industry (i) in each region (r), the ELQ is defined as:[19]

$$ELQ_{ir} = \frac{L_{ir}}{L_i} \bigg/ \frac{L_r}{L} = \frac{L_{ir}}{L_r} \bigg/ \frac{L_i}{L} \qquad (2.5)$$

If the ELQ is greater than unity, the region is considered to be specialised in that industry relative to all other regions; if it is less than unity, the region is assumed not to specialise in that activity. A matrix can be drawn up consisting of i rows and r columns, the elements of which are the ELQ_{ir}'s. The matrices for the years 1958 and 1963 are given in tables 2.A8 and 2.A9 of the appendix to the chapter. Assuming that the region will export the products of those industries in which it is relatively specialised, and import the products of industries for which the ELQ is less than unity, the column vectors of ELQs can be regarded as a proxy for the trading pattern of each region.[20] If the ELQs across any row are ranked from highest to lowest, the rankings should correspond to ordering the regions

[18] Specialisation may be measured in terms of employment or output. Since the rank correlation coefficient between these two measures is positive and significant at the 99 per cent confidence level for all regions, it should make no substantial difference to the results which measure is used.

[19] The ELQ is thus equivalent, in terms of ratios, to the components (expressed in terms of differences) of the measure of the *level* of regional specialisation and industrial localisation (see equations (2.1) and (2.2)).

[20] It should be remembered that attention is confined to manufacturing industry only.

by an exportation-importation scale for the products of that industry.[21]

The major defect of the location quotient approach in the present context is that it would be possible for all regions to be net importers of one product and net exporters of another, yet the ELQ measure must show some regions with an ELQ greater than unity in the first case and an ELQ less than unity in the second, thus possibly reversing the actual rankings within a region.[22] This defect is mitigated by two considerations: firstly, by the qualitative rather than quantitative use to be made of the quotients; and secondly, by the fact that the United Kingdom as a whole is a net exporter of the products of the industries with which we are concerned.[23]

THEORIES OF THE PATTERN OF REGIONAL SPECIALISATION BASED ON COMPARATIVE COSTS

(a) *The Heckscher-Ohlin theory*

Briefly stated, the Heckscher-Ohlin hypothesis is that economies will export goods which require for their production relatively large quantities of their most abundant factor of production, and import the products of those industries which are intensive in the relatively less abundant factor. Following extensive discussion in the literature over the influence of the composition of demand, and the resultant distinction between physical and 'economic' abundance,[24] the theorem has since been modified to predict production rather

[21] Emphasis is placed on 'rankings' and 'ordering' rather than on absolute magnitudes for a number of reasons. For example, it has been argued that the theory of comparative advantage predicts orderings rather than magnitudes. See R. W. Jones, 'Factor Proportions and the Heckscher-Ohlin Theorem', *Review of Economic Studies*, no. 1, 1956–7.

[22] An attempt has recently been made to overcome this problem in using location quotients to measure regional exports and imports. See F. J. B. Stillwell and B. D. Boatwright, 'A Method of Estimating Interregional Trade Flows', *Regional and Urban Studies*, vol. 1, 1971.

[23] Central Statistical Office, *Input-Output Tables for the United Kingdom 1963*, Studies in Official Statistics (HMSO, 1970).

[24] See in particular, S. Valavanis-Vail, 'Leontief's Scarce Factor Paradox', *Journal of Political Economy*, Dec 1954.

than trading patterns. Given the 'strong factor intensity' assumption, the theorem may be taken to state: 'Ordering the commodities with respect to the capital-labour ratios employed in production is to rank them in order of comparative advantage.'[25] Since the data we have available refers to specialisation in production rather than trade, the problem imposed by demand factors does not arise.[26]

Moroney and Walker in their study referred to earlier[27] examined the relationship between the relative capital intensity of (two-digit) manufacturing industries in the United States and the degree of specialisation in those industries in the South. Given that the South is a relatively low wage (labour abundant) region, the two-factor version of the Heckscher-Ohlin theorem predicts that the South should specialise in relatively labour intensive industries compared to the rest of the US. The particular hypothesis tested by Moroney and Walker is that there is an inverse rank ordering between capital-labour ratios and location quotients. In fact, they found the South specialising in relatively capital intensive industries, and rejected the hypothesis.

The Heckscher-Ohlin hypothesis was tested for the regions of the United Kingdom, for the years 1958 and 1963, using the procedures adopted by Moroney and Walker. Capital-labour ratios[28] were calculated for thirteen manufacturing orders[29] in the United Kingdom in 1960, using estimates of the capital stock made as part of the Cambridge Growth Project.[30] The industrial orders were then ranked from highest to lowest on the basis of the estimated capital-labour ratios. Assuming the order of these rankings to be preserved in the regions,[31] the rankings of the industries in terms of capital

[25] R. W. Jones, op. cit., p. 6.

[26] See Moroney and Walker, op. cit., for a review of tests of the Heckscher-Ohlin hypothesis, and the advantages of regional tests.

[27] Ibid.

[28] Labour is assumed to be homogeneous.

[29] SIC orders XI and XII were combined.

[30] G. Pyatt, *Capital, Output and Employment 1948–1960*, A Programme for Growth, vol. 4 (Department of Applied Economics, Cambridge, 1964). Data refers to the value of capital stock per employee in 1960.

[31] This amounts to the 'strong factor intensity assumption'.

TABLE 2.3 Relationship between relative capital intensity and regional specialisation patterns 1958 and 1963

	1958		*1963*	
Region	*Rank correlation coefficient*	*Index of earnings (UK = 100)*	*Rank correlation coefficient*	*Index of earnings (UK = 100)*
N	+0.01	103	−0.09	100
YH	+0.33	95	+0.35	93
EM	+0.14	96	+0.23	92
EA	−0.35	95	−0.32	93
SE	−0.30	108	−0.23	107
SW	−0.40	101	−0.32	101
WM	+0.11	104	+0.01	103
NW	+0.10	93	+0.30	96
W	+0.27	108	+0.33	108
S	+0.30	96	+0.27	95
NI	−0.31	75	−0.28	76

intensity were correlated with the rankings (from highest to lowest) of the column vectors of the ELQs (tables 2.A8 and 2.A9), and the rank correlation coefficients were computed. In high wage regions we expect specialisation in relatively capital intensive activities, and for the rank correlation coefficients to be positive. In low wage regions we expect the opposite. The estimates of the rank correlation coefficients are given in table 2.3, together with an index of average earnings per employee in total manufacturing in each region.

None of the rank correlation coefficients are significantly different from zero at the 95 per cent confidence level. It is interesting, however, to observe the sign of the coefficient for some individual regions. For example, the correlation coefficient for Northern Ireland is negative in both years indicating that there is some tendency for this low wage region to specialise in relatively labour intensive activities. The coefficient for Wales, a high wage region, is positive in both years, reflecting a tendency for resources to be concentrated in relatively capital intensive industries. The coefficient for the South East, however – a region short of labour with high wages – is negative in both years, a result which is inconsistent with the predictions of the Heckscher-Ohlin theory. As we progress from low wage to high wage regions we do not find, in fact, a smooth transition from negative coefficients (indicating specialisation in labour intensive industries) to positive coefficients (indicating specialisation in capital intensive industries). Overall, however, the evidence for the regions of the United Kingdom is more favourably inclined towards the Heckscher–Ohlin hypothesis than Moroney and Walker's results for the US.[32]

Two main explanations for the insignificant results[33] suggest themselves: one refers to the possibility of 'factor-reversal', the other refers to excluded variables. On the first point, the assumption that the ordering of capital-labour ratios is identical between regions may be invalid. If the elasticity of substitution differs between industries the ranking of industries by their capital-labour ratio will differ between the high wage and low wage regions. Consider two regions and two industries, one industry with an elasticity of substitution less than unity, the other with an elasticity of substitution greater than unity. The first industry will be less capital intensive than the second industry in the high wage region and more capital intensive than the second industry in the low wage region. Estimates of the elasticity of substitution at the SIC order level in United Kingdom manufacturing industry (see appendix 1) indicate that there are significant differences in the estimated elasticity of substitution between industries. This not only makes factor reversal possible, but also extremely likely, thus making the Heckscher-Ohlin theorem invalid even if all other assumptions of the model are fulfilled.

[32] A recent study using value added per employee as a measure of capital intensity reports results more favourable to the neoclassical hypothesis than those reported here. See B. Smith, 'Regional Specialisation and Trade in the United Kingdom', *Scottish Journal of Political Economy*, Feb 1975.

[33] Essentially the same results were obtained using Nicholson's estimates of the capital-labour ratio in ten industry groups for 1961. The results thus appear to be insensitive to alternative measures of the capital-labour ratio. See R. J. Nicholson, 'Capital Stock, Employment and Output in British Industry 1948–1964', *Yorkshire Bulletin of Economic and Social Research*, Nov 1966.

On the question of excluded variables, it is possible that more than two factors of production must be considered in conducting the analysis. For example, natural resources are often thought to be important as a determinant of comparative advantage, and their exclusion from analysis is often cited as the major contributor to poor results.[34] With manufacturing industry this consideration may not be so important as with other types of activity, although it could be an important factor in such industries as textiles and metal manufacture. An additional consideration is that no allowance has been made for differences in the skill and sex composition of the work-force between regions. A region specialising in relatively capital intensive industries may none the less have low wages because it has a high proportion of female and/or unskilled labour.

A different line of criticism is that of Brown who has argued (with others) that differences in the quality or efficiency of labour should be taken into account in testing the Heckscher-Ohlin theory.[35] Low money wages and abundant labour do not necessarily mean 'cheap' labour, if labour is inefficient. The hypothesis is easily reformulated to make differences in the efficiency of labour the proximate determinant of comparative advantage. Doing so has the advantage of retaining (implicitly) the importance of capital intensity as a variable but regarding it as only one determinant of differences in the 'efficiency wage'. Emphasis on the 'efficiency wage' is essentially an extension of the classical view that trade is based on comparative labour costs determined by comparative labour productivity.

(b) *Classical trade theory I: comparative labour productivity as the basis of specialisation*

A number of studies of the pattern of international trade have found empirical support for the classical hypothesis that differences in trading patterns, or shares of export markets, can

[34] Moroney and Walker use this explanation. Mention should also be made of market imperfections and returns to scale.

[35] A. J. Brown, 'Professor Leontief and the Pattern of World Trade'. *Yorkshire Bulletin of Economic and Social Research*, Nov 1957.

largely be explained by differences in comparative labour costs.[36] More recently, the importance of efficiency wage differences – differences in money wages relative to labour productivity – as a determinant of regional export performance and regional growth rate differences has been argued by Kaldor.[37]

A 'naive' version of the classical hypothesis is that there exists a relationship between specialisation and comparative labour productivity. This hypothesis is tested for the regions of the United Kingdom for the years 1958 and 1963. The method used to construct vectors of comparative labour productivity in manufacturing industries, in a manner consistent with the classical hypothesis, was as follows: firstly, the value of net output per employee was calculated for each industry in each region from the regional tables of the 1963 Census of Production.[38] This yields a matrix of *i* rows (industries) and *r* columns (regions) showing actual labour productivities in each region. Secondly, for each industry (row) in turn, labour productivity in each region was expressed as a proportion of the national average productivity in that industry. The derived matrices of comparative labour productivities are given in tables 2.A10 and 2.A11 in the appendix to the chapter. Regional comparative advantage is assumed to lie in the products of those industries for which regional productivity is highest relative to the nation. If regions specialise according

[36] G. D. A. MacDougall, 'British and American Exports: A Study Suggested by the Theory of Comparative Costs', *Economic Journal*, Dec 1951, and Sep 1952; R. Stern, 'British and American Productivity and Comparative Costs in International Trade', *Oxford Economic Papers*, Oct 1962; B. Balassa, 'An Empirical Demonstration of Classical Comparative Cost Theory', *Review of Economics and Statistics*, Aug 1963. A critical evaluation of these studies may be found in J. Bhagwati, 'The Pure Theory of International Trade: A Survey', *Economic Journal*, Mar 1964.

[37] N. Kaldor, 'The Case for Regional Policies', *Scottish Journal of Political Economy*, Nov 1970.

[38] Net output is defined as 'the value added to materials obtained by deducting from the gross output the cost of purchases adjusted for stock changes, payments for work given out to other firms and payments for transport'. 'Employees' includes: operatives, administrative, technical and clerical employees. Net output is measured in value terms. Regional price indices are not available.

TABLE 2.4 Rank correlation coefficients between comparative labour productivity and regional patterns of specialisation, 1958 and 1963

Region	*1958*	*1963*
N	+0.570*	+0.508*
YH	+0.311	+0.323
EM	−0.049	+0.059
EA	−0.096	−0.134
SE	−0.084	+0.086
SW	+0.242	+0.165
WM	−0.234	−0.130
NW	+0.148	+0.119
W	+0.131	−0.189
S	+0.191	−0.086
NI	+0.183	−0.042

* Indicates coefficient statistically significant at the 95 per cent confidence level.

to their comparative advantage, as defined above, we should expect to find a significant positive correlation between the rankings of the ELQs and the ranking of the productivity indices (both ranked from highest to lowest) down the corresponding columns of the matrices.[39,40] The rank correlation coefficients for each region are set out in table 2.4. Only one region, the North, exhibits a significant positive relation.

One obvious reason for the generally insignificant results is that product prices not only depend on factor productivity but also on the cost of inputs. Differences in wages may offset, or

[39] An alternative method is to deflate each column by the regional average and then to compare the relevant rows. The procedure adopted was preferred on intuitive grounds and also to facilitate 'absolute cost' comparisons to be made later.

[40] This amounts to a test of what Stigler has called a 'predictive' labour theory of value. See G. J. Stigler, 'Ricardo and the 93 per cent Labour Theory of Value', *American Economic Review*, June 1958. It appears that the classical economists were not alone in this view, as comments on the 'neo-classical' parable demonstrate. See P. Garegnani, 'Heterogenous Capital, the Production Function and the Theory of Distribution', *Review of Economic Studies*, July 1970.

more than offset, differences in labour productivity between regions and between industries within a region. A recent study by Woodward, using analysis of variance, reveals that while average product differs significantly between industries but not between regions, average earnings differ significantly between industries and between regions.[41] It seems desirable therefore to allow for this source of variation in the measure of comparative labour costs. This amounts to an analysis of efficiency wage differences (or unit labour costs) as the determinant of the observed pattern of regional specialisation.

(c) *Classical trade theory II: efficiency wage differences as the basis of specialisation*

Efficiency wages (or unit labour costs) were calculated for each industry in each region by dividing the gross wage and salary bill[42] by the value of net output. Comparative unit labour costs were then derived for each industry in each region in exactly the same way as comparative labour productivities, i.e. by dividing each row element in the unit labour cost matrix by the corresponding national average unit labour cost. The matrices of comparative unit labour costs are given in tables 2.A12 and 2.A13 in the appendix to the chapter. Ranking the indices down each column from highest to lowest is equivalent to ordering the industries in each region in terms of the opportunity cost to the region of using labour in each particular industry. The lowest unit labour cost industry relative to the nation represents the industry in which regional comparative advantage is greatest. If regions specialised according to their comparative advantage, measured by relative efficiency wages, we should expect to find a positive and significant correlation between the rankings of the ELQs, ranked from highest to lowest, and the rankings of the relative efficiency wage indices ranked from lowest to

[41] V. H. Woodward, *Regional Social Accounts for the United Kingdom*, NIESR Regional Papers 1 (Cambridge University Press, 1970).

[42] Gross wages and salaries are defined as amounts paid to operatives and to administrative, technical and clerical employees with no deduction made for income tax, insurances, contributory pensions, etc.

TABLE 2.5 Rank correlation coefficients between comparative efficiency wages (unit labour costs) and regional patterns of specialisation, 1958 and 1963

Region	*1958*	*1963*
N	+0.248	+0.194
YH	−0.022	−0.065
EM	−0.130	−0.350
EA	−0.701†	−0.557*
SE	−0.321	−0.045
SW	+0.501*	+0.130
WM	−0.365	−0.415
NW	+0.105	+0.048
W	−0.161	−0.570*
S	+0.262	+0.048
NI	−0.094	−0.355

* Indicates coefficient is statistically significant at the 95 per cent confidence level.

† Indicates significance at the 99 per cent confidence level.

highest down the corresponding columns of the matrices. The rank correlations are shown in table 2.5.

The results indicate that only one region, the South West in 1958, was specialising in industries in which it had a comparative advantage according to the efficiency wage criterion. Two regions were apparently specialising in industries in which they had a comparative disadvantage, i.e. East Anglia and Wales. In the other regions, no statistically significant relation is apparent. The hypothesis that regions specialise according to comparative advantage as measured by efficiency wage differences must be rejected on the evidence here.

If we are still willing to accept that specialisation and trade are determined by relative prices, and that efficiency wages are a good proxy for relative prices, there is the possibility that the poor results are due to the fact that the pattern of regional specialisation and trade is based not on comparative cost differences but on absolute cost differences. It is possible to test this hypothesis given the matrix of efficiency wages already derived.

(d) *Absolute unit labour costs as the basis of specialisation*
If regions specialise according to their absolute advantage (that is, if resources are industry, not regional, specific), and each industry is relatively concentrated in regions where the absolute unit labour cost in that industry is lowest, we should expect to find a significant positive correlation between the ELQs and the comparative unit labour cost indices, ranked *across* each corresponding row of the matrices.[43] Since the indices were derived by deflating actual unit labour costs in each row by a constant, the initial ordering of *absolute* costs (across each row) is preserved. The results of the absolute advantage test, relating specialisation and absolute unit labour costs by industry for each region, are set out in table 2.6. The results are not encouraging; in fact, there is some evidence that for many industries the degree of regional specialisation seems to be related to absolute disadvantage. It appears that the poor results of testing the efficiency wage hypothesis cannot be attributed to the original assumption of comparative advantage as the basis of specialisation and trade. If the test procedure is accepted we are left with two major possibilities. Either efficiency wages are not a good proxy for relative prices because of offsetting differences in other costs, or the pattern of specialisation and trade is not determined by relative price differences.

There are two grounds on which it can be argued that efficiency wages reflect relative prices, and against the objection that the poor results are due to other costs, particularly capital costs, offsetting unit labour cost differences. Firstly, what matters is not the absolute difference in capital costs between regions, but rather the comparative industrial rankings of capital costs for all industries in one region

[43] It is also possible to test the Heckscher-Ohlin theorem assuming resources are mobile between regions. Correlation coefficients could be computed between the ELQs and regional wage rates within each industry. If the Heckscher-Ohlin theorem is correct we should expect to find positive correlation coefficients for capital intensive industries and negative coefficients for labour intensive industries.

TABLE 2.6 Rank correlation coefficients between ELQs and unit labour costs by industry, 1958 and 1963

Industry	*1958*	*1963*
III	+0.227	+0.298
IV	+0.405	+0.041
V	+0.314	−0.048
VI	+0.064	−0.525
VII	−0.308	−0.500
VIII	−0.104	+0.348
IX	−0.357	−0.636*
X	−0.295	−0.634*
XI	+0.257	+0.831†
XII	+0.032	−0.570*
XIII	−0.557*	−0.551*
XIV	−0.057	−0.250
XV	−0.388	−0.020
XVI	−0.066	+0.527

* Indicates coefficient statistically significant at the 95 per cent confidence level.

† Indicates significance at the 99 per cent confidence level.

compared with another.[44] Secondly, numerous studies of locational decision making support the view that the minimisation of production costs is not accorded high priority by industrial decision makers in evaluating alternative locations.[45]

If it is accepted that efficiency wage differences can account for differences in relative prices, there is no alternative but to question the proposition that relative price differences determine the quantity composition of regional trade and the spatial pattern of resource allocation. Non-economic, or at least non-price determined, models appear to be necessary to understand the pattern of regional specialisation and the location of industry in the United Kingdom. An important factor affecting the results is likely to be that of locational

[44] This is discussed in S. J. Wells; *International Economics* (George Allen & Unwin, 1969).

[45] See G. McCrone, *Regional Policy in Britain* (George Allen & Unwin, 1969), pp. 169–91, and the references cited therein.

inertia. Clark, in a slightly different context, has put the matter this way: 'The essential concept of a free market is trial and error. . . . But can we say that this is a valid method of control in matters where you may have to wait two centuries before all the consequences of a decision are apparent?'[46]

The next chapter considers the element of inertia in resource allocation by examining the relation between structural or locational *change* and unit labour costs.

[46] C. Clark, 'Industrial Location and Economic Potential', *Lloyds Bank Review*, Oct 1966.

TABLE 2.A1 Standard industrial classification order numbers (1963)*

III	Food, drink and tobacco
IV	Chemicals and allied industries
V	Metal manufacture
VI	Engineering and electrical goods
VII	Shipbuilding and marine engineering
VIII	Vehicles
IX	Metal goods, n.e.s.
X	Textiles
XI	Leather, leather goods and fur
XII	Clothing and footwear
XIII	Bricks, pottery, glass and cement, etc.
XIV	Timber, furniture, etc.
XV	Paper, printing and publishing
XVI	Other manufacturing industries

* *Source:* Board of Trade, *Report on the Census of Production 1963* (London, HMSO, 1968), part 1, introductory notes.

TABLE 2.A2 Proportions of regional manufacturing employment by industry groups: 1958

Industry	*N*	*YH*	*EM*	*EA*	*SE*	*SW*	*WM*	*NW*	*W*	*S*	*NI*
III	7.2	8.6	7.2	22.3	9.7	15.1	6.0	8.9	6.3	12.4	14.8
IV	14.0	5.2	3.3	5.5	5.5	2.6	1.9	8.9	9.8	4.9	0.7
V	14.1	13.7	7.7	0.9	1.9	1.5	12.8	3.1	30.3	8.7	0.1
VI	22.6	17.0	19.1	30.7	29.0	20.2	22.8	19.4	13.3	20.1	11.7
VII	14.8	1.2	0.0	2.0	2.4	5.7	0.0	2.9	—	9.9	—
VIII	3.0	4.8	11.9	1.4	11.8	21.1	18.2	7.3	—	5.4	—
IX	2.4	7.1	2.8	1.4	5.0	2.3	16.9	3.9	8.0	3.6	0.8
X	3.8	23.3	20.3	2.8	1.6	4.2	3.3	22.3	6.1	14.1	30.6
XI	0.3	0.7	0.9	1.0	0.8	0.9	0.5	0.8	0.6	0.5	0.3
XII	6.6	6.9	14.7	11.7	7.2	6.8	1.9	7.4	4.3	4.1	14.1
XIII	3.9	3.6	3.3	3.9	3.2	2.6	7.6	3.5	4.2	3.0	2.3
XIV	2.6	2.6	2.7	5.6	5.1	4.2	1.9	2.1	2.6	3.1	2.2
XV	3.2	4.1	4.4	8.5	12.5	9.1	2.6	5.6	3.2	7.8	3.1
XVI	1.5	1.2	1.8	2.3	4.3	3.6	3.6	3.9	4.1	2.4	0.8
Total	100	100	100	100	100	100	100	100	100	100	100

Notes: Columns might not sum exactly to 100 due to rounding errors. (—) indicates data unavailable.

Source: Board of Trade, *Report on the Census of Production 1963* (London, HMSO, 1970), pp. 133–8, 133–5.

TABLE 2.A3 Proportions of regional manufacturing employment by industry groups: 1963

Industry	*N*	*YH*	*EM*	*EA*	*SE*	*SW*	*WM*	*NW*	*W*	*S*	*NI*
III	7.5	9.4	7.1	21.4	8.8	16.0	6.1	10.0	6.4	13.4	16.6
IV	14.3	5.2	3.6	4.5	5.7	2.2	1.7	8.5	8.0	4.9	1.4
V	13.0	13.6	7.5	0.7	2.2	1.5	12.7	2.9	30.6	7.4	0.2
VI	24.6	17.9	21.4	30.1	30.9	22.4	21.2	16.1	22.6	14.8	22.3
VII	10.1	0.9	0.1	1.7	2.0	5.2	0.2	2.3	—	6.8	—
VIII	2.4	4.6	8.8	7.8	10.9	18.2	18.1	9.2	—	5.2	—
IX	2.5	7.4	3.8	2.1	5.4	2.3	16.9	4.2	6.6	3.7	1.3
X	4.9	21.5	20.5	2.1	1.3	4.2	2.8	16.9	6.2	14.3	27.7
XI	0.4	0.7	0.8	0.7	0.8	0.9	0.5	0.7	0.5	0.5	0.4
XII	7.3	6.4	13.1	8.7	6.2	5.8	1.8	7.1	4.0	4.1	14.1
XIII	3.8	3.6	3.4	4.2	3.1	3.1	7.0	3.6	3.7	3.0	2.9
XIV	2.9	3.0	2.6	4.3	5.0	4.1	1.8	2.3	2.3	3.1	2.6
XV	3.6	4.3	4.4	8.7	12.6	9.5	2.7	6.6	3.6	8.6	3.7
XVI	2.9	1.5	2.8	2.8	4.9	4.5	4.1	4.4	4.7	2.5	1.2
Total	100	100	100	100	100	100	100	100	100	100	100

Notes: Due to rounding errors some columns may not sum exactly 100.

Source: Board of Trade, op. cit.

TABLE 2.A4 Proportions of industry work force, by region: 1958

Industry	*N*	*YH*	*EM*	*EA*	*SE*	*SW*	*WM*	*NW*	*W*	*S*	*NI*	*Total*
III	4.1	9.7	5.3	3.9	28.1	7.0	8.8	15.8	2.3	11.5	3.5	100
IV	12.9	9.6	4.0	1.6	26.2	1.9	4.6	25.8	5.7	7.4	0.3	100
V	10.1	19.7	7.2	0.2	6.9	0.9	23.8	7.0	13.9	10.3	0.0	100
VI	5.3	8.0	5.9	2.3	35.2	3.9	13.9	14.5	2.0	7.8	1.2	100
VII	22.0	3.6	0.1	0.9	18.5	7.0	0.2	13.6	—	24.4	—	100
VIII	1.6	5.0	8.1	0.2	31.6	9.1	24.6	12.0	—	4.6	—	100
IX	2.1	12.3	3.1	0.4	22.1	1.6	37.8	10.8	4.4	5.1	0.3	100
X	1.8	22.4	12.7	0.4	3.8	1.7	4.1	33.8	1.9	11.2	6.2	100
XI	2.4	10.5	8.5	2.4	31.8	5.5	10.1	18.2	2.9	6.6	1.1	100
XII	5.1	10.6	14.9	2.8	28.5	4.3	3.7	18.0	2.1	5.3	4.6	100
XIII	5.3	9.6	5.8	1.6	22.2	2.9	26.2	14.8	3.6	6.7	1.3	100
XIV	4.2	8.5	5.7	2.8	41.9	5.6	8.0	10.8	2.7	8.3	1.5	100
XV	2.4	6.2	4.3	2.0	48.6	5.7	5.1	13.5	1.5	9.7	1.0	100
XVI	2.4	4.0	3.8	1.2	36.5	4.9	15.3	20.5	4.3	6.5	0.5	100

Source: Board of Trade, op. cit.

TABLE 2.A5 Proportions of industry work force, by region: 1963

Industry	*N*	*YH*	*EM*	*EA*	*SE*	*SW*	*WM*	*NW*	*W*	*S*	*NI*	*Total*
III	3.9	10.2	5.2	4.4	25.9	7.4	9.0	16.7	2.4	11.3	3.7	100
IV	12.8	9.7	4.4	1.6	28.6	1.7	4.3	24.2	5.1	7.0	0.5	100
V	9.0	19.6	7.2	0.2	8.5	0.9	24.8	6.4	15.1	8.2	0.1	100
VI	5.1	7.7	6.1	2.4	35.8	4.1	13.7	14.0	2.4	7.5	1.3	100
VII	19.8	3.5	0.2	1.3	22.0	8.9	1.0	14.4	—	21.6	—	100
VIII	1.2	4.8	6.1	1.5	30.6	8.0	25.4	14.8	—	4.1	—	100
IX	1.9	12.0	4.1	0.6	23.4	1.6	37.1	10.5	3.7	4.6	0.4	100
X	2.5	23.4	14.9	0.4	3.9	1.9	4.2	28.3	2.3	12.1	6.1	100
XI	2.4	10.2	8.4	2.2	34.1	5.7	9.5	16.5	2.8	6.5	1.2	100
XII	5.8	10.7	14.5	2.7	27.7	4.0	4.1	18.1	2.3	5.3	4.8	100
XIII	4.9	9.6	6.1	2.1	22.6	3.5	25.4	14.7	3.4	6.2	1.6	100
XIV	4.3	9.3	5.5	2.5	42.3	5.5	7.7	11.2	2.5	7.4	1.7	100
XV	2.5	6.1	4.2	2.3	47.8	5.7	5.1	14.3	1.7	9.4	1.1	100
XVI	3.8	4.0	5.2	1.4	36.3	5.2	15.2	18.6	4.4	5.3	0.7	100

Source: Board of Trade, op. cit.

TABLE 2.A6 Proportions of total United Kingdom manufacturing employment within each region: 1958 and 1963

Region	*1958*	*1963*
N	5.3	5.0
YH	10.5	10.3
EM	6.9	6.9
EA	1.6	1.9
SE	27.0	27.9
SW	4.3	4.4
WM	13.6	14.0
NW	16.6	15.9
W	3.3	3.5
S	8.7	8.0
NI	2.2	2.1
UK	100.0	100.0

Source: Board of Trade, op. cit., Table 21.

TABLE 2.A7 Proportions of total United Kingdom manufacturing employment within each industry: 1958 and 1963

Industry	*1958*	*1963*
III	9.5	9.3
IV	5.6	5.7
V	7.2	7.3
VI	24.1	22.3
VII	2.6	3.5
VIII	10.0	10.1
IX	6.4	6.1
X	9.5	10.9
XI	0.7	0.7
XII	6.2	6.8
XIII	3.9	3.9
XIV	3.3	3.3
XV	7.3	7.0
XVI	3.8	3.2
UK	100.0	100.0

Source: Board of Trade, op. cit.

TABLE 2.A8 Employment location quotients:* 1958

Industry	*N*	*YH*	*EM*	*EA*	*SE*	*SW*	*WM*	*NW*	*W*	*S*	*NI*
III	76	91	76	235	102	159	63	94	66	131	156
IV	250	93	59	98	98	46	34	159	175	88	13
V	196	190	107	13	26	21	178	43	421	121	1
VI	94	71	79	127	120	84	95	80	55	83	49
VII	569	46	0	76	92	219	0	112	—	380	—
VIII	30	48	119	14	118	211	182	73	—	54	—
IX	38	111	44	22	78	36	264	61	125	56	13
X	40	245	213	29	17	44	35	235	64	148	322
XI	43	100	129	143	114	128	71	114	86	71	43
XII	106	111	237	189	116	110	31	119	69	66	227
XIII	100	92	85	100	82	67	195	90	108	77	59
XIV	79	79	82	170	154	127	58	64	79	94	67
XV	44	56	60	116	171	125	36	77	44	107	42
XVI	39	32	47	61	113	95	95	103	108	63	21

* $ELQ_{ir} = \left[\frac{L_{ir}}{L_r} \Big/ \frac{L_i}{L}\right] 100$

Source: Calculated from data presented in tables 2.A2–2.A7.

TABLE 2.A9 Employment location quotients:* 1963

Industry	*N*	*YH*	*EM*	*EA*	*SE*	*SW*	*WM*	*NW*	*W*	*S*	*NI*
III	78	99	75	232	93	168	64	105	69	141	176
IV	256	94	64	84	103	39	31	152	146	88	24
V	180	190	104	11	30	20	177	40	431	103	5
VI	102	75	88	126	128	93	98	88	69	94	62
VII	396	34	3	68	79	202	7	91	—	270	—
VIII	24	47	88	79	110	182	181	93	—	51	—
IX	38	117	59	32	84	36	265	66	106	58	19
X	50	227	215	21	14	43	30	170	66	151	290
XI	58	99	121	116	122	130	68	104	80	81	57
XII	116	104	210	142	99	91	29	114	66	66	229
XIII	98	93	88	111	81	80	181	92	97	78	76
XIV	86	90	80	132	152	125	55	70	71	93	81
XV	50	59	61	121	171	129	36	90	49	118	52
XVI	76	38	75	74	130	118	109	117	126	66	33

* $ELQ_{ir} = \left[\frac{L_{ir}}{L_r} \Big/ \frac{L_i}{L}\right] 100$

Source: Calculated from data presented in tables 2.A2–2.A7.

TABLE 2.A10 Indices of comparative net output per employee: 1958*

Industry	*N*	*YH*	*EM*	*EA*	*SE*	*SW*	*WM*	*NW*	*W*	*S*	*NI*
III	84	83	110	84	106	116	98	101	83	105	88
IV	114	91	78	83	105	80	81	106	86	92	80
V	102	98	101	62	102	73	91	93	129	93	41
VI	104	100	99	100	100	95	95	102	100	103	77
VII	113	102	162	112	96	89	98	109	—	95	—
VIII	65	95	90	317	109	93	107	86	—	87	—
IX	95	95	112	138	116	89	92	99	96	102	91
X	105	111	107	93	119	135	114	88	211	94	69
XI	96	94	120	78	105	113	75	96	110	101	84
XII	91	88	108	100	119	98	102	90	88	88	72
XIII	95	111	102	107	119	90	74	115	100	101	86
XIV	92	88	89	94	113	88	95	92	75	88	94
XV	89	87	81	89	110	93	86	93	93	88	75
XVI	85	83	107	67	96	142	102	103	102	93	58

* Element $= \left[\frac{NO_{ir}}{L_{ir}} \Big/ \frac{NO_i}{L_i}\right] 100$

where NO = net output
L = employment

Source: Board of Trade, op. cit., pp. 133–8, 133–5.

TABLE 2.A11 Indices of comparative net output per employee: 1963*

Industry	*N*	*YH*	*EM*	*EA*	*SE*	*SW*	*WM*	*NW*	*W*	*S*	*NI*
III	85	87	107	98	101	107	96	101	92	113	97
IV	112	82	75	112	105	83	78	107	82	99	122
V	91	95	106	92	100	88	97	92	118	97	92
VI	92	95	107	84	105	98	96	92	113	99	92
VII	99	95	126	87	107	100	164	111	—	91	—
VIII	69	82	69	110	118	97	101	89	—	96	—
IX	93	97	107	120	111	102	95	94	96	98	86
X	175	104	97	103	115	157	117	83	201	92	77
XI	91	109	111	91	107	125	71	93	103	91	65
XII	101	88	107	92	112	122	94	94	91	90	71
XIII	99	104	105	109	119	90	76	112	100	100	93
XIV	95	93	95	96	110	87	93	94	86	90	89
XV	85	84	82	93	112	88	83	94	107	87	73
XVI	95	88	90	86	98	120	109	101	99	98	58

* Element = $\left[\frac{NO_{ir}}{L_{ir}} \Big/ \frac{NO_i}{L_i}\right] 100$

Source: Board of Trade, op. cit., pp. 133–8, 133–5.

TABLE 2.A12 Indices of comparative unit labour cost: 1958*

Industry	*N*	*YH*	*EM*	*EA*	*SE*	*SW*	*WM*	*NW*	*W*	*S*	*NI*
III	105	110	93	120	103	90	105	98	110	90	103
IV	95	103	110	115	93	118	118	98	120	105	78
V	100	104	98	80	102	138	107	102	89	100	182
VI	98	97	100	93	100	98	105	97	92	97	111
VII	90	100	65	84	106	106	97	94	—	103	—
VIII	134	93	108	54	98	103	97	106	—	106	—
IX	102	102	117	83	91	107	103	102	103	97	78
X	90	95	98	103	93	103	102	111	64	98	108
XI	109	105	89	138	100	92	100	98	89	97	117
XII	102	105	102	109	95	103	89	103	108	109	105
XIII	110	95	97	114	95	110	112	93	100	97	88
XIV	100	105	105	97	100	103	98	102	117	103	71
XV	93	100	97	98	100	102	102	103	93	102	91
XVI	93	108	86	95	102	75	105	100	92	107	97

* Element = $\left[\frac{W_{ir}}{NO_{ir}} \Big/ \frac{W_i}{NO_i}\right] 100$

where W = wage and salary bill.

Source: Board of Trade, op. cit., pp. 133–8, 133–5.

TABLE 2.A13 Indices of comparative unit labour cost: 1963*

Industry	*N*	*YH*	*EM*	*EA*	*SE*	*SW*	*WM*	*NW*	*W*	*S*	*NI*
III	108	105	92	103	108	97	103	95	100	82	95
IV	97	114	111	94	94	117	126	97	129	100	86
V	102	104	95	98	104	114	102	104	96	93	88
VI	109	100	95	107	96	98	105	109	84	104	93
VII	99	103	68	103	97	99	79	93	—	105	—
VIII	127	107	127	76	92	103	103	105	—	95	—
IX	102	102	94	85	96	94	104	106	104	100	96
X	64	100	102	94	96	72	98	117	68	98	104
XI	111	98	102	93	94	91	111	107	98	106	148
XII	93	107	105	108	97	90	97	102	90	102	107
XIII	102	100	96	106	94	107	111	98	100	100	96
XIV	102	100	98	100	98	107	98	98	105	102	97
XV	102	104	100	104	98	106	106	104	85	102	102
XVI	90	98	106	96	98	88	100	104	94	106	121

* Element $= \left[\dfrac{W_{ir}}{NO_{ir}} \Big/ \dfrac{W_i}{NO_i}\right]100$

Source: Board of Trade, op. cit., pp. 133–8, 133–5.

3 Relative Costs as a Determinant of Changes in the Pattern of Regional Specialisation and Industrial Location

The evidence in the last chapter referred to the existing pattern of specialisation and location at a point in time, reflecting decisions made in past periods in the light of prices, factor availabilities and technology then ruling or expected to rule. In contrast, the determinants of resource allocation and the decision rules or economic models which explain allocation refer to a 'planning function' (or 'book of blueprints') which contain only the 'best practice' decisions in each *current* period.[1] In examining the spatial structure of industry at a point in time we are really contemplating the fossilised history of the regions. There is a clear analogy here between models of locational structure and change and the vintage approach to the study of economic growth. The view embodied in vintage models is well illustrated by a quotation from Salter, one of the pioneers of the vintage approach to economic growth: 'An economy in the process of growth is, so to speak, sandwiched between its past history and its expected future. From the past it has inherited a capital stock, the physical form of which reflects past investment and technique decisions. From the future, expectations are thrown back about new techniques, variations in factor prices and new demand conditions. And in the present itself, new technical knowledge, new savings and perhaps new labour, are

[1] J. A. S. Schumpeter, *History of Economic Analysis* (George Allen & Unwin, 1954).

available to be incorporated into the economy.'[2]

Leaving aside the question of static efficiency at any point in time, it seems reasonable that any test of the relationship between relative costs and resource allocation should refer to current allocative decisions rather than to the total existing resource mix.[3] In an attempt to remove the influence of history we investigate in this chapter the relationship between current labour costs and the pattern of resource *reallocation* (including the assignment of new resources). We shall accept the hypothesis that relative price differences are reflected in differences in unit labour costs, and examine whether any association can be found between various measures of changes in the pattern of regional specialisation and industrial location and the observed pattern of unit labour costs over the period 1958 to 1963.

Any study of these relationships cannot neglect the role of expectations and time lags in decision making. To the extent that allocation decisions reflect relative prices and costs they are likely to be based on *expected* economic conditions as much as on existing or past economic conditions. But expected economic conditions cannot be observed. One solution to this problem would be to accept an extrapolative expectations model in which recent experience is assumed to be the dominant factor in shaping future expectations. If this procedure was acceptable it would then be valid to consider locational change as somehow related to economic conditions as they presented themselves in the base period. In this case, base period costs could be used as a proxy for expected cost relationships, and we could reasonably test for a relationship between structural change over the period 1958 and 1963 and cost conditions prevailing in 1958. Unfortunately, the existence of time lags between market signals, arriving at a decision and implementing it, make the use of this hypothesis

[2] W. E. G. Salter, 'Productivity Growth and Accumulation as Historical Processes', in E. A. G. Robinson (ed.), *Problems in Economic Development* (Macmillan, 1965).

[3] V. R. Fuchs, 'Statistical Explanations of the Relative Shift of Manufacturing Among Regions of the United States', *Regional Science Association Papers and Proceedings*, vol. XIII, 1962.

unacceptable. What evidence we have suggests that allocation changes in any period are probably related to economic conditions experienced at least three to four years prior to the observed structural change.[4] Since the data on structural change at our disposal relates to 1958 to 1963, this would mean that the relevant economic conditions to consider would be those prevailing in 1954 to 1959. Unfortunately the earliest cost data available to us refers to the year 1958. The only reasonable alternative is to assume that current cost conditions in 1958 and 1963 accurately reflect the conditions that were expected to prevail in those years. In other words, we reverse the expectations hypothesis and assume that expectations, as represented by cost conditions prevailing after the decision is made, are fulfilled. An additional problem which should be mentioned is that the relevant costs to be considered are those costs facing new firms rather than the average cost conditions of established firms. However, it will be assumed that the existing cost ratios for all established firms within an industry adequately reflect the cost ratios of marginal plants. For this assumption to be acceptable it is not necessary to assume that 'marginal' plants possess cost curves which are identical to established plants within each industry and region, but only that the difference between the two is in the same proportion between industries and regions such that the relative rankings of cost ratios are preserved.

Bearing in mind the data limitations and the assumptions outlined above, we examine the relation between resource reallocation and both comparative and absolute costs, which reflect different assumptions as to the specificity of resources. Assumptions about the nature of resource mobility are likely to be fairly crucial in considering structural change. Considerable attention will be devoted to alternative measures of regional structural change.

[4] Data on industrial movement, and on building approvals and completions, suggests that the decision-implementation lag alone is some two years. On industrial movement see, Board of Trade, *The Movement of Manufacturing Industry in the United Kingdom 1945–1965*, HMSO, 1968; on industrial building area approved and completed see, *Monthly Digest of Statistics*, HMSO.

TABLE 3.1 Rank correlation coefficients between changes in location quotients within each region and comparative unit labour costs, 1958–63

Region	*1958*	*1963*
N	+0.193	+0.315
YH	−0.470*	+0.183
EM	+0.075	+0.250
EA	+0.492*	+0.198
SE	+0.040	+0.155
SW	+0.440	+0.138
WM	+0.077	+0.243
NW	−0.150	−0.065
W	+0.549*	+0.718*
S	+0.501*	−0.192
NI	+0.227	+0.102

* Indicates that coefficient is statistically significant at the 95 per cent confidence level.

SPECIALISATION CHANGE AND COMPARATIVE UNIT LABOUR COSTS

In this section the hypothesis is examined that resources were reallocated within each region over the period 1958 to 1963 in the light of comparative unit labour costs prevailing, or expected to prevail, at the beginning and end of the period.[5] In other words, we initially assume that resources are regional specific.

The static analysis of the previous chapter measured specialisation using the employment location quotient (ELQ_{ir}). In the first instance it would seem natural to measure changes in specialisation by the absolute change in the location quotient between the beginning and end of the period. If the extent and direction of reallocation within each region is based on the pattern of comparative unit labour costs (as a proxy for relative prices), and the pattern of reallocation is adequately measured by the ordering of changes in the ELQs, we should expect to find a positive rank correlation between the ordering of com-

[5] An alternative procedure would be to relate changes in specialisation to *changes* in comparative labour costs over the period. The existence of time lags makes this impracticable.

parative unit labour costs in the industries of each region (ranked from lowest to highest), and the ordering of changes in the location quotient (ranked from highest to lowest). The coefficients of rank correlation between these two measures are shown in table 3.1. In general, the results are not inconsistent with the hypothesis. Eighteen out of the twenty-two coefficients (eleven for each year) are positive, although only four are statistically significant at the 95 per cent confidence level.

The absolute change in the location quotient, however, is probably not the best measure of specialisation change to take. It suffers from the defect that the change may simply be due to a change in the base ratio, that is in the proportion of the national workforce employed within the region. This can be demonstrated by totally differentiating the ELQ as defined in equation (2.5), and holding L_{ir} and L_i constant, which yields approximately:[6]

$$\mathrm{dELQ}_{ir} = \mathrm{d}L\left(\frac{L_{ir}}{L_i}\cdot\frac{1}{L_r}\right) - \mathrm{d}L_r\left(\frac{L_{ir}}{L_i}\cdot\frac{L}{L_r^2}\right)$$

$$= \left(\frac{\mathrm{d}L}{L} - \frac{\mathrm{d}L_r}{L_r}\right)\frac{L}{L_r}\frac{L_{ir}}{L_i} \qquad (3.1)$$

It is clear from equation (3.1) that it is possible for the measure of specialisation to change simply because of a change in L_r/L. Furthermore the effect of this variation will differ between the industries within the region. Although the bracketed term of equation (3.1) will be the same for all industries in a given region, the term outside the brackets will not be the same for each industry. It follows that the rankings of specialisation, and specialisation change, as measured by first differences in the ELQ, will not be invariant with respect to changes in the ratio of regional to national employment – the degree of sensitivity depending on the proportion of each industry's employment to be found in the region. This difficulty may be overcome by using proportionate changes in the location quotient as the measure of specialisation change which leaves

[6] Here, as elsewhere in the work, second order terms will be omitted.

TABLE 3.2 Rank correlation coefficients between percentage changes in location quotients within each region and comparative unit labour costs, 1958–63

Region	*1958*	*1963*
N	+0.318	+0.498*
YH	−0.341	+0.150
EM	+0.257	+0.269
EA	+0.530*	+0.178
SE	+0.085	+0.304
SW	+0.210	+0.320
WM	+0.506*	+0.713*
NW	+0.066	+0.489*
W	+0.432	+0.967*
S	+0.345	+0.325
NI	+0.110	+0.239

* Indicates coefficient is significant at the 95 per cent confidence level.
† Indicates significance at the 99 per cent confidence level.

the rankings of change unaltered by a change in the base ratio.[7]

A more acceptable test of a relationship between specialisation change and comparative labour costs would appear to be to take percentage changes in the ELQs as the measure of reallocation. Rank correlation coefficients were therefore calculated between percentage changes in the industry location quotients within each region (ranked from highest to lowest) and comparative unit labour costs (ranked from lowest to highest). These coefficients are reported in table 3.2. The evidence in table 3.2 is even more favourable to the hypothesis being tested than the evidence in table 3.1. With the exception of the coefficient for Yorkshire and Humberside in 1958, all the rank correlations are positive, and six of the coefficients are statistically significant.

It may reasonably be concluded that there is some evidence

[7] This is presumably what Moroney and Walker were referring to when they say '... the rankings [of ELQs] and the rankings of *percentage* changes are ... not affected by the change in base', op.cit. p. 583n.

of a fairly close relationship between changes in the pattern of regional specialisation and regional comparative advantage as measured by comparative unit labour costs.

The proportionate rate of change in the ELQ is given by:

$$\frac{\mathrm{d}(\mathrm{ELQ}_{ir})}{\mathrm{ELQ}_{ir}} = \frac{\mathrm{d}L_{ir}}{L_{ir}} - \frac{\mathrm{d}L_i}{L_i} + \frac{\mathrm{d}L}{L} - \frac{\mathrm{d}L_r}{L_r} \tag{3.2}$$

It is clear that inter-industry variations in this measure of structural change within a region arise not because of differences in the rate of growth of the region compared to the nation but because of differences in the relative rates of expansion of an industry in the region compared to the expansion of the industry as a whole. In short, ranking the industries in each region according to the magnitude of the proportionate change in the location quotient is equivalent to ranking industries according to the magnitude of the term $((\mathrm{d}L_{ir}/L_{ir}) - (\mathrm{d}L_i/L_i))$ in equation (3.2). The fairly close association (reported earlier) between the proportionate change in location quotients and comparative unit labour costs may therefore have its origin either in a close relationship between comparative costs and the rates of growth of individual industries in the region $(\mathrm{d}L_{ir}/L_{ir})$, or in a close relation between *relative* rates of growth $((\mathrm{d}L_{ir}/L_{ir}) - (\mathrm{d}L_i/L_i))$ and comparative unit labour costs. The rank correlations reported in table 3.2 measure the latter relation. To measure the former relation, rank correlation coefficients were computed relating the ordering of rates of growth of employment within each industry in the region and comparative unit labour costs (see table 3.3). Many of the coefficients are found to be smaller in magnitude than the coefficient estimates in table 3.2. A comparison of the results indicates that the association between comparative advantage and structural change is not simply a reflection of different rates of industrial expansion within the region but also a reflection of different *relative* rates of expansion of industries within the region compared with the industry as a whole. In other words, the structural change which has taken place has not only taken the form of *intra-regional* differences in growth rates, but also reflects *intra-industry* (inter-regional) differences in growth rates. The

TABLE 3.3 Rank correlation coefficients between the rates of growth of industry employment within each region[1] and comparative unit labour costs[2]: 1958–63

Region	*1958*	*1963*
N	+0.275	+0.270
YH	−0.410	+0.392
EM	−0.100	+0.112
EA	+0.569*	+0.214
SE	+0.100	−0.032
SW	+0.361	+0.111
WM	+0.140	+0.325
NW	−0.106	+0.025
W	+0.511*	+0.818†
S	+0.417	−0.208
NI	+0.283	+0.472

[1] Ranked from highest to lowest.
[2] Ranked from lowest to highest.
* Indicates coefficient is significant at the 95 per cent confidence level.
† Indicates significance at the 99 per cent confidence level.

finding that not only rates of industrial growth within regions are associated with the pattern of comparative unit labour costs, but also differential rates of regional growth in the same industry, is favourable to the hypothesis under study.

The difference between the rate of growth of an industry in a region and the total growth of the industry $((dL_{ir}/L_{ir}) - dL_i/L_i))$, however, is not a very adequate measure of structural change, in the sense that two industries within a region may have the same growth rate yet because of differences in their absolute size they make vastly different claims on resources within the region. The larger the proportion of the regional workforce in any industry, the greater will be the reallocation of regional manpower resources to that industry for any given rate of growth. This leads to a consideration of structural change as measured by relative rates of growth weighted by the proportion of regional employment engaged in the industry concerned in the base year. The weighted relative rate of growth for any industry in any region (WRG_{ir}) is thus defined as:

$$\text{WRG}_{ir} = \frac{L_{ir}}{L_r}\left(\frac{\text{d}L_{ir}}{L_{ir}} - \frac{\text{d}L_i}{L_i}\right) \tag{3.3}$$

This measure is one measure of the growth component used in shift-share analysis of interregional differences – what we called the effect of 'within' industry (or regional specific) differences in chapter 1 (see pp. 9–11 and equation (1.2) in particular).[8]

As far as differences in regional employment growth are concerned, shift-share models adopt as their starting point a definitional relationship involving three terms: the national rate of employment growth, the rate of growth in an industry within the region, and the rate of growth of the industry in all regions taken together. We have:

$$\frac{\text{d}L_{ir}}{L_{ir}} = \frac{\text{d}L_{ir}}{L_{ir}} + \frac{\text{d}L}{L} - \frac{\text{d}L}{L} + \frac{\text{d}L_i}{L_i} - \frac{\text{d}L_i}{L_i},$$

which, rearranging, gives:

$$\frac{\text{d}L_{ir}}{L_{ir}} - \frac{\text{d}L}{L} = \left(\frac{\text{d}L_i}{L_i} - \frac{\text{d}L}{L}\right) + \left(\frac{\text{d}L_{ir}}{L_{ir}} - \frac{\text{d}L_i}{L_i}\right) \tag{3.4}$$

The last term on the R.H.S. of equation (3.4) is the unweighted relative growth term referred to earlier. Multiplying each side by the proportion of employment in a region engaged in each industry, *i*, and summing over industries gives:

$$\frac{\text{d}L_r}{L_r} - \frac{\text{d}L}{L} = \sum_i \frac{\text{d}L_i}{L_i}\left(\frac{L_{ir}}{L_r} - \frac{L_i}{L}\right) + \sum_i \frac{L_{ir}}{L_r}\left(\frac{\text{d}L_{ir}}{L_{ir}} - \frac{\text{d}L_i}{L_i}\right) \tag{3.5}$$

The L.H.S. measures the difference between the regional and national growth rates of employment, and represents (in terms of growth) the 'total shift'. The first term on the R.H.S. is a measure of the influence of differential structure and is variously called the 'mix', 'composition' or 'structural' effect. The second term on the R.H.S. represents the effect of

[8] For the methodology of shift-share analysis see H. S. Perloff, E. S. Dunn, E. E. Lampart and R. F. Muth, *Regions, Resources and Economic Growth* (Johns Hopkins Press, 1960); and A. P. Thirlwall, 'A Measure of the Proper Distribution of Industry', *Oxford Economic Papers*, Mar 1967. See also our more extensive discussion in chapter 8.

differential growth in the same industry, and is variously called the 'rate', 'growth' or 'competitiveness' effect.[9] Regional employment may grow rapidly relative to employment in the nation as a result of two forces. Firstly it may specialise in industries which are expanding rapidly in the nation as a whole. Secondly the region's share of individual industries may increase because employment growth in the industry in the region is faster than the growth of the industry as a whole (i.e. $(\mathrm{d}L_{ir}/L_{ir}) > (\mathrm{d}L_i/L_i)$). It is this latter effect which is of particular interest at this point because it is this 'growth' or 'competitiveness' effect which is identical to the sum of the 'weighted relative rate of growth' terms for the region (equation (3.3) above).

Perloff and others claim that: 'The differential [i.e. 'growth'] effect arises out of the fact that some regions gain over time a differential advantage (*vis-à-vis* other regions) in their access to important markets and inputs for each of one or more specific activities.'[10] Later they explain that '... when we speak of access ... we refer ... to all the cost elements inherent in the production of the commodity'.[11] Other authors[12] also indicate that the 'growth' effect is a reflection of the locational advantage of the region. Given the association of the 'growth' effect with competitiveness and locational advantage, it is of some interest to test the hypothesis of whether, in fact, the 'growth' effect in shift-share analysis does reflect competitiveness, and as such may be interpreted as an indicator of regional advantage in a cost sense. To the extent that the 'growth' effect

[9] It should be emphasised that the components of differential growth in equation (3.5) represent only one of a number of possible methods of decomposition, as should have been clear from equations (1.1) to (1.5) in chapter 1. The discussion to follow, however, provides some grounds for regarding the 'growth' or 'competitiveness' component in equation (3.5) as having some basis in theory. The measurement of the 'structural' effect and the possibility of interaction between 'structural' and 'growth' effects, whilst important in another context, is irrelevant for the present discussion. See chapter 8 for a fuller discussion of these measurement problems.

[10] H. S. Perloff, *et alia*, op.cit., p. 74.

[11] Ibid., p. 87.

[12] e.g. G. McCrone, *Regional Policy in Britain* (George Allen & Unwin, 1969), chapter 7.

TABLE 3.4 Rank correlation coefficients between weighted relative rate of growth terms and comparative unit labour costs, 1958–63

Region	*1958*	*1963*
N	+0.240	+0.543*
YH	−0.446	+0.050
EM	−0.057	+0.142
EA	+0.190	+0.077
SE	+0.217	+0.280
SW	+0.424	+0.196
WM	+0.359	+0.340
NW	−0.012	+0.500*
W	+0.565*	+0.669*
S	+0.118	+0.240
NI	+0.235	+0.383

* Indicates coefficient is significant at the 95 per cent confidence level.

for each industry reflects comparative advantage, we should expect to find a positive correlation between the weighted relative rate of growth term (equation 3.3) for each industry in the region (ranked from highest to lowest) and comparative unit labour costs (ranked from lowest to highest). The rank correlations for each region are reported in table 3.4.

The preponderance of positive coefficients suggests that the 'growth' effect, and thus resource reallocation, may reflect the pattern of regional comparative advantage, and that the differential growth component in shift-share analysis may reflect the operation of what may loosely be termed 'competitiveness factors'. Given the exclusion of variables such as transport costs, and the coarseness of the industrial classification, the results may be considered to be consistent with the hypothesis under study.

LOCATIONAL CHANGE AND ABSOLUTE UNIT LABOUR COSTS

The above analysis has been concerned with changes in the pattern of regional specialisation on the assumption that resources are regional specific, so that measures of change were related to comparative costs. To the extent that resources are mobile at all, however, we would expect locational change *within any industry* to be related to *absolute* unit labour cost differences between regions. In this section on locational change, therefore, we examine the relation between measures of locational change within an industry and the regional pattern of unit labour costs prevailing in that industry in both 1958 and 1963.

The most obvious measure of locational change to take for comparison with the regional rankings of unit labour costs in that industry is the absolute first difference of the location quotient. It has already been demonstrated in the previous section, however, that the absolute first difference is an inferior measure to the proportionate change in the location quotient. We shall therefore take this latter measure of locational change first.

As before, the proportionate change in the location quotient may be expressed as:

$$\frac{\mathrm{d}(\mathrm{ELQ}_{ir})}{\mathrm{ELQ}_{ir}} = \frac{\mathrm{d}L_{ir}}{L_{ir}} - \frac{\mathrm{d}L_r}{L_r} - \frac{\mathrm{d}L_i}{L_i} + \frac{\mathrm{d}L}{L} \qquad (3.6)$$

Ranking the percentage change of the location quotients *across* regions *within* an industry is equivalent to ranking the *differential* rates of growth of the industry in each individual region (i.e. the industry growth in the region compared with the rate of growth of all industries in the region), since the last two terms on the R.H.S. of equation (3.6) will be constant for any industry group. It follows that in examining the relationship between the proportionate change in the location quotients and absolute unit labour costs, a relationship is being sought between the performance of an industry in a region relative to all industries and the costs of industry locating in that region.

Assuming that the proportionate change in the location quotient is an adequate measure of locational change, and that these changes are related to the pattern of unit labour costs, we should expect to find a positive correlation between the rate of growth of location quotients (ranked from highest to lowest) and absolute unit labour costs (ranked from lowest to highest). The results are given in table 3.5. Twenty-one of the

TABLE 3.5 Rank correlation coefficients between proportionate changes in location quotients and unit labour costs for each industry, 1958 and 1963

Industry	*1958*	*1963*
III	+0.205	+0.275
IV	+0.752†	+0.580*
V	−0.613*	−0.127
VI	−0.140	+0.185
VII	+0.072	+0.466
VIII	+0.625*	+0.467
IX	+0.506	+0.520
X	+0.650*	+0.438
XI	−0.222	−0.417
XII	+0.072	+0.140
XIII	+0.260	+0.215
XIV	+0.223	+0.338
XV	+0.180	−0.040
XVI	+0.564*	+0.172

* Indicates coefficient is statistically significant at the 95 per cent confidence level.
† Indicates significance at the 99 per cent confidence level.

28 coefficients are positive and six of them are significant at the 95 per cent confidence level.

If a region is a low cost location for one industry, it may be a low cost location for all industries in which case there would be no tendency for any one industry to grow faster than all others. In other words, there may be a closer association between the regional rankings of unit labour costs and dL_{ir}/L_{ir}, than between unit labour costs and $(dL_{ir}/L_{ir}) - (dL_r/L_r)$. This turns out to be the case. In sixteen out of the twenty-eight cases there is a higher degree of association between the regional growth rates in an individual industry and absolute unit labour costs between regions in that industry, than between the differential growth between the industry in the region and all industries and the regional rankings of absolute unit labour costs in the industry.

Ordering the growth of employment in an industry across regions (i.e. ordering the dL_{ir}/L_{ir}'s within an industry) is equivalent to ranking regions by their performance relative to the national growth of the industry. That is, it is equivalent to ranking regions according to the magnitude of $[(dL_{ir}/L_{ir}) - (dL_i/L_i)]$ which, as we saw in the previous section, is closely related to regional comparative advantage. The results of this section, therefore, are consistent with the hypothesis that resource reallocation was primarily regional in character and related to comparative advantage as measured by comparative unit labour costs.[13]

MOVEMENT PATTERNS AND UNIT LABOUR COSTS

If a manufacturer decides to locate in one region rather than another, the basis for decision-making seems relatively clear. To the extent that location decisions reflect cost considerations, it is absolute costs not comparative costs that matter to the firm. An analysis of the relationship between industrial movement and labour costs, therefore, should enable more precise conclusions to be drawn about the importance of unit labour costs as a factor affecting location decisions, and also of the implications for economic efficiency of diverting firms from central locations to sites in the peripheral regions.

As part of a Board of Trade research programme into the movement of manufacturing industry over the period 1945 to 1965,[14] data was collected (though not published) on the number of establishments, and the associated employment involved, which 'moved' from one area to another over the period. A 'move' is defined in the Report as '...the opening of new manufacturing establishments in new locations...in which the firm in question had not manufactured previously'.[15] The Department of Trade and Industry have

[13] Some evidence of the magnitude of *intra*-regional, as opposed to *inter*-regional, labour mobility may be found in A. J. Brown, *The Framework of Regional Economics in the United Kingdom* (Cambridge University Press, 1972), p. 218.

[14] See Board of Trade, *The Movement of Manufacturing Industry in the United Kingdom 1945–1965* (HMSO, 1968).

[15] Ibid., p. 3.

supplied data which provide a breakdown, by industry and region of destination, of the number of establishments[16] involved in moves over the period 1960 to 1965. The data are summarised in table 3.A1 of the appendix to the chapter. What we wish to examine here is whether there is any association between the regional pattern of 'destinations' within an industry and the ordering of regions by the magnitude of unit labour costs in existing establishments in that industry in 1958 and 1963.

The pattern of movement can be measured by the proportion of the total number of moves in each industry destined for each region (m_{ir}).

i.e. $$m_{ir} = \frac{M_{ir}}{M_i}$$

where M_{ir} is number of moves in industry (i) with destination in region r.

and M_i is total number of moves in industry i.

To the extent that this is an adequate measure of the pattern of movement within an industry we should expect to find a positive association between the m_{ir}'s ranked from highest to lowest across regions for each industry and the ordering of unit labour costs between regions ranked from lowest to highest. In fact, over one-half of the twenty-eight rank correlation coefficients (fourteen for each year) are negative. Clearly, there is no discernable relation between patterns of movement, as measured above, and absolute unit labour costs. Before reaching conclusions about the resource waste that this would seem to imply, however, two possible factors accounting for the results need to be considered. Firstly, it is possible that the quantity of moves is influenced by the size of regions. Secondly, the influence of the government's distribution of industry policy cannot be ignored. Attempts to standardise for the size of regions did not alter the results. Attempts to isolate the effects of government policy, by analysing movement within assisted regions only, did not alter the qualitative nature of the results either.

[16] Unfortunately, a sufficiently detailed breakdown of moves measured in terms of employment is not available.

We are left with the conclusion that the relative costs of alternative locations are not an important consideration in the location decision.[17] This conclusion is consistent with the findings of other research.[18] These findings on the movement of industry are not inconsistent with our earlier finding of a relation between changes in the pattern of localisation and unit labour costs because changes in localisation are determined not only by the movement of firms but also by the differential growth of industries within the regions.

The main policy implication from the analysis of this chapter and the previous one is that there would seem to be a great potential for productivity gain from intra-regional resource reallocation. This potential can only be realised by more flexible and imaginative policies on the part of government. There is no guarantee that private enterprise will seek out its least cost location.

In reaching any firm policy conclusions, however, the defects of the analysis must not be overlooked. Apart from limitations such as the level of aggregation, and the relatively short time period, both of which arise in the main from data deficiencies, the main reservations of the analysis are related to three important assumptions: (1) that relative prices and profitability are reflected in unit labour costs: (2) that observed unit costs adequately reflect expectations as to these costs; and (3) that average cost conditions of existing firms are those experienced by new entrants. Also, many relevant factors have been inadequately represented: demand conditions, transport costs, externalities and the location of other firms. Despite these defects, the methods of analysis we have used are of general applicability and warrant use in other contexts, and the conclusions we have drawn do not appear to be unreasonable in the sense that they are supported by other evidence using different research methods and data.

[17] The likely explanation for this is that relative unit labour costs are a poor proxy for relative profitability. But to say this is not very helpful without saying why.

[18] In particular that of: W. P. Luttrell, *Factory Movement and Industrial Location* (NIESR, 1962); G. C. Cameron and B. D. Clark, *Industrial Movement and the Regional Problem* (Oliver and Boyd, 1966); and B. J. Loasby, 'Making Location Policy Work', *Lloyds Bank Review*, Jan 1967.

TABLE 3.A1 Number of firms in each industry moving into the regions 1960–65* (i.e. no. of cases)

I \ R	*N*	*YH*	*EM*	*EA*	*SE*	*SW*	*WM*	*NW*	*W*	*S*	*NI*	*Total*
III	4	7	4	8	13	2	6	7	2	12	4	69
IV	4	2	2	8	30	3	5	11	6	7	3	81
V	2	2	2	1	3	2	5	7	0	6	0	30
VI	23	8	20	26	122	42	15	37	24	41	17	375
VII	0	0	0	0	2	1	0	0	0	0	0	3
VIII	7	0	4	6	16	3	2	6	5	12	2	63
IX	3	5	2	6	25	12	22	5	11	10	4	105
X	2	6	3	2	1	3	2	17	9	9	12	66
XI	1	0	1	2	4	2	0	3	0	0	0	14
XII	7	7	7	3	15	12	4	13	13	29	3	113
XIII	8	4	3	2	9	5	5	6	2	9	1	52
XIV	5	1	1	6	17	7	6	7	4	4	0	58
XV	7	3	2	5	21	5	3	10	5	3	1	65
XVI	8	3	1	10	22	2	6	16	5	8	4	85
Total	81	48	52	85	300	101	81	145	86	150	52	1181

* Enumerated by region of destination.

Source: Data supplied by the Department of Trade and Industry.

4 Types of Unemployment: Cyclical v. Non-cyclical Unemployment

TYPES OF UNEMPLOYMENT

At the macro level it is conventional to distinguish three main types of unemployment existing at any one time: frictional unemployment; structural unemployment, and demand-deficient unemployment which may include a cyclical and seasonal component. Frictional unemployment is associated, as its name suggests, with frictions in the labour market, including barriers to mobility and lack of information. Its essential characteristic is that in principle there are jobs available for the unemployed if the frictions can be overcome. Structural unemployment on the other hand is associated with a lack of matching between the location and characteristics of the unemployed and the location and characteristics of unsatisfied labour demand. Jobs are not available for the structurally unemployed unless they are willing to migrate considerable distances and/or retrain. Demand-deficient unemployment is associated with a general deficiency of demand for labour. Under the influence of classical economic thinking demand-deficient unemployment used to be thought of as primarily cyclical, but following Keynes, it is now recognised as something that may be more permanent. The distinction between cyclical and permanent demand-deficient unemployment should be made clear from the start. Cyclical unemployment is measured against the underlying trend level of unemployment, but the trend may contain within it unemployment which arises from the fact that the demand for labour is permanently depressed. Theoretically and empirically cyclical and total demand-deficient unemployment are different concepts. Cyclical unemployment will always be a minimum estimate of demand-deficient unemployment, and non-cyclical unemployment will always be a maximum estimate of non demand-deficient unemployment (comprising structural and frictional elements).

The purpose of the next two chapters is to analyse interregional differences in unemployment by measuring types of unemployment using a number of different procedures. In this chapter an attempt is made to distinguish cyclical from non-cyclical unemployment and also to analyse the sensitivity of regional unemployment to changes in national unemployment. In the following chapter we attempt to distinguish demand-deficient from non demand-deficient unemployment, and then to separate non demand-deficient unemployment into frictional unemployment on the one hand and structural unemployment on the other. Each of the different approaches is directed at the same question of whether interregional differences in the percentage level of unemployment are caused primarily by differences in demand pressure (cyclical and/or permanent) or primarily by differences in the level of structural and frictional unemployment. To anticipate the conclusions, we find that there are differences between regions in the extent of cyclical unemployment; in their sensitivity to national unemployment, and in the magnitude of structural and frictional unemployment, but the primary cause of interregional differences in the percentage level of unemployment is persistent differences in the demand for labour between regions. Of course, this conclusion provides no explanation of interregional unemployment rate differences in a causal sense, because what causes differences in demand pressure is not explained. In chapter 10, however, a model is developed which makes regional output growth, and *a fortiori* labour demand, a function of the rate of growth of exports. We believe the model to be generally applicable, but in particular to depressed regions where output growth is obviously not constrained by a lack of factor supplies. On the basis of the model, we would ascribe lack of labour demand and high levels of demand-deficient unemployment to the poor export performance of the regions concerned and to the consequent lack of induced demand in the form of investment and the demand for ancillary services.

To measure the average amount of non-cyclical unemployment a trend line is fitted to the unemployment data for each region, leaving cyclical unemployment as the residual difference between total unemployment and the measure of non-cyclical unemployment. An 'evaluation of inner products' (see chapter 1) can then be performed to see whether variation in the cyclical component of regional unemployment contributes more to the total variation in unemployment than variation in the non-cyclical component. To measure the unemployment sensitivity of regions we regress each region's rate of unemployment on the national rate of unemployment and use the deviations between the value of the regression coefficient and unity as a basis for measuring the contribution of a region's sensitivity to interregional differences in unemployment. It should be emphasised again that neither approach implies anything about the contribution of demand differences in the aggregate to the persistence of regional unemployment rate differences.

CYCLICAL V. NON-CYCLICAL UNEMPLOYMENT

Suppose for each of a set of regions we have a time series of unemployment which exhibits cycles. There is no reason to expect that either the floor of unemployment or the amplitude of the fluctuations will be the same in each region. On the contrary, if the unemployment rate differs between industries, and each region has a different industrial composition, the region's unemployment floor will tend to differ and so will its sensitivity to changes in business conditions in the country as a whole. Even if each region was a microcosm of the country as a whole, factors peculiar to the region may still cause the floor to differ and for the unemployment sensitivity of the same industry to differ between regions.

The time series graphs of unemployment in the various regions over the period 1951–72, and the minimum unemployment rates achieved, can be seen in figures 5.4 to 5.11 in the next chapter. It is clear from the graphs that the minimum unemployment rates achieved in some parts of the country – notably the South and Midlands – are much lower than in other parts, and that the variations in unemployment in relation to a time trend based on the first minimum unemployment rate also differ. Let us examine the extent of these differences.

To measure non-cyclical unemployment let total unemployment (U) equal the sum of cyclical unemployment (U_C) and non-cyclical unemployment (U_{NC}):

$$U = U_C + U_{NC} \tag{4.1}$$

Now let

$$U_{NC} = a_o + b_1 t \tag{4.2}$$

where a_o is the level of U_{NC} in time period O (calculated by extrapolation back from the first minimum unemployment rate), b_1 is the regression coefficient of U on t and t is a time trend, 1951 to 1972. Assuming that the measure of cyclical unemployment is linearly independent of time we can write:

$$U = U_C + a_o + b_1 t \tag{4.3}$$

The average non-cyclical component of total unemployment is measured as:

$$\bar{U}_{NC} = a_o + b_1 \bar{t} \tag{4.4}$$

where ($\bar{\ }$) denotes the average value of a variable.

The average cyclical component is measured as:

$$\bar{U}_C = \bar{U} - (a_o + b_1 \bar{t}) \tag{4.5}$$

The time trends on which the average measures of non-cyclical unemployment are based (using quarterly data 1951–72) are as follows (standard errors in brackets):

SE	: $U = 0.787 + \underset{(0.002)}{0.013t}$	: $r^2 = 0.344$
SW	: $U = 1.055 + \underset{(0.002)}{0.021t}$	: $r^2 = 0.506$
M	: $U = 0.412 + \underset{(0.003)}{0.028t}$	: $r^2 = 0.446$
NW	: $U = 1.586 + \underset{(0.004)}{0.018t}$	: $r^2 = 0.199$
N	: $U = 1.597 + \underset{(0.004)}{0.040t}$	: $r^2 = 0.498$
S	: $U = 2.564 + \underset{(0.004)}{0.022t}$	: $r^2 = 0.274$
W	: $U = 2.085 + \underset{(0.004)}{0.028t}$	: $r^2 = 0.424$
GB	: $U = 1.086 + \underset{(0.003)}{0.021t}$	: $r^2 = 0.446$

There has been a statistically significant increase in the percentage level of unemployment in all regions over time. In Great Britain as a whole the trend rate of increase has been 0.021 per quarter or nearly 0.1 percentage point per year over the period under review. The trend rate of increase has been highest in the northern region, Wales and Scotland.

Using these time trends, the calculations of the average level of cyclical and non-cyclical unemployment, as in equations (4.4) and (4.5), are shown in table 4.1.[1]

It is clear from table 4.1 that the predominant component of unemployment in all regions is unemployment which persists independently of fluctuations in the demand for labour. This is not to say, however, that demand is unimportant in determining the level of unemployment. In regions with high unemployment, the trend rate of unemployment almost certainly contains an element of permanent demand-deficient unemployment. In these regions, the percentage contribution of non-cyclical unemployment undoubtedly exaggerates the

[1] Note that the constant term, a_o, in equations (4.4) and (4.5) is not the constant term in the time trend equations. It is estimated by extrapolation.

TABLE 4.1 Average measures of cyclical and non-cyclical unemployment

				% contribution to $\bar{U}$ of:	
	$\bar{U}$	$\bar{U}_{NC}$	$\bar{U}_C$	$\bar{U}_{NC}$	$\bar{U}_C$
SE	1.34	0.91	0.43	68	32
SW	1.98	1.31	0.67	66	34
M	1.60	1.17	0.43	73	27
NW	2.34	1.74	0.60	74	26
N	3.41	2.36	1.05	70	30
S	3.62	2.62	1.00	73	27
W	3.38	2.17	1.21	64	36
GB	2.10	1.40	0.70	67	33

amount of unemployment not associated with the state of demand in the labour market. The contributions of non-cyclical unemployment to total unemployment in the South East and South West, however, are probably fairly reasonable estimates of the relative importance of demand-deficient and non demand-deficient unemployment. The figure of a 68 per cent contribution of non-cyclical unemployment to total unemployment in the South East is very close, as we shall see in chapter 5, to the estimated contribution of non demand-deficient unemployment to total unemployment using vacancy statistics to separate demand-deficient from non demand-deficient unemployment.

In terms of the cyclical–non-cyclical distinction, the major source of variation in unemployment rates between regions is variations in the degree of non-cyclical unemployment. An 'evaluation of inner products'[2] applied to table 4.1 shows that approximately 54 per cent of the total interregional variation in $\bar{U}$ can be explained in terms of variations in $\bar{U}_{NC}$, and only 6 per cent in terms of $\bar{U}_C$ – the interaction between $\bar{U}_{NC}$ and $\bar{U}_C$ accounting for 40 per cent. Without further evidence about the make-up of non-cyclical unemployment, however, it would be wrong to conclude that interregional variations in the pressure of demand are a minor source of interregional differences in unemployment rates.

[2] See chapter 1, p. 11.

THE SENSITIVITY OF REGIONAL TO NATIONAL UNEMPLOYMENT

The second approach mentioned above to the analysis of interregional unemployment rate differences is to regress each region's unemployment rate on the national rate of unemployment and to use the difference between the regression coefficient and unity as the basis for measuring the contribution of differential sensitivity to interregional differences. In contrast to the earlier approach, the sensitivity coefficient will pick up the influence of cycle and trend, which is important if it is believed that at least a part of a region's trend rate of unemployment is endogenous. The results of regressing regional unemployment on the national unemployment rate over the period 1951 to 1972, using the Cochrane Orcutt iterative technique to transform the data for strong serial correlation in the residuals, are shown in table 4.2.

TABLE 4.2 The sensitivity of regional unemployment

Region (*r*)	$U_r = a + b(U_{GB})$	r^2
SE	$U_{SE} = 0.250 + 0.535\,(U_{GB})$ (0.034)	0.932
SW	$U_{SW} = 1.236 + 0.602\,(U_{GB})$ (0.094)	0.697
M	$U_{M} = -0.262 + 1.013\,(U_{GB})$ (0.083)	0.893
NW	$U_{NW} = 0.302 + 1.030\,(U_{GB})$ (0.134)	0.766
N	$U_{N} = 0.599 + 1.413\,(U_{GB})$ (0.193)	0.749
S	$U_{S} = 1.374 + 1.096\,(U_{GB})$ (0.120)	0.823
W	$U_{W} = 0.537 + 1.389\,(U_{GB})$ (0.107)	0.903

In the South East and South West regions, the sensitivity coefficients are significantly less than unity, and in the North and Wales significantly greater than unity. In the Midlands, North West and Scotland, the coefficients do not differ significantly from unity at the 95 per cent confidence level. An 'evaluation of inner products' shows that differences in the sensitivity coefficient between regions contributes 57 per cent to the total interregional variation in unemployment rates. On this evidence it seems that the average unemployment experience of regions would be less disparate if the overall sensitivity of regions to unemployment was more equal. The results and conclusions of this section differ from those of the last because the measures of sensitivity here pick up the influence of divergent trends in unemployment between regions which are excluded from the earlier calculations.

BRECHLING'S MODEL

A similar model to the above has been developed and tested by Brechling for the period 1952 to 1963.[3] He distinguishes three components of regional unemployment: (1) an aggregative cyclical component; (2) a structural component, and (3) a cyclical component peculiar to the region (obtained as a residual). Brechling specifies his model as linear in logarithms, but he also tests an arithmetically linear version which enables our results to be compared. The aggregative cyclical component (A_{rt}) is defined as the cyclical sensitivity of regional unemployment to national unemployment, i.e. $A_{rt} = U_{Tt}^{\alpha_r}$, or in arithmetically linear form, $A_{rt} = a_r U_{Tt}$.[4] The parameter a_r is the same as our measure of the sensitivity of regional unemployment reported in table 4.2. The structural component (S_{rt}), which is peculiar to the region and depends on the structural characteristics of the region, is assumed to be the product of a constant and a quadratic time trend, which allows S_r to change through time, i.e. $S_{rt} = C_r e^{\beta_r t + \gamma_r t^2}$, or in arithmetically linear form, $S_{rt} = C_r' + b_r t + d_r t^2$, where C_r or C_r' is the level of structural unemployment at the beginning of the period. The regional cyclical component (R_{rt}) is obtained as a residual. Thus, the log-linear specification of the model is:

[3] F. Brechling, 'Trends and Cycles in British Regional Unemployment', *Oxford Economic Papers*, Mar 1967.

[4] Brechling allows U_T to be lagged in some regions to allow for the lack of synchronisation between the national and regional cycles. We shall ignore this refinement in discussing his model.

$$U_{rt} = C_r U_{Tt}^{\alpha_r} e^{\beta_r t + \gamma_r t^2} R_{rt} \tag{4.6}$$

and the arithmetically linear specification is:

$$U_{rt} = a_r U_{Tt} + C'_r + b_r t + d_r t^2 + R'_{rt} \tag{4.7}$$

For all regions to have the same unemployment rate as the nation requires that $C_r = \alpha_r = R_r = 1$ and $\beta_r = \gamma_r = 0$ in equation (4.6), and that $a_r = 1$ and $C'_r = b_r = d_r = R'_r = 0$ in equation (4.7). These requirements give some standard against which to judge the actual parameter values when (4.6) and (4.7) are fitted to the data. Equation (4.7) is very close to our own model specification except that we used an ordinary linear time trend. Our equation was put to rather different use, however; a_r and b_r were estimated separately and C'_r was not estimated freely but by extrapolation back from the first minimum unemployment rate in the region. It is interesting, nevertheless, to compare Brechling's estimates of a_r with our own, and also an average of his estimates of the structural component (our non-cyclical component) of regional unemployment derived from the log-linear model (see table 4.3).

If the London and South and East regions are combined, and also the Ridings and Midlands regions, it can be seen that the ordering of the regions according to their average level of structural unemployment is virtually identical to the ordering of regions according to their level of non-cyclical unemployment in table 4.1. The absolute magnitude of the estimates differ because of the differences in estimation techniques and differences in the time period studied. There is also a close similarity between his aggregative cyclical coefficients and our sensitivity estimates even though his estimates exclude the effects of trend. The southern regions appear as cyclically insensitive, while the northern regions, including Wales and Scotland, appear as cyclically sensitive. It is also apparent that if an evaluation of inner products was to be performed on Brechling's results, the major source of interregional variation in unemployment rates would be variation in the structural component. It should be stressed again, however, although Brechling does not, that this does not imply that differences in the pressure of labour demand are

TABLE 4.3 Brechling's estimates of structural (non-cyclical) unemployment and aggregative cyclical coefficients

	Average structural unemployment	*Aggregative cyclical coefficients*
London	0.71	0.614
South and East	0.76	0.715
Wales	1.54	0.742
South West	0.87	0.965
Ridings	0.61	1.073
North Midlands	0.44	0.886
Midlands	0.50	0.961
North West	1.13	1.319
North	2.19	1.213
Scotland	2.21	1.535

not important in explaining interregional unemployment rate differences. Brechling's use of the term 'structural' is misleading without qualification because a good deal of the unemployment in the northern regions which is defined as structural is almost certainly the result of a permanent deficiency of demand for labour. It should not be concluded from Brechling's work that structural unemployment, in the normal sense of unemployment caused by a lack of job matching, is the major source of regional unemployment rate discrepancies.

THE SOURCES OF VARIATIONS IN THE SENSITIVITY OF REGIONAL TO NATIONAL UNEMPLOYMENT

Given that differences in the sensitivity of regions to unemployment are an important source of interregional variations in unemployment, it is interesting to enquire into why unemployment should be more sensitive to changes in national demand conditions in some regions than in others. In the first instance, the unspecified causes of the observed variations may be grouped under two heads, which will be referred to here as inter-industry factors and intra-industry factors. The first group relates to the fact that fluctuations in the rate of unemployment are not the same in all industries, so that regional differences in industrial structure will tend to produce interregional variations in unemployment sensitivity. The second group of factors relates to the possibility that fluctuations in unemployment in a given industry may differ between regions. In the analysis to follow an attempt will be made to measure the contribution of these two groups of factors to each region's sensitivity to unemployment. The time period taken, and hence the estimates of sensitivity, differs from the estimates reported earlier in table 4.2 because it was impossible to obtain data on unemployment by industry and region on a consistent regional basis for the whole period 1951 to 1972. We therefore use estimates published elsewhere for the period 1949 to 1964, and analyse these results.[5] Measurement will be based on the standardisation procedures discussed in chapter 1. In interpreting the results it must be understood that the two factors in themselves are not the fundamental causes of the observed interregional variations in sensitivity; rather, the two sets of factors represent logical or convenient groups of (unidentified) causes whose contribution to the total variation can be quantified. The relative importance of each of the two factors can then be assessed for each region, and between regions as a whole. Subsequently, if desired, the fundamental causes which determine the manner and extent to which the factors operate in each region can be investigated where the initial analysis undertaken shows that either or both of the factors have made significant contributions to differences in sensitivity.

If U_r is the rate of unemployment in a region, its value is given by

$$U_r = \sum_i p_i r_i$$

where p_i is the proportion of the region's workforce in industry i, and r_i is the region's rate of unemployment in

[5] See A. P. Thirlwall, 'Regional Unemployment as a Cyclical Phenomenon', *Scottish Journal of Political Economy*, June 1966, and C. P. Harris and A. P. Thirlwall, 'Interregional Variations in Cyclical Sensitivity to Unemployment', *Bulletin of the Oxford Institute of Statistics*, Feb 1968.

the same industry. Similarly, if U is the national rate of unemployment then

$$U = \sum_i p'_i r'_i$$

where the superscript (′) indicates the corresponding national values. The contribution that a given industry makes to a region's rate of unemployment and the national rate, respectively, may differ because $p_i \neq p'_i$ and/or because $r_i \neq r'_i$. The effects of these two inequalities on the difference between a region's rate of unemployment and the national rate can be measured by standardising for 'proportions' and 'rates' separately. Standardisation for 'proportions' involves substituting the national proportions of the workforce in each industry (i.e. the p'_i series) for the actual regional values (the p_i series) to obtain a hypothetical rate of unemployment for the region based on the assumption that it has the same industrial structure as the nation. If U_r^* is defined as the rate of unemployment resulting from this substitution, its value is given by

$$U_r^* = \sum_i p'_i r_i$$

U_r^* may be called a region's *composition-constant* rate of unemployment. Likewise, standardisation for 'rates' involves substituting the national unemployment rates in each individual industry (the r'_i series) for the actual regional values (the r_i series) to obtain a second hypothetical rate of unemployment for the region based on the assumption that the rate of unemployment in each individual industry located in the region is the same as that in the nation. If this alternative standardised rate of unemployment for a region is denoted as U_r^{**}, its value is given by

$$U_r^{**} = \sum_i p_i r'_i$$

U_r^{**} may be called a region's *rate-constant* rate of unemployment. The estimated contribution of the two differences, $(p_i - p'_i)$ and $(r_i - r'_i)$, to the total difference between a region's rate of unemployment and the national rate will depend on the weighting system employed, as outlined in equations (1.1) to (1.5) in chapter 1:

$$U_r - U = \sum_i r_i(p_i - p_i') + \sum_i p_i'(r_i - r_i')$$

$$U_r - U = \sum_i r_i'(p_i - p_i') + \sum_i p_i(r_i - r_i')$$

$$U_r - U = \sum_i r_i(p_i - p_i') + \sum_i p_i(r_i - r_i') + \sum_i (p_i - p_i')(r_i' - r_i)$$

$$U_r - U = \sum_i r_i'(p_i - p_i') + \sum_i p_i'(r_i - r_i') + \sum_i (p_i' - p_i)(r_i' - r_i)$$

$$U_r - U = \sum_i \tfrac{1}{2}(r_i + r_i')(p_i - p_i') + \sum_i \tfrac{1}{2}(p_i + p_i')(r_i - r_i')$$

Using these weighting procedures, the interregional variations in unemployment sensitivity can be readily analysed according to composition (inter-industry) and rate (intra-industry) differences between regions. The first step is to calculate the sensitivity of unemployment in each region using the series of U_r, U_r^* and U_r^{**} separately. The actual sensitivity of the region (b) can then be compared with (1) the sensitivity of the region assuming the region possessed the same industrial structure as the nation (b^*), i.e. the regression coefficient of U_r^* on U, and (2) the sensitivity of the region assuming the region experienced the same rate of unemployment in each of its industries as the nation (b^{**}), i.e. the regression coefficient of U_r^{**} on U. The estimates of b, b^* and b^{**} for the period 1949 to 1964 are shown in table 4.4.

To use the estimates in table 4.4 to measure the contribution of inter-industry and intra-industry factors to a region's sensitivity to unemployment involves the same weighting problems as attached to the analysis of the absolute difference between a region's rate of unemployment and the national rate. That is, either regional or national weights may be used, or a mixture, or an average, of both. To analyse the source of sensitivity (or insensitivity) we examine deviations from unity. This is the obvious standard to take since if a region had the same industrial composition as the nation and also the same rate of unemployment in each of its individual industries as in the nation, then b would be unity. The five estimates of the contribution of inter-industry and

TABLE 4.4 Indices of sensitivity to unemployment

Old standard regions	*Actual sensitivity* (b)	*Composition-constant sensitivity* (b^*)	*Rate constant sensitivity* (b^{**})
London and South East	0.450	0.451	0.690
East and South	0.543	0.561	0.723
South West	0.534	0.526	0.830
Midland	0.535	0.524	0.814
North Midland	0.798	0.622	1.253
East and West Ridings	1.298	0.823	1.395
Wales	1.134	1.336	0.799
Scotland	1.066	1.225	0.991
North	0.873	1.213	0.773
North West	2.410	1.513	1.439

Source: C. P. Harris and A. P. Thirlwall, op. cit.

intra-industry factors to a region's sensitivity, corresponding to the five weighting schemes outlined earlier, can be obtained from the following five formulae:

(i) $b-1 = (b-b^*)+(b^*-1)$

(ii) $b-1 = (b^{**}-1)+(b-b^{**})$

(iii) $b-1 = (b-b^*)+(b-b^{**})+[(b^{**}-1)+(b^*-b)]$

(iv) $b-1 = (b^{**}-1)+(b^*-1)+[(1-b^{**})+(b-b^*)]$

(v) $b-1 = \frac{1}{2}[(b-b^*)+(b^{**}-1)]+\frac{1}{2}[(b-b^{**})+(b^*-1)]$

In each form (i) to (v) the first term gives the contribution of inter-industry factors (composition differences) to a region's sensitivity; the second term gives the contribution of intra-industry factors (rate differences) to a region's sensitivity, and the third term in forms (iii) and (iv) is the interaction term between composition and rate differences. Thus the contribution of inter-industry factors to a region's sensitivity, excluding interaction terms, can be measured by $(b-b^*)$, $(b^{**}-1)$, or by the average of these two terms. Likewise the contribution of intra-industry factors to a region's sensitivity to unemployment can be measured by (b^*-1), $(b-b^{**})$ or by the average of these two terms. The variation that the form selected

TABLE 4.5 Contributions of inter-industry and intra-industry factors to the sensitivity of regions to unemployment

Regions	*Forms*				
	(i)	(ii)	(iii)	(iv)	(v)
	(*a*) *Inter-industry factors – composition differences*				
London and South East	−0.001	−0.310	−0.001	−0.310	−0.155
East and South	−0.018	−0.277	−0.018	−0.277	−0.147
South West	0.008	−0.170	0.008	−0.170	−0.081
Midland	0.011	−0.186	0.011	−0.186	−0.087
North Midland	0.176	0.253	0.176	0.253	0.215
East and West Ridings	0.475	0.395	0.475	0.395	0.435
Wales	−0.232	−0.201	−0.232	−0.201	−0.217
Scotland	−0.159	−0.009	−0.159	−0.009	−0.084
North	−0.340	−0.227	−0.340	−0.227	−0.284
North West	0.897	0.439	0.897	0.439	0.668
	(*b*) *Intra-industry factors – rate differences*				
London and South East	−0.549	−0.240	−0.240	−0.549	−0.395
East and South	−0.439	−0.180	−0.180	−0.439	−0.310
South West	−0.474	−0.296	−0.296	−0.474	−0.385
Midland	−0.476	−0.279	−0.279	−0.476	−0.378
North Midland	−0.378	−0.455	−0.455	−0.378	−0.417
East and West Ridings	−0.177	−0.097	−0.097	−0.177	−0.137
Wales	0.366	0.335	0.335	0.366	0.351
Scotland	0.225	0.075	0.075	0.225	0.150
North	0.213	0.100	0.100	0.213	0.157
North West	0.513	0.971	0.971	0.513	0.742

Source: Calculated from the estimates of b, b^* and b^{**} in table 4.4.

makes to the estimates of the contributions of these two factors is shown in table 4.5.

There are only two instances in table 4.5 where the signs of the values given by the three weighting systems are not the same. These are the contributions of the inter-industry factors in the South West and the Midland regions. In both regions the positive values are small and are given by the use of regional weights, while the negative values given by the national weights are considerably larger, so that the average contributions (form v) are negative.

Differences between the magnitudes of the contributions given by the regional and national weights respectively are much more important than the differences in signs. For the inter-industry factors (composition differences), the use of national weights in place of regional weights makes the contributions larger in London and South East, East and South, South West, Midland, and North Midland, and smaller in the other five regions, and the changes are fairly substantial. On the other hand, the substitution of national for regional weights in calculating the contribution of the intra-industry factors (rate differences) increases the magnitude of the contributions in only two regions, North Midland and North West. Thus, on balance, the use of national rather than regional weights makes little difference to the general significance of the inter-industry factors (although the effect in each region is altered), but it makes a substantial reduction in the relative importance of the intra-industry factors.

RESULTS OF THE ANALYSIS[6]

In discussing the main results of our analysis, only those given by form (v) in table 4.5 will be referred to. The results will be examined in two ways. First, the position in sensitive and insensitive regions will be compared. Secondly, any differences between regions with rates of unemployment persistently above and below the national average will be discussed.

The regions which were sensitive and insensitive to unemployment over the period are distinguished in table 4.4. Of the six regions which were insensitive to unemployment over the period, the contributions of both the inter-industry and intra-industry factors were in the same direction in the London and South East; East and South; South West and Midland

[6] In interpreting the results it must be remembered that the calculations have been based on the use of the twenty-four industrial orders of the SIC, which represent a high level of industry aggregation. The orders contain many sub-orders (minimum list headings), the importance of which may vary between regions and whose economic behaviour may be different from that of the order as a whole. It cannot be said for certain, however, how the results would differ if it was possible to undertake the analysis at a lower level of industry aggregation. The contributions of the inter-industry and intra-industry factors to a region's sensitivity could increase or decrease together, or move in opposite directions.

regions. In the other two insensitive regions, however, the contributions of these two factors were in opposite directions. In the North Midlands, inter-industry factors would have made the region sensitive to unemployment had it not been for the greater offsetting influence of intra-industry factors. In the North Region, on the other hand, intra-industry factors would have caused the region to be sensitive to unemployment had it not been for the greater offsetting influence of inter-industry factors. With regard to the relative size of the contributions of the inter-industry and intra-industry factors, it can be seen that in five of the six regions the value of the intra-industry factors was greater than that of inter-industry factors.

Of the four regions which were sensitive to unemployment over the period, only in the North West region did the two sets of factors operate in the same direction. In this region, which was the most sensitive of all regions over the period, the contributions of both intra-industry factors and inter-industry factors to total sensitivity were large – the magnitude of the former being slightly greater than the latter. In the remaining three regions which were sensitive, the contributions of the two factors were in opposite directions. In Wales and Scotland the contribution of inter-industry factors was negative (i.e. would have made the regions insensitive), but this was more than counter-balanced by the effects of intra-industry factors. The position in the East and West Ridings was the reverse of that in Wales and Scotland. In this region, sensitivity was due to the effect of inter-industry factors. Therefore, in three of the four regions which were sensitive to unemployment, intra-industry factors were of greater importance than inter-industry factors in determining the degree of sensitivity.

With regard to the influence of inter-industry factors as a whole, it can be said that three of the ten regions under study specialised in industries in which the rate of unemployment fluctuated by more than the average in all industries. These regions were the North Midlands, East and West Ridings, and the North West. On balance, therefore, the other seven regions specialised more in industries which were insensitive. When the influence of intra-industry factors is considered, it can be seen from table 4.5 that four regions specialised more in industries in which the degree of unemployment sensitivity within those regions was greater than in all regions together. These regions were the North West, North, Wales and Scotland. In the other six regions, the industrial structure was more heavily weighted by industries which were less sensitive to unemployment in those regions than in all regions together.[7]

The influence of inter-industry and intra-industry factors may also be examined in relation to their effects in regions with rates of unemployment persistently above and below the national mean. Regions with rates above the mean were the North West, North, Wales and Scotland, and those with rates of unemployment below the mean were London and South East; East and South; South West; Midlands; North Midlands, and East and West Ridings. In all four regions with higher than average rates of unemployment over the period 1949 to 1964, the independent influence of intra-industry factors would have made *all* the regions *sensitive* to unemployment. This is in contrast to the regions with lower than average rates of unemployment over the same years, where the influence of intra-industry factors would have made *all* the regions *insensitive* to unemployment.

However, with regard to differences in the influence of inter-industry factors between regions with high and low rates of unemployment, no consistent pattern is evident. The sign indicating the direction of influence of inter-industry factors is positive and negative within both groups of regions. In one-half of the regions the sign of the contribution of inter-industry factors was different from the sign of the actual sensitivity index of the regions.

[7] The effect of the two factors in a given region depends on the relative size of a particular industry in that region. An industry which is sensitive to unemployment in the nation as a whole will make a large contribution to a region's sensitivity only if a significant part of the region's workforce is in that industry. Similarly, the contribution of an industry which is more sensitive to unemployment in the region than the nation will make a large contribution to a region's sensitivity only if it has a significant share of the region's workforce.

It would appear, therefore, that interregional variations in sensitivity to unemployment over the period 1949 to 1964 were due more to interregional differences in the sensitivity of individual industries to unemployment than to regional differences in industrial structure. An 'evaluation of inner products' indicates that 47 per cent of the variation in the sensitivity coefficient between regions can be accounted for by interregional differences in intra-industry factors, while only 28 per cent can be accounted for by interregional differences in industrial composition.

Some comment is necessary on the association found between regions with higher than average rates of unemployment and intra-industry factors conducive to sensitivity, and between regions with lower than average rates of unemployment and intra-industry factors conducive to insensitivity.

One possible explanation is that manufacturers have hoarded labour in regions where labour has been continually in short supply, whereas labour has been more readily dismissed by manufacturers in regions where the supply of labour has always tended to be plentiful relative to demand.

Another explanation might be connected with differences in the nature of industrial units between regions. There is some evidence, for instance, that in periods when industry develops spare capacity, production is slowed down in branch plants before being run down in the main plant.[8] If regions with higher than average rates of unemployment contain a larger proportion of their workforce in branch plants than other regions – a situation which might even be attributable to government policies to influence the distribution of new industry – unemployment might be expected to fluctuate more in industries in these regions than in the same industries elsewhere.

A third explanation concerns the possibility that unemployed labour in regions with high rates of unemployment might be less occupationally or geographically mobile than in other regions, through a relative lack of new employment opportunity, a greater unwillingness to move, or because

[8] See the evidence contained in B. J. Loasby, 'Making Location Policy Work', *Lloyds Bank Review*, Jan 1967.

unemployed labour is more specific in these regions.

Whatever the causes of regional differences in the sensitivity of individual industries to unemployment, however, the evidence suggests that intra-industry factors made the major contribution to interregional variations in sensitivity to unemployment over the years 1949 to 1964. For future work in this field, therefore, detailed analyses of interregional variations in the performance of individual industries would seem more relevant than studies of the industrial composition of regions.

5 Types of Unemployment: Demand-deficient v. Non Demand-deficient Unemployment

The classification of unemployment into demand-deficient and non demand-deficient is more contentious than the distinction between cyclical and non-cyclical unemployment or the measurement of sensitivity because the classification can either be made on a causal (*ex-ante*) basis, or on a cure (*ex-post*) basis. The use of vacancy statistics, which we adopt later, is essentially a causal basis of classification and, as such, leads to minimum estimates of non demand-deficient unemployment.

Classification according to cures

The fact that vacancy statistics are not always available has led, particularly in the United States, to the practice of classifying unemployment according to the possible means of reducing it, assuming certain constraints on action. Using a 'cure' basis for classification gives *ex-post* measures of each type of unemployment; that is, measures of the types of unemployment depending on the success of various policies in reducing unemployment within the constraints laid down. The approach leaves much to be desired, however. It is arbitrary, and leads to inconsistencies in measurement because the constraints on action have been variously defined by investigators according to subjective preferences. For example, the distinction has long been made between unemployment that could be eliminated by expanding demand without causing 'intolerable' inflation, and unemployment that could not be so eliminated. Opinions have differed widely, however, as to what constitutes 'intolerable' inflation.

The price constraint is introduced in recognition of the fact that if the demand for labour was strong enough almost all unemployment could probably be eliminated (as in war time), but only at the cost of substantial upward pressure on wages and prices. If relative price stability is a goal of economic policy a certain rate of inflation must clearly be included as a constraint in the measurement of demand-deficient unemployment. For example, suppose the trade-off curve between the rate of increase in prices and unemployment is given as in figure 5.1.

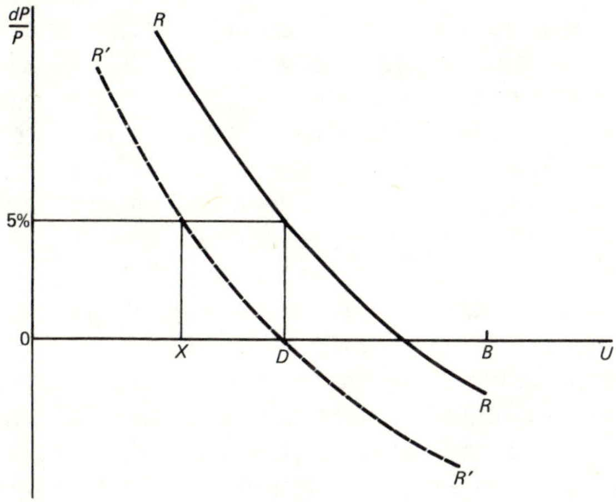

FIGURE 5.1

If there was a general consensus that a 5 per cent annual rate of price increase is just tolerable, then demand-deficient unemployment would be the difference between the actual amount of unemployment (say *B*) and the amount of unemployment associated with price increases of 5.0 per cent – *D* in figure 5.1.

Within this framework, frictional and structural unemployment, which together constitute non demand-deficient unemployment, is a residual after the amount of demand-deficient unemployment has been determined – *OD* in figure 5.1. The problem then is how to distinguish frictional and structural unemployment on a 'cure' basis. One possibility is to measure structural unemployment as that amount of unemployment removable through labour market policies of the retraining variety, thus permitting the economy to operate at a higher level of employment without violating the price constraint. For example, if labour market policies could displace the existing trade-off curve, *RR*, to *R'R'* in figure 5.1, unemployment *XD* could be regarded as structural. The remainder of unemployment, *OX*, would be frictional. Alternatively, structural unemployment could be defined, as Lipsey[1] has done, as that amount of unemployment that can be removed by structural cures 'some of which pay for themselves on an analysis of money costs and money benefits and some of which are justified because the non-pecuniary social benefits are judged to justify the net money costs of the schemes'. In Lipsey's model, the *RR* curve in figure 5.1 is shifted to the left by a specified amount after a cost-benefit analysis of structural cures. The amount of structural unemployment then depends on the new point of tangency of the *RR* curve and the policy maker's preference curve between the discommodities inflation and unemployment (i.e. a concave indifference curve between dP/P and U).[2] A third possibility would be to define structural unemployment as the difference between non demand-deficient unemployment and the minimum rate of unemployment experienced over the period as a measure of the frictional minimum below which unemployment cannot fall. The problem here is to know whether the minimum experienced is truly a frictional minimum. Further criteria for distinguishing frictional and structural unemployment on a 'cure' basis could no doubt be given. It should already be clear, however, that a classification of unemploy-

[1] R. Lipsey, 'Structural and Demand-Deficient Unemployment Reconsidered', in A. Ross (ed.), *Employment Policy and the Labour Market* (University of California Press, 1965).

[2] Lipsey uses a preference curve in his analysis as a substitute for an absolute price constraint. The logic of this is presumably that policy makers are unlikely to be indifferent to a rise in the rate of unemployment even though a decision has been reached on what constitutes a tolerable rate of inflation.

ment based on its remedies, subject to constraints, can easily lead to different estimates of the types of unemployment, and hence to a good deal of confusion.

CLASSIFICATION ACCORDING TO CAUSES: THE USE OF VACANCY STATISTICS

Using a 'causal' basis for classification offers much more hope for objectivity provided data are available relating to the amount and structure of labour demand. Classifying unemployment according to its causes gives *ex-ante* measures of each type of unemployment; that is, measures of the types of unemployment before appropriate remedies are applied which may or may not have the desired effect on reducing any particular type of unemployment. For example, demand-deficient unemployment could be said to exist when total expenditures in an economy are not sufficient to generate jobs for all those willing to work at the equilibrium wage: demand-deficient unemployment being that amount of unemployment in excess of the demand for labour. There can be no guarantee, however, that if the demand for labour expands, unemployment will fall by exactly the same amount. This will depend on the type of labour in demand in relation to the skills of the unemployed labour force.

If the demand for labour is not deficient, but is at least equal to the supply of labour available, the unemployment existing is commonly referred to as frictional and structural unemployment. Frictional unemployment consists of the unemployed who have the right skills to meet the labour demand and who are in the process of moving to new jobs. Frictional unemployment may increase or decrease with increases in the demand for labour according to whether the increase in unemployment due to more voluntary job changing is greater or less than the reduction in unemployment due to the greater ease of finding new work.

If the unemployed are not of the right type to match the demand for labour, causing concentrations of unemployment to arise in particular social groups or in particular geographic areas, the unemployment is called structural. The difference between frictional and structural unemployment is that whereas frictional unemployment arises from a lack of instant job mobility, structural unemployment arises through the inability or the failure of labour to adapt to changes in the composition of demand so that unemployment becomes concentrated for long periods of time among specific occupational groups in particular areas, while elsewhere employers are seeking workers but of a different type with different qualifications to the unemployed. The amount of structural unemployment therefore depends on how smoothly the labour market functions; how well the skills, experience and qualifications of redundant workers match the specifications of available jobs; how willing and able unemployed workers are to change their residence and occupations; how adequate the facilities are for retraining and education, and how rapidly certain jobs are being destroyed through economic change.

Classifying unemployment in this 'causal' way requires not only a measure of the demand for labour, but also knowledge of the characteristics of labour in demand and supply. In Great Britain, there are vacancy statistics available on both a regional and an occupational basis, and also by occupation within regions. The existence of such data provides the possibility of establishing a framework for measuring objectively types of unemployment by region on a consistent basis. It has already been argued that for separating demand-deficient unemployment (U_{DD}) from all other types of unemployment (non demand-deficient unemployment (U_{NDD})) one obvious criterion as an objective dividing line would be the point of balance between the available supply of labour and the unsatisfied demand for labour. The amount of unemployment in excess of the point of balance could justifiably be called demand-deficient unemployment, and unemployment at the point of balance could be called non demand-deficient unemployment. The major practical difficulty in using this criterion lies in identifying the level of unemployment at which the labour supply available equals unsatisfied demand. An approximate solution to the problem is to equate unemployment itself with the supply of labour available for employment, and to use unfilled vacancy statistics as a proxy measure of unsatisfied demand for labour. On this basis, the amount of unemployment at which unemployment equalled the number of vacancies would be non demand-deficient unemployment, and unemployment in excess of this amount would be demand-deficient unemployment. The important question is whether it is reasonable to equate unemployment with the supply of labour available, and unfilled vacancies with the unsatisfied demand for labour. On the supply side, it would have to be admitted that a proportion of the unemployed are unemployable; but offsetting this, there will be people available for work but who are not registered as unemployed. On the demand side there are also two problems. One is the possibility of vacancy over-reporting by manufacturers when there is a chronic shortage of labour; the other is general under-reporting of vacancies through official channels because many employers prefer to advertise job vacancies through other media which are not then recorded in the official vacancy statistics. Even if the *net* statement error is small in the aggregate, there is the additional problem in a comparison of types of unemployment between markets that the statement error may vary from market to market according to such factors as the pressure of demand, the efficiency of local employment exchange offices, and so on. These considerations must be borne in mind in interpreting the results later.

It should be readily apparent that unfilled vacancy statistics can be used as a means of breaking down non demand-deficient unemployment into structural (U_S) and frictional (U_F) unemployment, if the skill composition of vacancies and unemployment are both known. Given the composition of the unemployed, total vacancies (V) could be split into those which are of the right type (V_R) and those which are of the wrong type (V_W) to absorb the unemployed. Taking the two extremes, if all vacancies exactly matched the characteristics of the unemployed, all non demand-deficient unemployment would be frictional; on the other hand, if there was no matching at all, all non demand-deficient unemployment would be structural.

Using vacancy figures, therefore, it is possible to construct a complete framework for the classification of unemployment in any geographic labour market with the three types of unemployment, as defined above, adding up to total unemployment (U), i.e.

$$U = U_{DD} + U_F + U_S \tag{5.1}$$

Note, however, that where $V > U$, U_F and U_S cannot add up to total vacancies. In measuring the components of total unemployment in practice, therefore, two cases must be distinguished (a) where $U > V$, and (b) where $V > U$.

(a) *Measurement when aggregate unemployment exceeds aggregate vacancies*

When aggregate unemployment exceeds total vacancies we have:

$$U_{DD} = U - V \tag{5.2}$$

from which it follows from equation (5.1) that:

$$U_S + U_F = V \tag{5.3}$$

Unemployment is frictional if there are suitable vacancies for the unemployed to fill, and structural if the vacancies are not suitable. Hence:

$$U_F = V - V_W = V_R$$

and

$$U_S = V - V_R = V_W$$

where V_W is the number of vacancies of the wrong type
V_R is the number of vacancies of the right type
and $V = V_W + V_R$

This classification is applicable to any labour market if unemployment and vacancy data are available on a disaggregated basis by occupation. Assuming for the moment perfect geographic mobility within the labour market (i.e. ignoring the geographic component of structural unemployment), vacancies of the right type consists of the total sum of vacancies in occupations where unemployment exceeds vacancies plus the total sum of unemployment in occupations where vacancies exceed unemployment. Thus:

$$\begin{aligned} U_F = V_R = &\sum_{i=1}^{n} V_i \quad (\text{where } U_i > V_i) \\ &+ \sum_{i=n+1}^{T} U_i \quad (\text{where } V_i > U_i) \end{aligned} \tag{5.4}$$

where n is the number of occupations in which $U_i > V_i$
$T-n$ is the number of occupations in which $V_i > U_i$
and T is the total number of occupations.

Vacancies of the wrong type consist of the excess of vacancies over unemployment in occupations where $V_i > U_i$, when in other parts of the labour market $U_i > V_i$ (and $U > V$, of course). In other words, unemployment is structural if the unemployed in occupations where $U_i > V_i$ do not have the characteristics of the labour demand in the occupations where $V_i > U_i$. The magnitude of structural unemployment will depend on the size of the gap between vacancies and unemployment in shortage occupations. Thus:

$$U_S = V_W = \sum_{i=n+1}^{T} (V_i - U_i) \tag{5.5}$$

It is easily shown that $V_W + V_R = U_S + U_F = V$. Summing equations (5.4) and (5.5) gives:

$$\begin{aligned} U_F + U_S &= \sum_{i=1}^{n} V_i + \sum_{i=n+1}^{T} U_i + \sum_{i=n+1}^{T} V_i - \sum_{i=n+1}^{T} U_i \\ &= \sum_{i=1}^{n} V_i + \sum_{i=n+1}^{T} V_i \\ &= \sum_{i=1}^{T} V_i \\ &= V \end{aligned}$$

(b) *Measurement when aggregate vacancies exceed aggregate unemployment*

When aggregate vacancies exceed unemployment there is no demand-deficient unemployment by definition; all unemployment is either frictional or structural:

$$U = U_F + U_S \tag{5.6}$$

Frictional unemployment is measured as before:

$$U_F = \sum_{i=1}^{n} V_i + \sum_{i=n+1}^{T} U_i \tag{5.7}$$

Since all unemployment is accounted for in equation (5.7) except for the excess of unemployment over vacancies in the occupations where $U_i > V_i$, it follows that structural unemployment must be measured as:

$$U_S = \sum_{i=1}^{n} (U_i - V_i) \tag{5.8}$$

It is easily verified that $U_S + U_F = U$ by summing equations (5.7) and (5.8).

Whether $U > V$ or $V > U$, the easiest approach to the measurement of the two types of non demand-deficient unemployment is first to measure structural unemployment and to obtain frictional unemployment as a residual. In the case where $U > V$, structural unemployment is measured as $\sum_i (V_i - U_i)$ in occupations where $V_i > U_i$, so that $U_F = V - U_S$. Where $V > U$, structural unemployment is measured as $\sum_i (U_i - V_i)$ in occupations where $U_i > V_i$, so that $U_F = U - U_S$.

The dependence of structural and frictional unemployment on the pressure of demand

Inherent in the above classification of types of unemployment, based on the level and composition of vacancies, is the dependence of the measure of non demand-deficient unemployment on the pressure of demand for labour, and the fact that structural unemployment will be a feature of good times rather than bad. The dependence of total non demand-deficient unemployment on the pressure of demand for labour arises from the fact that unless the demand for labour consists entirely of the people with the skills (and in the locations) represented by the unemployed, unfilled vacancies are bound to rise at the same time unemployment is falling. As long as $U > V$, a rise in V is equivalent to an increase in non demand-deficient unemployment. A simple diagram illustrates the point.

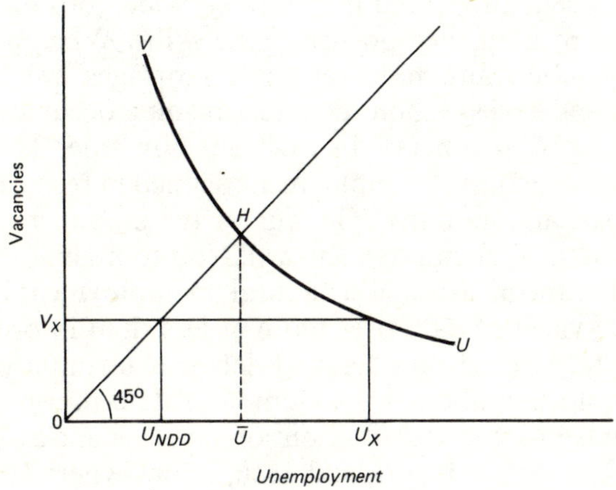

FIGURE 5.2

In figure 5.2 VU represents the relationship between V and U. V_X is the prevailing level of vacancies and U_X the prevailing level of unemployment. When $U > V$, non demand-deficient unemployment is defined as unemployment existing at the point of equality between V and U, i.e. OU_{NDD} in figure 5.2. Demand-deficient unemployment is the excess of unemployment over vacancies – $U_{NDD}U_X$. It is clear from the shape of the VU relation, however, that $U_{NDD}U_X$ overstates the number of jobs that need to be created by increasing demand to equate supply and demand in the labour market. If demand expands there is a movement up the VU curve from U_X, and the equality of V and U occurs at $\bar{U}$. Clearly the increased demand for labour has not consisted entirely of the demand for people with the skills of the unemployed. 'True' demand-deficient unemployment is $\overline{U}U_X$ and 'true' non demand-deficient unemployment is $\overline{U}$.

The dependence of structural unemployment on the tightness of the labour market will be a feature of any measure of structural unemployment defined on the basis of an excess demand for labour in particular sectors of the economy while unemployment exists elsewhere in the economy. When the aggregate economy is depressed, there are likely to be few shortage occupations and therefore very few jobs for the unemployed to fill if they possessed the skills. When aggregate demand is buoyant, however, skill shortages are likely to develop, and excess labour demand in some occupations and excess supply in others will exist side by side. This is the essence of structural unemployment defined in terms of a lack of occupational mobility. The tighter the labour market, the more structural unemployment will tend to manifest itself.

Whether the measure of structural unemployment based on the use of vacancy data rises more or less than in proportion to the total level of non demand-deficient unemployment as the demand for labour rises cannot be determined *a priori*. It depends on the distribution of new vacancies between occupations where $V_i > U_i$ and occupations where $U_i > V_i$.

Methods to overcome the dependence of the measurement of non demand-deficient (and structural) unemployment on the pressure of demand

To overcome the dependence of the measurement of total non demand-deficient unemployment on the pressure of demand, four approaches to measurement suggest themselves. One is to plot the number of vacancies and unemployment on a time series graph and to take an average of the numbers (or per cent) unemployed at which the two curves intersect. At the points at which vacancies have matched unemployment there can be no doubt that the unemployment existing is truly non demand-deficient. The difficulty here is that the two series might rarely, if ever, cross. As we shall see later, however, it is possible to adopt this procedure for some of the regions of the British economy, with interesting results.

Another approach is to regress the percentage level of unemployment against the excess demand for labour ($V-U$ or $\%V-\%U$) over time and to use the constant term in the linear regression equation as the measure of non demand-deficient unemployment. This approach is illustrated in figure 5.3 with the dependent variable on the X axis.

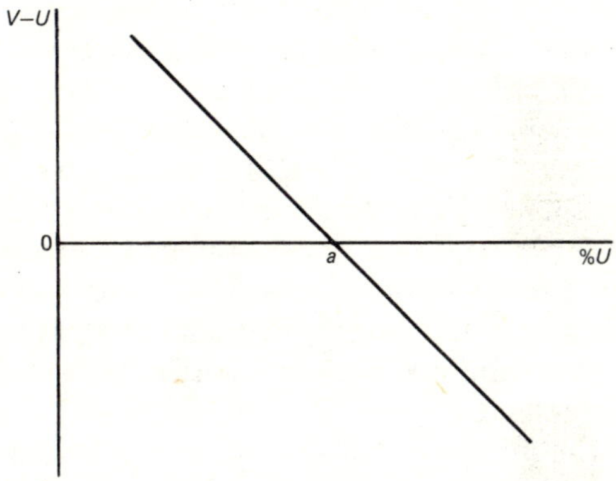

FIGURE 5.3

The value of the intercept term, a, gives the rate of unemployment at which $V-U=0$ and this is a measure of non demand-deficient unemployment independent of demand pressure. Even if V had never reached the level of U, the standard error of a would give some measure of confidence in the estimate.

A third approach, similar to the above, is to plot the trade-off curve between unfilled vacancies and unemployment (as a percentage of the workforce) for any market over time and to calculate the percentage level of unemployment at which a least squares regression line fitted to the observations cuts the 45° line from the origin as in figure 5.2. At any point on the 45° line $V=U$ or $V-U=0$. What form the function fitted to the data should take must depend on the nature of the observed relation between the two variables $\%V$ and $\%U$. The general presumption is one of a convex relation since unemployment will be decreasingly sensitive to increases in demand. As we shall see in practice, however, an arithmetically linear relation is often a closer approximation to the data. The percentage level of unemployment at which $V-U=0$ can be estimated by extrapolation if V has never matched U.

A further approach is to take the classificatory scheme outlined in equations (5.1) to (5.8), apply it to the data year by year and then take an average of the measures of non demand-deficient unemployment. The problem with this approach, however, is that in measuring the average we would be confined to points on the 45° line between O and H in figure 5.2 because non demand-deficient unemployment can never exceed total unemployment. Indeed, if U was always greater than V, all the points of U_{NDD} would be below H so that a 'true' measure of U_{NDD} could never be obtained. Measuring U_{NDD} in this way will inevitably give a downward bias compared with the other approaches. Interregional comparisons in particular will be invalidated because of differences in the average pressure of demand.

As far as the measure of structural unemployment by itself is concerned there is no easy solution. For an individual labour market the best that can be done is either to take an average of the measures at different pressures of demand, or choose a level of demand pressure arbitrarily and measure structural unemployment at that level. For example, it is conceivable that policy makers might wish to know the magnitude of bottlenecks in a labour market at some desired level of unemployment they wish to maintain. But clearly, interregional comparisons of structural unemployment cannot be meaningfully made unless the measures are standardised to allow for differences in the average pressure of demand or unless comparisons are made when the pressure of demand has been the same in each of the labour markets under study. First let us show, however, the dependence of our measures of non demand-deficient and structural unemployment on the pressure of demand (as measured by vacancies) and then see what conclusions emerge when the approaches mentioned above are adopted to avoid the 'dependence' problem.

RESULTS

Applying the unemployment classification outlined in equations (5.1) to (5.8) to the regions of Great Britain, and to the country as a whole, over the period 1963 to 1972 gives the results as shown in table 5.A1 of the appendix to the chapter.[3] The dependence of the measures of non demand-deficient unemployment, and structural unemployment, on the pressure of demand is readily apparent. The measure of frictional unemployment, on the other hand, tends to be relatively stable for both males and females. When comparing regions of different size, of course, the absolute figures of non demand-deficient and structural unemployment are not very meaningful. The figures need to be adjusted for the size of the region by dividing the estimates by the size of the regional labour force. The percentage levels of types of unemployment will also vary, however, with the pressure of demand. We therefore leave the conversion of the absolute numbers to percentages until we take *average* measures and adjust the average estimates for each region for differences in the pressure of demand between regions (see table 5.8).

Our first suggested approach to the measurement of non demand-deficient unemployment in the regions, which overcomes the pressure of demand problem, is to plot the percentage level of unemployment and vacancies on a time series graph, and to take an average of the levels of unemployment at which the two curves cross. This is a feasible approach providing the two curves cross at least once. In figures 5.4 to 5.11, unemployment and vacancy rates are plotted for the regions of the country and Great Britain over the period 1951 to 1972. In the case of the North region, Scotland and Wales the two series have never crossed; in the remaining regions, the average level of unemployment at which the two series have crossed are: South 1.3 per cent; South West 1.5 per cent; Midlands 1.3 per cent; North West 1.4 per cent; Great Britain 1.5 per cent. The rates are clearly close to one another. They

[5] Estimates assume perfect geographic mobility *within* each labour market. The analysis is confined to 1963–72 because published data on unemployment and vacancies by occupation and region are not available prior to 1963.

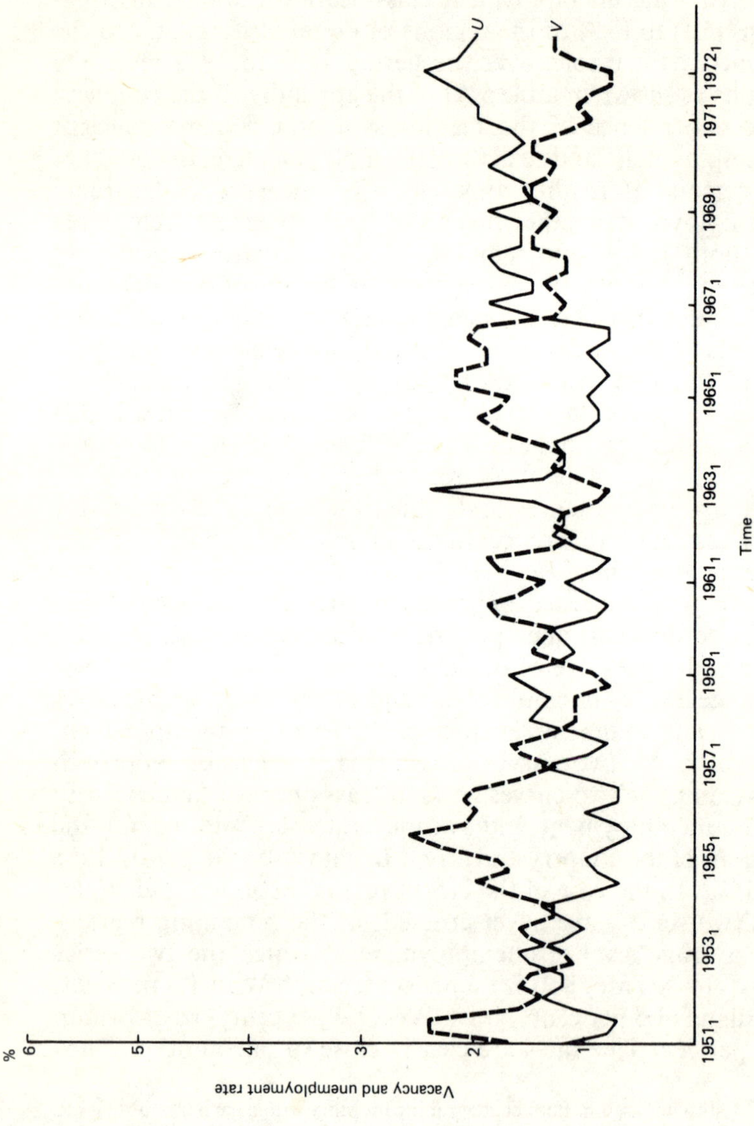

FIGURE 5.4 Unemployment and vacancy rates 1951–72 – SOUTH

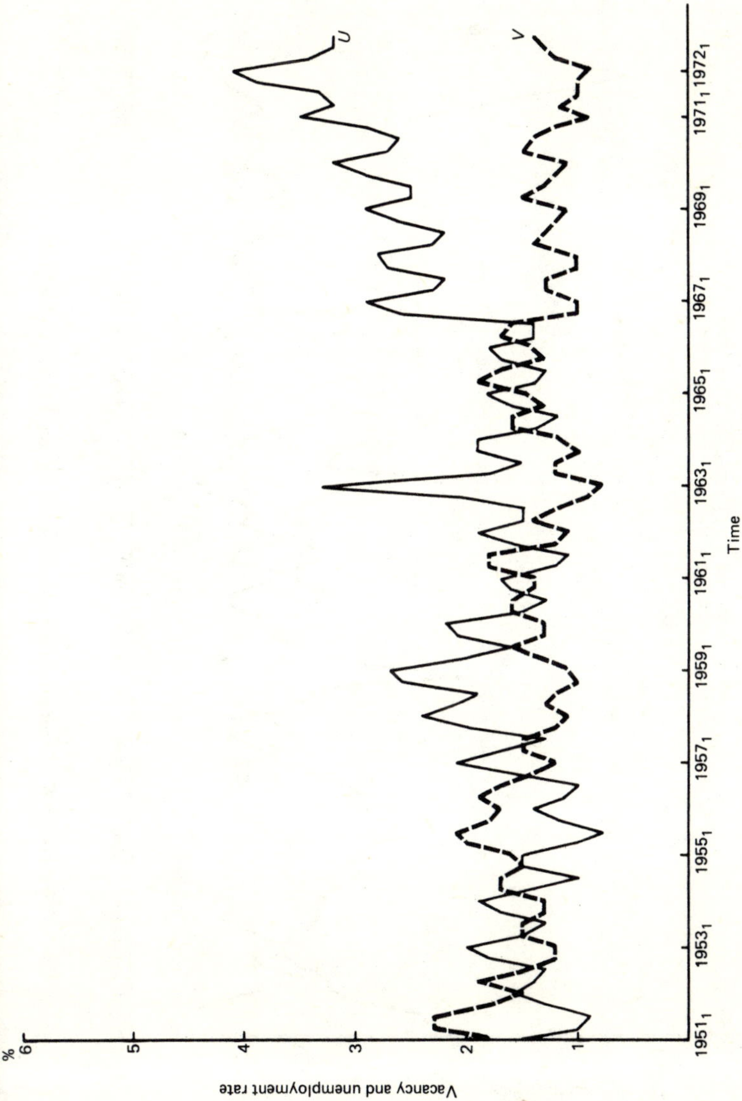

FIGURE 5.5 Unemployment and vacancy rates 1951–72 – SOUTH WEST

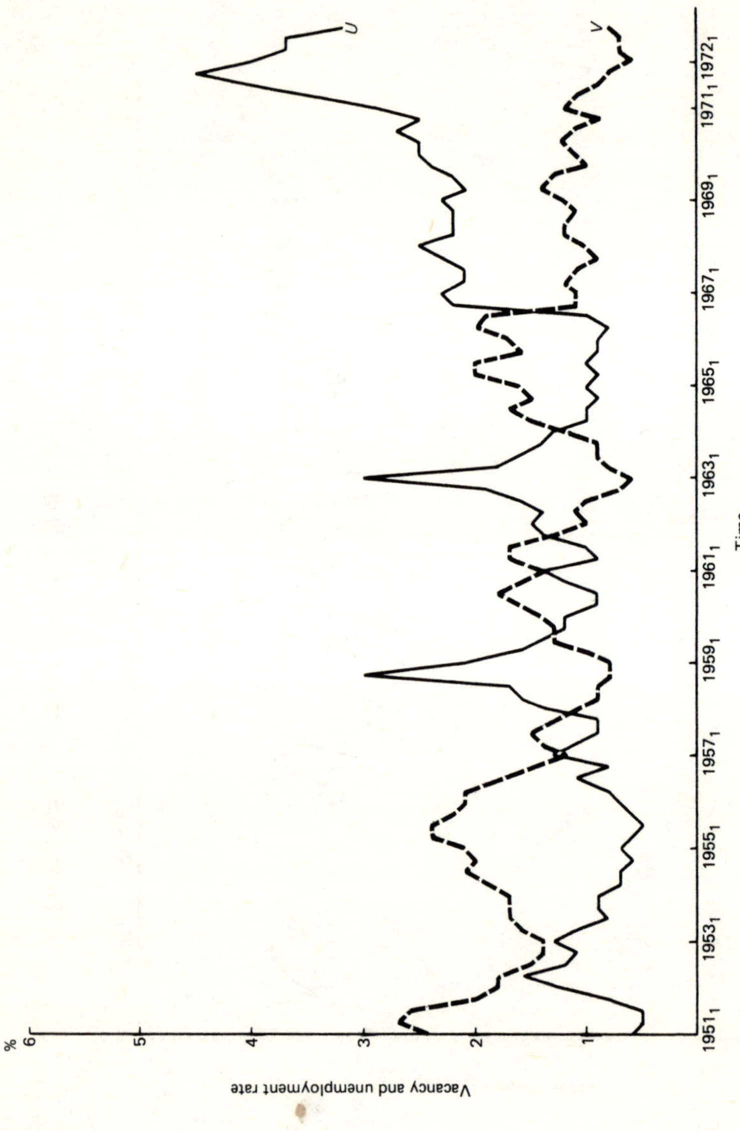

FIGURE 5.6 Unemployment and vacancy rates 1951–72 – MIDLANDS

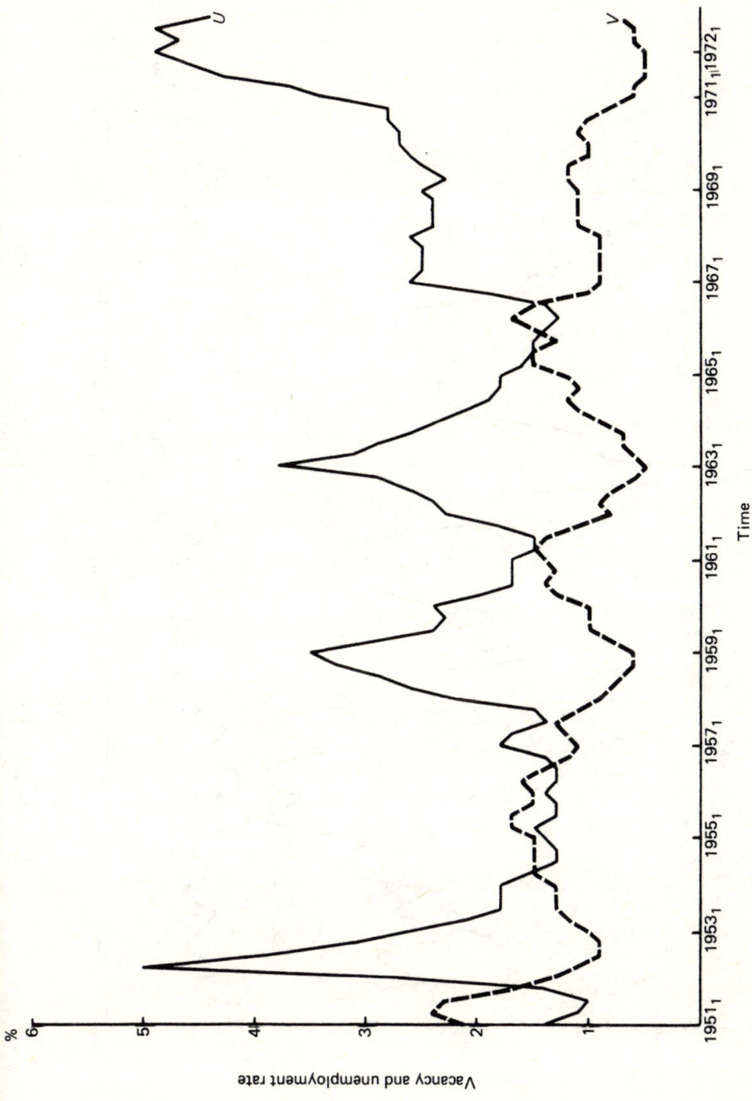

FIGURE 5.7 Unemployment and vacancy rates 1951–72 – NORTH WEST

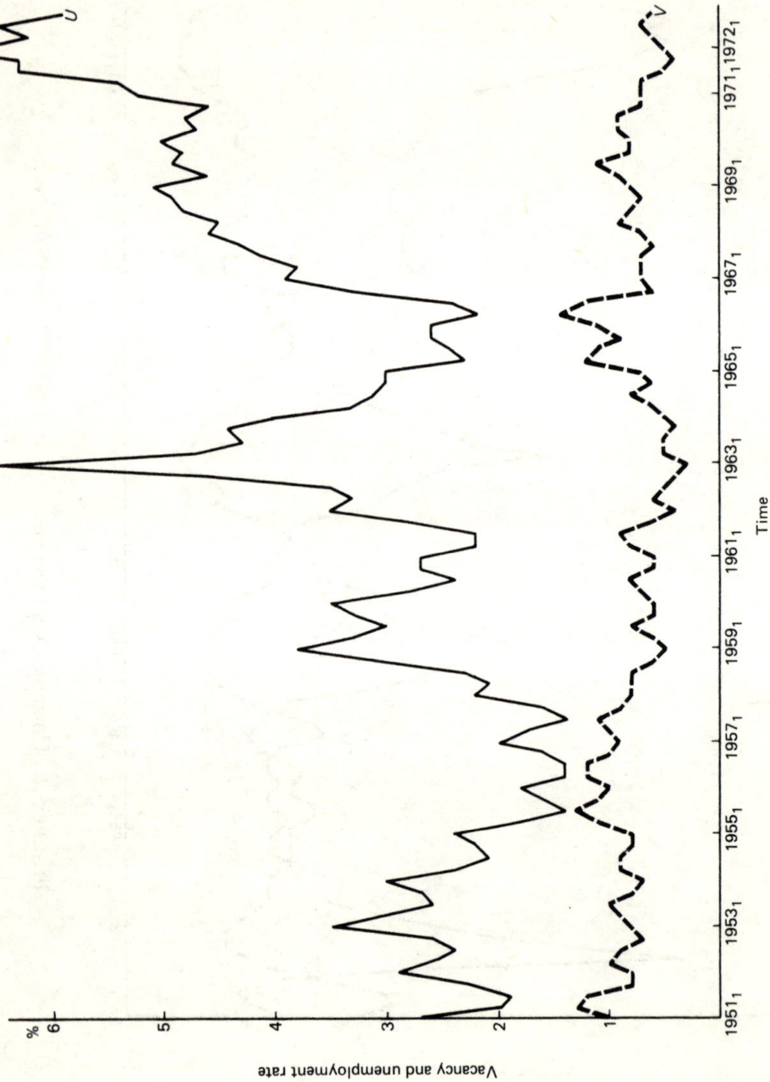

FIGURE 5.8 Unemployment and vacancy rates 1951–72 – NORTH

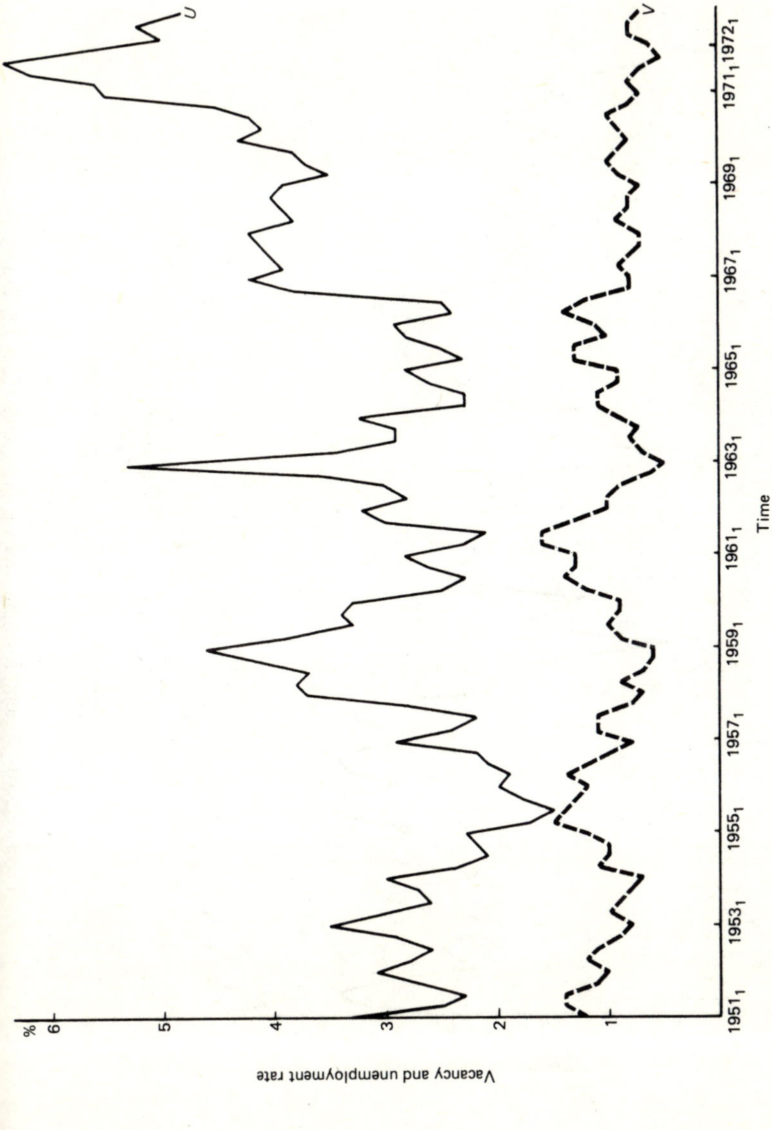

FIGURE 5.9 Unemployment and vacancy rates 1951–72 – WALES

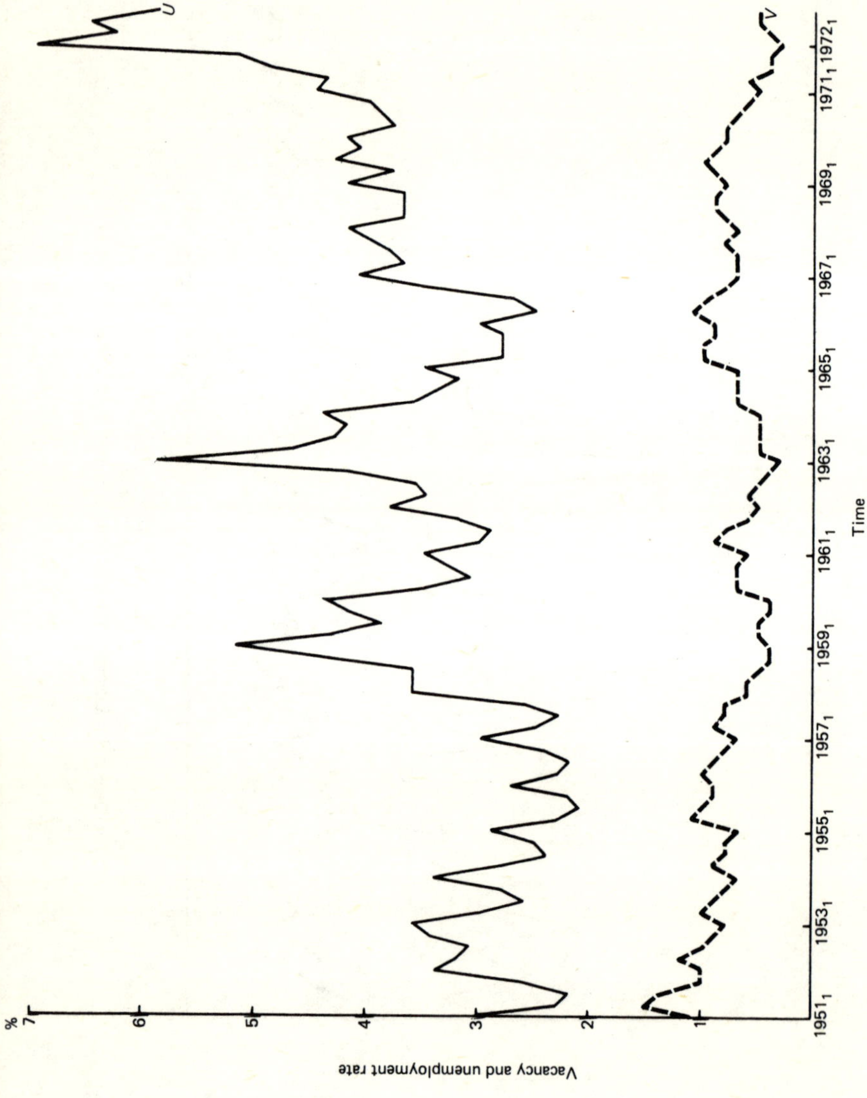

FIGURE 5.10 Unemployment and vacancy rates 1951–72 – SCOTLAND

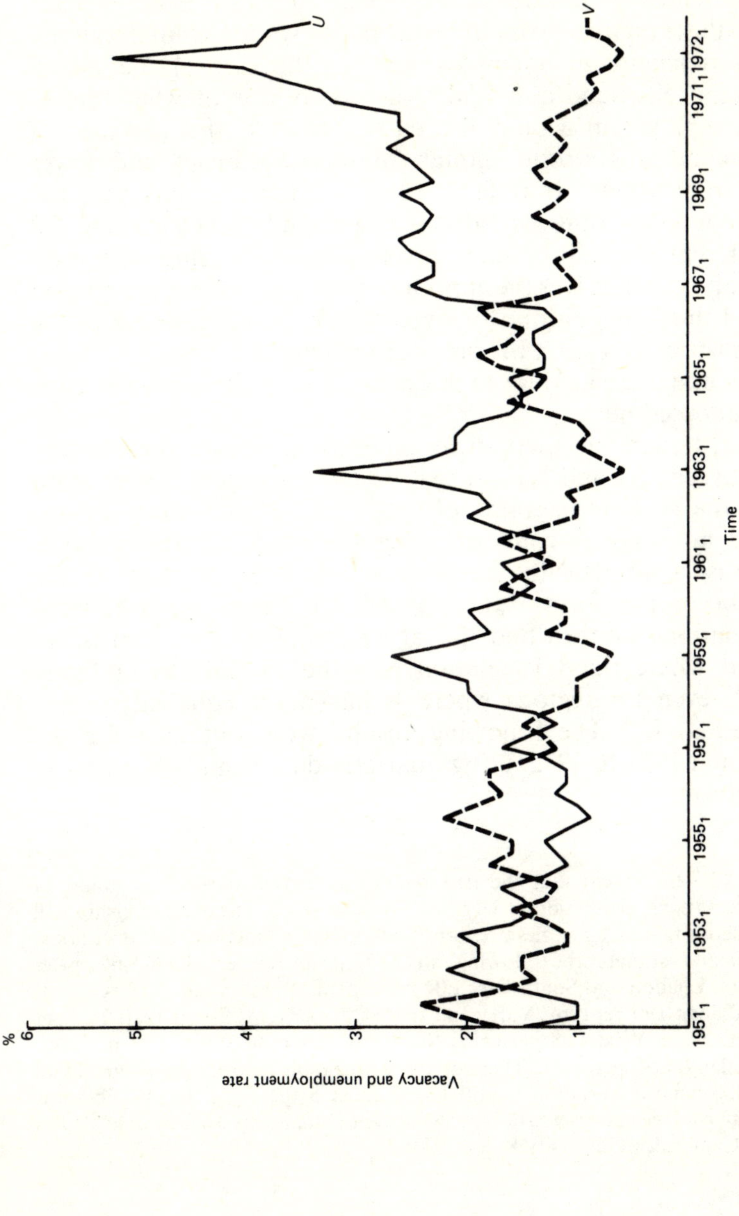

FIGURE 5.11 Unemployment and vacancy rates 1951–72 – GREAT BRITAIN

are certainly much closer than the average unemployment rates experienced over the period, which suggests that differences in non demand-deficient unemployment – at least for these regions – cannot be the major source of interregional discrepancies in unemployment. In the case of the North region, Scotland and Wales the question is at what rate of unemployment would the curves cross if the pressure of demand was strong enough to raise vacancies and lower unemployment. It is fairly clear from the graphs that the hypothetical rates would lie somewhere between 1.5 and 2.0 per cent. We can be more precise, however, using regression analysis, which was the approach mentioned under our second and third suggestions for overcoming the dependence of the measure of U_{NDD} on the pressure of demand. Since approaches two and three amount to the same thing, only approach three is adopted here.

Although the theoretical expectation is that the relation between $\%U$ and $\%V$ is negative and non-linear, observation of the scatter diagrams of $\%U$ and $\%V$ for most regions did not suggest convexity over the range of observations. Thus, arithmetically linear functions were applied to the data of the form: $\%U = a + b(\%V)$. From the estimated equations we then find $\%U$ at which $\%U = \%V$. That is, we find where the UV relation cuts the 45° line as in figure 5.2 – even for regions where V has never equalled (or exceeded) U.[4] The following results were obtained for the period 1951 to 1972, using quarterly data (standard errors in brackets):

[4] To the extent that the true relation is convex outside the range of observations, estimation of U_{NDD} on the basis of the linear relationship will underestimate U_{NDD}. Cheshire has fitted log-linear functions to the regional data and estimates the following rates of U_{NDD} for the period 1962–65 (males only): London and South East 1.04 per cent; East and South 1.18 per cent; Midlands 0.90 per cent; Yorks and Lincs 1.01 per cent; South West 1.23 per cent; North West 1.28 per cent; North 1.62 per cent; Wales 1.77 per cent; Scotland 1.68 per cent. There is more variation here in the estimates of U_{NDD}, but the variation is still less than in actual $\%U$. See P. Cheshire, *Regional Unemployment Differences in Great Britain*, NIESR Regional Papers II (Cambridge University Press, 1973).

TABLE 5.1 1951 to 1972 (quarterly data)

Region	$\%U = a + b(\%V)$	r^2	$\%U$ *when* $\%U = \%V$
SE	$U = 2.821 - 0.985(V)$ (0.103)	0.517	1.421
SW	$U = 4.553 - 1.848(V)$ (0.171)	0.578	1.599
M	$U = 3.749 - 1.514(V)$ (0.164)	0.502	1.491
NW	$U = 4.578 - 1.985(V)$ (0.173)	0.608	1.534
N	$U = 6.181 - 3.607(V)$ (0.530)	0.352	1.342
S	$U = 5.927 - 3.207(V)$ (0.352)	0.494	1.409
W	$U = 6.318 - 3.112(V)$ (0.310)	0.542	1.536
GB	$U = 4.138 - 1.656(V)$ (0.137)	0.134	1.558

The striking feature of the results in table 5.1 is the apparent degree of uniformity in the level of non demand-deficient unemployment between regions. There is no consistent tendency for high unemployment regions to have higher percentage levels of non demand-deficient unemployment than low unemployment regions. Indeed, regions such as Scotland and the North appear to have lower percentage levels of non demand-deficient unemployment than the South East and Midlands. Again the conclusion is reached that the major cause of high unemployment in the depressed regions is a deficiency of demand. This is most clearly seen if we take each region and solve for the percentage vacancy rate which would equalise regional unemployment rates at, say, 2 per cent. The results show a very similar vacancy rate in each region: South 0.83 per cent; South West 1.38 per cent; Midlands 1.15 per cent; North West 1.30 per cent; North 1.16 per cent; Scotland 1.22 per cent; and Wales 1.40 per cent. The fact that roughly the same vacancy rate would equalise unemployment rates suggests that the major cause of unemployment

TABLE 5.2 1951 to 1966 (quarterly data)

Region	$(\%U) = a+b(\%V)$	r^2	$\%U$ when $\%U = \%V$
SE	$U = 2.128 - 0.640(V)$ (0.046)	0.755	1.298
SW	$U = 3.441 - 1.232(V)$ (0.101)	0.705	1.542
M	$U = 2.516 - 0.867(V)$ (0.074)	0.686	1.348
NW	$U = 3.868 - 1.497(V)$ (0.166)	0.567	1.549
N	$U = 5.087 - 2.882(V)$ (0.278)	0.635	1.310
S	$U = 5.173 - 2.495(V)$ (0.245)	0.626	1.480
W	$U = 4.893 - 1.990(V)$ (0.223)	0.562	1.636
GB	$U = 3.144 - 1.074(V)$ (0.075)	0.766	1.516

differences must be differences in the vacancy rates.[5] If demand was to expand in depressed regions, unemployment would respond (as can be seen from the size of the regression coefficients in table 5.1) such that at zero excess demand, the level of unemployment would be no higher in the depressed regions than elsewhere in the country.

The time series graphs of $\%U$ and $\%V$ in figures 5.4 to 5.11 show a marked break in the UV relation in 1967. The level of vacancies since 1967 appears to have been associated with a much higher level of unemployment than the same level of vacancies before 1967. This changed relationship is sometimes interpreted as an increase in the level of structural and frictional unemployment (i.e. non demand-deficient unemployment). If $\%U$ is regressed on $\%V$ for the two separate

[5] The pattern of vacancy rates outlined here (as an expression of demand pressure) will not necessarily equalise unemployment in practice, because regions are interdependent and an increase in demand for labour in one region will have effects on unemployment in others. At the end of the chapter an interdependent system is specified in which unemployment in one region is linked to demand in all others. The model is then solved simultaneously for the pattern of vacancies that would, hypothetically, equalise unemployment.

TABLE 5.3 1967 to 1972 (quarterly data)

Region	$(\%U) = a + b(\%V)$	r^2	$\%U$ *when* $\%U = \%V$
SE	$U = 4.222 - 1.780(V)$ (0.432)	0.447	1.519
SW	$U = 5.388 - 2.067(V)$ (0.529)	0.421	1.757
M	$U = 7.015 - 4.043(V)$ (0.938)	0.470	1.391
NW	$U = 6.488 - 3.802(V)$ (0.505)	0.730	1.351
N	$U = 7.676 - 3.753(V)$ (1.678)	0.192	1.615
S	$U = 7.848 - 5.171(V)$ (1.094)	0.516	1.272
W	$U = 8.834 - 5.376(V)$ (1.221)	0.480	1.386
GB	$U = 5.991 - 2.930(V)$ (0.375)	0.744	1.524

time periods 1951–66 and 1967 to 1972, however (using quarterly data), the $\%U$ at zero excess demand in the various regions is not markedly different from one period to the other. In Great Britain as a whole, the rate of U_{NDD} is unchanged. The results are shown in tables 5.2 and 5.3. In some regions the $\%U$ at zero excess demand is higher post 1967, in others lower; for Great Britain as a whole the rate is 1.5 per cent in both periods. Those who have argued that the changed relation between U and V is the result of an increase in the level of non demand-deficient unemployment have been confusing more unemployment at the same level of vacancies with an increase in non demand-deficient unemployment when U_{NDD} is measured on the 45° line in the UV plane. It is quite possible for there to be a general upward shift in the UV relation but for the UV relation to cut the 45° line at roughly the same point because the slope of the relation has changed. This is what seems to have happened, but the 'true' effect of either of these changes cannot be ascertained from the equations in tables 5.2 and 5.3 without the use of dummy variables.

If $\%U$ is regressed on $\%V$ for the whole period 1951 to 1972, with the inclusion of a shift dummy which takes on values of zero for 1951 to 1966 and values of unity for 1967 to 1972, the shift dummy emerges as statistically significant and substantial in magnitude, as can be seen from table 5.4.

TABLE 5.4

Region	$(\%U) = a+b(\%V)+c(D)$	r^2
SE	$U = 2.291-0.742(V)+0.617(D)$ (0.083) (0.075)	0.731
SW	$U = 3.564-1.316(V)+0.932(D)$ (0.121) (0.085)	0.826
M	$U = 2.800-1.049(V)+1.090(D)$ (0.152) (0.167)	0.670
NW	$U = 4.183-1.755(V)+0.516(D)$ (0.178) (0.156)	0.653
N	$U = 5.170-2.982(V)+1.943(D)$ (0.364) (0.192)	0.708
S	$U = 5.538-2.968(V)+0.797(D)$ (0.319) (0.170)	0.599
W	$U = 5.133-2.221(V)+1.190(D)$ (0.261) (0.150)	0.738
GB	$U = 3.417-1.269(V)+0.820(D)$ (0.106) (0.090)	0.815

Using the equations in table 5.4, the $\%U$ at zero excess demand in the two periods is given in table 5.5.

TABLE 5.5 $\%U$ at zero excess demand using 'shift' dummies

	1951–66	*1967–72*
SE	1.315	1.669
SW	1.539	1.941
M	1.367	1.898
NW	1.518	1.706
N	1.298	1.786
S	1.396	1.597
W	1.594	1.963
GB	1.506	1.867

Without exception the results in table 5.5 show an upward shift in the *UV* relation, holding the slope of the relations constant. But the fact that the level of U_{NDD} has not changed significantly in the regions as shown in tables 5.2 and 5.3 suggests that there must have been an offsetting change in the slope of the *UV* curve at the same time. Higher unemployment is associated with the same level of vacancies, but unemployment has become more responsive to changes in vacancies.[6] Of course, this is merely a description of what seems to have happened; it is not an explanation. There is still the puzzle of why, suddenly in 1967, the level of unemployment associated with a given level of vacancies should have increased. No attempt will be made to answer this question here. We merely repeat that the occurrence of more unemployment at the same vacancy level cannot be interpreted as a rise in the level of non demand-deficient unemployment. To know the level of U_{NDD} we must know where the *UV* relation cuts the 45° line. The evidence is that the point at which the new *UV* relation cuts the 45° line is not substantially different from the old point of intersection.

Another suggested approach to the measurement of U_{NDD} is to take the estimates for each individual year using the classification outlined in equations (5.1) to (5.8), and reported in table 5.A1 of the appendix, and to average them over the years. It was argued earlier, however, that in making interregional comparisons this has the weakness that the average estimates will be affected by the average pressure of demand. It is none the less interesting to examine the extent of non demand-deficient unemployment in individual regions and the components of U_{NDD}. Then when the absolute numbers are converted into percentage rates, the rates can be adjusted for differences in the pressure of demand between regions to see whether a rough uniformity emerges. The contribution of structural unemployment to total unemployment in the various regions can be examined in the same way. The average

[6] A part of this effect may be spurious to the extent that no allowance is made for the fact that the *UV* relation may not be linear outside the range of observations. If the relation is non-linear the estimated difference in the level of U_{NDD} between the two periods might be somewhat greater.

regional levels of non demand-deficient unemployment, and its components, are given in table 5.6, together with the levels of U_{NDD} as a percentage of the workforce.

TABLE 5.6 Average levels of U_{NDD}, structural and frictional unemployment in the regions 1963–72

	Average structural		*Average frictional*		*U_{NDD} as % of workforce*	
	Males	*Females*	*Males*	*Females*	*Males*	*Females*
LSE, E & S	13538	2162	33800	14447	1.6	1.0
SW	1531	1502	5280	3609	0.8	1.1
M, YH	7830	3835	16245	10064	0.7	1.7
NW	2415	4066	8094	6451	0.6	0.9
N	734	973	3609	2549	0.5	0.8
W	1548	677	2868	2016	0.6	0.9
S	759	1626	4785	4277	0.4	0.8
GB*	26151	19336	86290	56969	0.8	0.9

* Note the estimate for Great Britain will not be the sum of the regional estimates. The estimate for GB is based on the assumption of complete geographic mobility. The regional estimates treat the regions as if they were self contained labour markets with no mobility between them.

Source: Table 5.A1 of the appendix to the chapter.

The average level of non demand-deficient unemployment in Great Britain as a whole over the period has been approximately 190,000, which constitutes just over one-third of the average stock of unemployment or 0.8 per cent of the workforce. The dependence of the percentage level of U_{NDD} in the regions on regional demand pressure is quite apparent from table 5.6. When adjustment is made for differences in demand pressure much greater uniformity is shown, reinforcing our earlier conclusion.

The average number of structurally unemployed males and females in Great Britain has averaged 45,000 or 15 per cent of the average number of unemployed over the period. This gives some measure of the extent of structural imbalances in the labour market as a whole (ignoring geographic immobility) at the pressure of demand that has prevailed in the economy over the period 1963 to 1972. In the years of the highest pressure of demand for male and female labour (1965 and 1967, respectively), we calculate that approximately 100,000 job vacancies existed in shortage occupations. Thus we estimate that approximately one-fifth of the average unemployment stock over the last decade would require retraining for a once-for-all reduction in the structural component of unemployment. What the flow of new trainees would then have to be to keep structural unemployment from rising again would depend on the extent of structural change in the labour market.

The average contribution of structural unemployment to total unemployment in each region, without adjustment for differences in demand pressure, is shown in table 5.7.

TABLE 5.7 Structural unemployment as a % of total unemployment

	Males	*Females*
LSE	18.1	11.8
ES	26.3	8.8
SW	9.0	25.5
M	19.2	22.1
YH	13.5	24.0
NW	6.0	25.0
N	2.5	15.4
W	7.8	11.1
S	1.6	10.2
GB	10.2	22.5

Apart from the problem of regional differences in demand pressure, the estimates on a regional basis are subject to the possibility of both underestimate and overestimate. Since regions are treated as independent labour markets, structural unemployment may be overstated because some of the unemployed classified as structural could possibly move to vacancies in other regions. On the other hand, structural unemployment may be underestimated by the assumption of complete geographic mobility *within* the region. The realism of these assumptions may vary from region to region affecting the realism of the estimates accordingly.

In making interregional comparisons, table 5.7 presents the same problem as we encountered before in estimating the percentage level of U_{NDD}, namely that the relative importance of each type of unemployment in each region is not independent of the region's pressure of demand. Ideally what we wish to know is whether structural unemployment is more of a problem in region *X* than in region *Y* at the same pressure of demand in both regions. One way of overcoming the difficulty is to adjust each region's structural unemployment by the extent to which its pressure of demand (as measured by the percentage level of unemployment[7]) has fallen short of, or exceeded, the average pressure of demand for all regions; the adjustment factor being based on the regression coefficient relating the percentage of structural unemployment to the percentage level of unemployment in each region. A second approach is simply to find years when the pressure of demand has been the same in each region, and to compare the relative contribution of structural unemployment on this basis. There is no one year when all regions had the same percentage level of unemployment but a year can be found for each region when unemployment was approximately 2.5 per cent. The results of both exercises are shown in table 5.8.

It can be seen from the first column of table 5.8, in comparison with table 5.7, that when adjustment is made for differences in regional demand pressure the contribution of structural unemployment to total unemployment varies very little between regions. The exceptional regions are the South West and North West where the pressure of demand as measured by unemployment has been relatively strong but where vacancies relative to unemployment have been low. Adjustment makes the measure of structural unemployment lower.

The more interesting and revealing calculations, however, are those which show the percentage contribution of structural

[7] Taking unemployment as a measure of demand pressure is legitimate if the degree of non demand-deficient does not vary significantly between regions, which, we have argued, it does not.

TABLE 5.8 Structural unemployment in the regions adjusted for differences in regional demand pressure

	Average structural unemployment as a % of total unemployment adjusted for differences in the pressure of demand (using regression analysis)	*Structural unemployment as a % of total unemployment when regional unemployment = 2.5% (unless otherwise stated)*
London and South East	9.8	4.0 (at $U = 2.2\%$)
East and South	17.3	5.0 (at $U = 2.1\%$)
South West	6.9	3.2
Midlands	13.7	4.3 (at $U = 2.4\%$)
Yorkshire and Humberside	12.1	3.2
North West	5.3	4.3
North	13.6	8.9
Wales	14.7	17.5
Scotland	11.3	3.9 (at $U = 2.7\%$)

unemployment to total unemployment in each region when the percentage level of unemployment has been close to 2.5 per cent. Although there is some bias in the figures because Scotland's unemployment has never fallen to 2.5 per cent, and unemployment in the South has never approached 2.5 per cent, it is difficult to escape the conclusion that the extent of structural imbalance in relation to the size of regions does not vary markedly between regions of the country (with the exception perhaps of Wales). The major source of inter-regional differences in the percentage level of unemployment must be differences in the pressure of labour demand. The additional interesting finding here is that the labour market bottlenecks that would emerge in depressed regions if demand was expanded to achieve 2.5 per cent unemployment would be no greater than in the prosperous regions operating at 2.5 per cent unemployment. At levels of unemployment in excess of 2.5 per cent of the labour force in the depressed regions, unemployment appears extremely responsive to demand expansion. The major problem confronting policy would seem to be that the interregional pattern of demand is such that when depressed regions operate at 2.5 per cent unemployment, unemployment elsewhere falls to a very low level indeed, and chronic labour shortages develop in the prosperous regions. The focus of policy if interregional unemployment rate discrepancies are to be narrowed must be on policies to expand demand in the depressed regions in activities with high local linkages so as to insulate the rest of the economy from their effects.

The geographic dimension of structural unemployment

So far it has been assumed that workers are completely mobile geographically; that unemployed workers in one geographic labour market are frictionally unemployed provided there are vacancies in the same occupation in another part of the same labour market regardless of the distance between the location of the unemployed and the location of unsatisfied labour demand. It is usual, however, to recognise that structural unemployment has a geographic dimension; that for unemployment to be truly frictional there must exist vacancies not only in the right occupation but within reasonable travelling distance as well. The fact that not all vacancies occur in the locations of the unemployed means that our previous measure of frictional unemployment will overstate the true extent of frictional unemployment and understate the true extent of structural unemployment. The boundary between frictional and structural unemployment depends, in short, not only on how finely occupations are classified but also on how geographic labour markets are defined. In general, the greater the number of different occupations and localities distinguished as separate markets, the smaller the frictional component of unemployment and the larger the structural component. It does not follow, however, that the greater the degree of disaggregation the better. To argue for the finest disaggregation possible would be to assume a degree of immobility between regions and between occupations which may not be warranted. Workers may be quite mobile within a fairly large occupational grouping or within a fairly broad region. Later we measure the geographic dimension of structural unemployment in the country as a whole, using the old Standard Regions as labour markets. These are much larger than travel to work areas, which means that we shall probably be underestimating the extent of structural unemployment associated with geographic immobility. We cannot estimate the geographic dimension of structural unemployment *within* the Standard Regions because the data required are not available at the sub-regional level. The basis of measurement would be exactly the same, however.

To obtain a measure of the geographic dimension of structural unemployment within a labour market, the classificatory scheme outlined in equations (5.1) to (5.8) can be applied to unemployment and vacancies in the *same* occupation *between* areas within the labour market, so that 'geographic' structural unemployment is the sum of the excess of vacancies over unemployment in an occupation in each area, when in the occupation as a whole $U_i > V_i$, plus the sum of the excess of unemployment over vacancies in an occupation in each area, when in the occupation as a whole $V_i > U_i$. Frictional unemployment is measured as a residual in the normal way. Hence, total structural unemployment associated with geographic immobility is given by:

$$\sum_{n}\sum_{irm}(v_{ir}-u_{ir})+\sum_{m}\sum_{irn}(u_{ir}-v_{ir}) \qquad (5.9)$$

where n is the number of occupations in which $U_i > V_i$
m is the number of occupations in which $V_i > U_i$
irm is the number of areas in which vacancies exceed unemployment (when in the occupation as a whole $U_i > V_i$)
and irn is the number of areas in which unemployment exceeds vacancies (when in the occupation as a whole $V_i > U_i$).

This measure of the geographic dimension of structural unemployment plus the earlier occupational measure of structural unemployment given by equation (5.5) gives *total* structural unemployment when $U > V$ in the labour market.

When $V > U$ in the aggregate, *total* structural unemployment is given by the sum of equations (5.9) and (5.8).

It is interesting to note that our total measure of structural unemployment when $U > V$ is equal to

$$\sum_{i}\sum_{irm}(v_{ir}-u_{ir})$$

where $i = n+m$. To see this, add equations (5.5) and (5.9) which gives:

$$\sum_{m}(V_i-U_i)+\sum_{n}\sum_{irm}(v_{ir}-u_{ir})+\sum_{m}\sum_{irn}(u_{ir}-v_{ir}) \qquad (5.10)$$

Now

$$\sum_{m}(V_i-U_i)+\sum_{m}\sum_{irn}(u_{ir}-v_{ir})=\sum_{m}\sum_{irm}(v_{ir}-u_{ir}) \qquad (5.11)$$

so that equation (5.10) may be written:

$$\sum_{n}\sum_{irm}(v_{ir}-u_{ir})+\sum_{m}\sum_{irm}(v_{ir}-u_{ir}) \qquad (5.12)$$

Since $n+m = i$, we have total structural unemployment equal to:

$$\sum_{i}\sum_{irm}(v_{ir}-u_{ir}) \qquad (5.13)^{8}$$

In other words, structural unemployment due to occupational mismatch and geographic immobility is the sum over all occupations of the excess demand for labour in particular occupations in all the geographic areas that make up the labour market under study.

The application of equation (5.9) to data for the British economy gives the results shown in table 5.9.

It can be seen from table 5.9 that the estimates of the numbers unemployed associated with the inability of workers within an occupation to move from a region where there is excess labour supply in that occupation to a region where there is excess demand are lower than the measures of structural unemployment previously ascribed to occupational immobility. There is a contrast, however, between the results

[8] This measure has been suggested by Perlman but without formal derivation. See R. Perlman, *Labour Theory* (John Wiley and Son, 1969).

TABLE 5.9 The geographic dimension of structural unemployment in Great Britain

	Males	*Females*
1963	7949	14268
1964	10248	15778
1965	8930	20612
1966	5344	10324
1967	5946	11082
1968	5926	9071
1969	6068	8741
1970	5304	8595
1971	1992	7423
1972	6660	9189

for males and females in the sense that the two measures of structural unemployment for females are much closer than for males. It should also be noted that the measure of 'geographic' structural unemployment for females is higher than for males. The year to year measures are again sensitive to the overall pressure of demand, but maximum estimates can be obtained. For males the figure is 10,000, compared with over 20,000 for females. This contrast is despite the fact that the average number of females unemployed is only roughly one-fifth of the average number of males unemployed at any one time.

Comparing the amount of structural unemployment resulting from geographic immobility with that resulting from occupational immobility, two conclusions stand out. The first is that in general, and for males in particular, the regional distribution of the supply and demand for labour within occupations is much more balanced than the distribution of the supply and demand for labour between occupations in the country at large. This would suggest that equilibrium tendencies, such as mobility, are more powerful in equalising the regional dispersion of the supply and demand for labour within occupations than in equalising the supply and demand for labour between occupations. In short, occupational immobility is more of a 'problem' than geographic immobility. The second conclusion is that given the greater amount of structural unemployment among females associated with geographic immobility, it seems that the equilibrating tendencies in the female labour market are much weaker than in the male labour market, presumably due to a greater reluctance to move.

Adding the occupational and geographic dimensions of structural unemployment gives a measure of total structural unemployment. If we take the maximum male and female totals for each component, we obtain a total figure of 130,000 as the measure of structural unemployment in the British economy during the period 1963 to 1972 when the pressure of demand in the labour market was strongest.

Given the size of the regions used in the analysis, it could be argued that our measure of structural unemployment associated with geographic immobility is understated. Some of the unemployed classified as frictionally unemployed within a large region may, in fact, be quite immobile between one part of the region and another. An analysis of the geographic dimension of structural unemployment by travel to work areas (or any smaller geographic unit) would inevitably reveal a greater amount of structural unemployment the way we have defined it. It is not the case, however, that the greater the degree of disaggregation the better. Too great a degree of disaggregation may grossly underestimate the degree of mobility between regions and therefore exaggerate the amount of structural unemployment associated with geographic immobility. The optimum-sized geographic area from this point of view would seem to be that in which immobility within the region was in exact balance with mobility between itself and other regions.

The implications of the analysis for policy are fairly clear. Given the predominant cause of structural unemployment, it makes sense for manpower policy to devote the major part of its resources to schemes for occupational training and retraining as opposed to schemes for encouraging labour mobility from one region to another, especially when labour mobility usually means migration to the southern half of the country where the social costs imposed on the community by immigrants tend to be highest. From all points of view, the most useful manpower policies of all would be those which made workers more occupationally mobile within their own region. Labour shortages could be eased; workers would not have to uproot themselves, and the drift to prosperous areas, generating even further prosperity, would be curtailed.

EQUALISATION OF REGIONAL UNEMPLOYMENT RATES

It has been argued that the major cause of the persistence of interregional discrepancies in unemployment has been persistent differences in the pressure of demand between regions. The question arises of what demand pressure would be required, expressed in terms of vacancies, to equalise unemployment rates bearing in mind that expanding demand in one region will have repercussions on unemployment in other regions. One approach to answering this question is to formulate an explanatory model of regional unemployment which relates each region's unemployment rate to demand in all other regions as measured by regional vacancy rates, and then to determine the pattern of vacancies that would hypothetically equalise unemployment at some given percentage in this 'general equilibrium' framework.

For each region, let the unemployment rate be a function of the demand for labour within the region, as measured by the region's own vacancy rate, and also a function of the state of demand in the economy as a whole as measured by the aggregate unemployment rate. It is useful on two counts to use aggregate unemployment as a separate argument in the regional unemployment function. First, a measure of aggregate demand is needed to capture the possibility that the supply of labour to and from a region, and therefore a region's unemployment rate, may respond to demand conditions outside the region. The region's own vacancy rate may not be a good proxy for the state of demand outside the region (i.e. V_r and U_{GB} may vary independently). Secondly, it is convenient to use aggregate unemployment as an explanatory variable in each region in order to link up regions by using the identity that aggregate $\%U$ is a weighted sum of the regional rates of unemployment. Hence for each region we specify:

$$U_t^r = f(V_t^r, U_t^{GB}) \quad (5.14)$$

It is further hypothesised that the adjustment of unemployment to changes in the demand for labour within and outside a region does not take place instantaneously but is a distributed lag function of past demand, so that we may write (5.14) in linear estimating form as:

$$U_t^r = a_o + bV_t^r + b_1 V_{t-1}^r + b_2 V_{t-2}^r + \ldots + cU_t^{GB} + c_1 U_{t-1}^{GB} + c_2 U_{t-2}^{GB} + \ldots + \varepsilon_t \quad (5.15)$$

where ε_t is a disturbance term.

To facilitate estimation we assume the Koyck specification that the coefficients on each explanatory variable decline geometrically, and also that the distributions on both variables have the same parameters, λ, so that: $b_k = b\lambda_1^k$ and $c_k = c\lambda_2^k$ $(k = 0, 1 \ldots)$ and $0 < \lambda_1 = \lambda_2 < 1$. Substitution of b_k and c_k into (5.15) and some manipulation gives the Koyck transformation which has only three parameters to be estimated:[9]

$$U_t^r = a_o^* + bV_r^t + cU_t^{GB} + \lambda U_{t-1}^r + \varepsilon^* \quad (5.16)$$

where $a_o^* = a_o(1-\lambda)$
and $\varepsilon^* = \varepsilon_t - \lambda\varepsilon_{t-1}$.

The model is simultaneous in the sense that U_t^{GB} is a weighted sum of U_t^r $(r = 1 \ldots 7)$. The model thus consists of seven behavioural equations and one identity giving eight equations in eight unknowns. The system may be written as follows:

$$U_t^{SE} = a_1 + \gamma_{11} V_t^{SE} + \gamma_{12} U_{t-1}^{SE} + \gamma_{13} U_t^{GB} + z_{1t}$$
$$U_t^{SW} = a_2 + \gamma_{21} V_t^{SW} + \gamma_{22} U_{t-1}^{SW} + \gamma_{23} U_t^{GB} + z_{2t}$$
$$U_t^{M} = a_3 + \gamma_{31} V_t^{M} + \gamma_{32} U_{t-1}^{M} + \gamma_{33} U_t^{GB} + z_{3t}$$
$$U_t^{NW} = a_4 + \gamma_{41} V_t^{NW} + \gamma_{42} U_{t-1}^{NW} + \gamma_{43} U_t^{GB} + z_{4t}$$
$$U_t^{N} = a_5 + \gamma_{51} V_t^{N} + \gamma_{52} U_{t-1}^{N} + \gamma_{53} U_t^{GB} + z_{5t}$$
$$U_t^{S} = a_6 + \gamma_{61} V_t^{S} + \gamma_{62} U_{t-1}^{S} + \gamma_{63} U_t^{GB} + z_{6t}$$

[9] If the λ parameter is different for each explanatory variable, the Koyck transformation would contain more lagged variables and more parameters to be estimated.

$$U_t^{\mathrm{W}} = a_7 + \gamma_{71} V_t^{\mathrm{W}} + \gamma_{72} U_{t-1}^{\mathrm{W}} + \gamma_{73} U_t^{\mathrm{GB}} + z_{7t}$$

$$U_t^{\mathrm{GB}} = w_1 U_t^{\mathrm{SE}} + w_2 U_t^{\mathrm{SW}} + w_3 U_t^{\mathrm{M}} + w_4 U_t^{\mathrm{NW}} + w_5 U_t^{\mathrm{N}} + w_6 U_t^{\mathrm{S}} + w_7 U_t^{\mathrm{W}}$$

where the *w*'s in the last equation are the weights measuring the proportional importance of a region in the nation in terms of the workforce.

The system may be written in matrix form as:

$$\Gamma Y + \beta X + Z = 0 \tag{5.17}$$

where Y is an $m \times T$ matrix of endogenous variables
X is a $k \times T$ matrix of predetermined variables (i.e. exogenous and lagged endogenous)
Γ is an $m \times m$ matrix of coefficients on the endogenous variables
β is an $m \times k$ matrix of coefficients on the predetermined variables
Z is an $m \times T$ matrix of error terms
T is the number of observations
m is the number of endogenous variables
and k is the number of predetermined variables.

The solved reduced form for each of the endogenous variables is:

$$Y = -\Gamma^{-1} \beta X \tag{5.18}$$

The direct or fitted reduced form obtained simply by regressing each endogenous variable on all predetermined variables in the system may be written:

$$Y = \Pi X \tag{5.19}$$

where Π is an $m \times k$ matrix of least squares regression coefficients.

We shall use (5.19) here since we expect the direct reduced form to have the least residual variance. For one region in the system (say the South East) the direct reduced form gives:

$$U_t^{SE} = a_1 + b_1 V_t^{SE} + b_2 V_t^{SW} + b_3 V_t^{M} + b_4 V_t^{NW} + b_5 V_t^{N} + b_6 V_t^{S} + b_7 V_t^{W} + c_1 U_{t-1}^{SE} + c_2 U_{t-1}^{SW} + c_3 U_{t-1}^{M} + c_4 U_{t-1}^{NW} + c_5 U_{t-1}^{N} + c_6 U_{t-1}^{S} + c_7 U_{t-1}^{W}$$

To determine the pattern of vacancies that would equalise the U^rs at some level of unemployment (say 2 per cent), set $U_t^{r1} = U_t^{r2} = \ldots U_t^{r7} = U_{t-1}^{r1} = U_{t-1}^{r2} = \ldots U_{t-1}^{r7} = 2$. This gives a new matrix $Y = \Pi^* X^*$, where Π^* is now of dimension $m \times m$ and X^* is of dimension $m \times T$. Hence $X^* = \Pi^{*-1} Y$ gives the value of the V^rs, which equalise unemployment in each region at 2 per cent. The results obtained are shown in table 5.10, and compared with the vacancy rates that would appear to be necessary to equalise unemployment at 2 per cent assuming no interdependence between regions (derived from table 5.1). The average vacancy rates which have actually prevailed over the sample period are also shown.

TABLE 5.10

	Required V^rs to equalise regional unemployment at 2 per cent assuming interdependence between regions	*Required V^rs to equalise regional unemployment at 2 per cent assuming no interdependence between regions*	*Actual vacancy rates (av. 1951 to 1972)*
SE	−0.34	0.83	1.50
SW	1.52	1.38	1.40
M	0.76	1.15	1.42
NW	2.95	1.30	1.13
N	1.95	1.16	0.80
S	1.55	1.22	0.75
W	2.57	1.40	0.98

The results show that the pattern of demand required to equalise unemployment rates is virtually the reverse of that which has prevailed in the past – as measured by vacancy rates. The regions with the highest vacancy rates require the least demand pressure to achieve 2 per cent unemployment; whereas those regions with the lowest vacancy rates require the greatest demand pressure. The North West and Wales in particular seem to require a very high demand pressure for unemployment to be reduced to 2 per cent. The differential demand pressure required for the equalisation of unemployment rates is a reflection of three main factors: firstly, differences in the amount of unemployment in a region which exists independently of the pressure of demand; secondly, differences in the responsiveness of unemployment to demand within the region, and thirdly, differences in the repercussions that demand in one region has on others. We have already seen, however, that the rate of unemployment which is independent of the pressure of demand does not differ markedly between regions and that the sensitivity of unemployment to demand is, if anything, higher in high unemployment regions than in low unemployment regions. It would seem, therefore, that the differential pattern of required vacancy rates outlined in table 5.10 is mainly a reflection of interregional labour demand relations. In the South East region, for example, the fact that the pressure of demand would apparently have to be such that the vacancy rate was negative is almost certainly due to the strong repercussions that extra labour demand outside the south would have on the demand for labour in the south, because of the quantity of inputs the north purchases from the south. On the other hand, the feedback effects of the south on the north are probably much less. Obviously this will be to a certain extent a function of the industrial composition and openness of regions.

It is also seen that the differential demand pattern between regions to equalise unemployment is substantially different from that indicated earlier, taking each region in isolation without considering interregional linkages and the repercussions that the expansion of demand in one region has on others. The regional demand problem is more serious than appears on the surface in the sense that to equalise unemployment it would not be sufficient merely to raise demand in the 'north' to the level in the 'south'. A higher level would be required than in the 'south' because the 'north' apparently makes much heavier demands on the 'south' than the 'south' does on the 'north'. All this leads to the conclusion that if a really serious attempt is to be made to narrow regional unemployment rate discrepancies, demand must be severely curtailed in the south while demand is expanded in the north. This does not spell depression for the south; the demand contraction is necessary to nullify the expansionary effects on the south of demand expansion in the north.

TABLE 5.A1 Types of Unemployment

LONDON AND SOUTH EAST

	Males				Females			
	Total	*Demand-deficient*	*Structural*	*Frictional*	*Total*	*Demand-deficient*	*Structural*	*Frictional*
1963	47541	20708	9671	17162	12132	0	1814	10318
1964	35058	0	17525	19533	9102	0	397	8705
1965	35227	0	13823	21404	7841	0	424	7417
1966	38901	4714	14308	19879	7358	0	421	6937
1967	72262	48154	3360	20748	11167	0	1072	10095
1968	70042	44531	3742	21769	10088	0	948	9140
1969	66840	37407	7250	22183	9519	0	1156	8363
1970	67908	39162	5216	23530	8963	0	1170	7793
1971*	126200	94897	2216	29087	17905	0	5017	12888
1972	128706	83344	6241	39121	18853	0	2918	15935

* Figures refer to the South East region after 1971.

EAST AND SOUTH

1963	21523	6472	5752	9299	5572	0	1130	4442
1964	16986	0	7031	9955	9102	0	209	8893
1965	16936	0	6498	10438	3880	0	67	3813
1966	21202	0	9425	11777	4316	0	142	4174
1967	35113	16778	5018	13317	6503	0	690	5813
1968	35563	16394	5192	13997	5717	0	520	5197
1969	38013	16398	7010	14605	5398	0	494	4904
1970	40864	19475	5039	16350	6279	0	901	5378
1971*	15704	13938	92	1674	2436	746	460	1230
1972	12847	9835	487	2525	2357	0	836	1521

* Figures refer to East Anglia after 1971.

SOUTH WEST

	Males				*Females*			
	Total	*Demand-deficient*	*Structural*	*Frictional*	*Total*	*Demand-deficient*	*Structural*	*Frictional*
1963	14156	8635	1747	3774	4059	0	1084	2975
1964	12273	4499	3494	4280	3334	0	664	2670
1965	13682	5910	3025	4747	3370	0	531	2839
1966	16350	10329	1922	4099	3646	0	865	2781
1967	23388	18017	750	4621	4637	0	1243	3394
1968	24101	18892	672	4537	4459	0	1034	3425
1969	27253	21795	806	4652	4878	0	1259	3619
1970	27762	22047	799	4916	4890	0	1426	3464
1971	35744	31031	189	4524	6666	1596	1626	3444
1972	34111	26833	952	6326	6587	199	2646	3742

MIDLANDS

1963	34825	24009	3220	7596	10719	1463	3671	5585
1964	19069	0	9922	9147	6379	0	1191	5188
1965	19729	0	9672	10057	5940	0	621	5319
1966	23650	0	12858	10792	6242	0	842	5400
1967	53100	38474	3174	11452	11061	1046	3555	6460
1968	57073	40735	3583	12755	9277	0	2560	6717
1969	55214	37906	4582	12726	8740	0	2406	6334
1970	62778	47469	2729	12580	11123	919	3439	6765
1971*	93618	84323	1178	8117	15190	8137	2175	4878
1972	97564	86315	1228	10021	17362	9174	2138	6050

* Figures refer to the combined East and West Midlands after 1971, and the Midlands and North Midlands prior to 1971.

Yorkshire and Humberside

	Males				Females			
	Total	Demand-deficient	Structural	Frictional	Total	Demand-deficient	Structural	Frictional
1963	23527	18029	1613	3885	6395	0	2796	3599
1964	16549	6398	5258	4893	4836	0	1326	3510
1965	14929	2912	6915	5099	3812	0	445	3367
1966	16678	5653	5720	5305	4023	0	660	3363
1967	32022	25431	1442	5149	5867	0	1855	4012
1968	41893	36108	875	4910	5532	0	1562	3970
1969	42184	34313	1922	5949	6082	0	1705	4377
1970	46215	37945	1504	6766	6441	0	1922	4519
1971*	65173	60543	236	4394	9212	4606	1129	3477
1972	65022	59252	337	5433	10906	5852	1176	3879

* Figures prior to 1971 refer to East and West Ridings.

North West

1963	51091	44800	743	5448	17327	8049	2828	6450
1964	37263	26666	2977	7620	11325	0	4052	7273
1965	31683	17143	5836	8704	9019	0	2576	6443
1966	31282	16799	6277	8206	7939	0	2128	5811
1967	54025	45094	1200	7731	11645	1576	3379	6690
1968	56567	46354	1406	8807	8636	0	2371	5265
1969	58411	47434	2544	8433	8384	0	2677	5707
1970	65081	55039	1494	8548	9486	0	3674	5812
1971	96769	91209	157	5403	14421	7867	1538	5016
1972	110700	104662	16	6022	17696	11806	866	5024

NORTH

	Males				Females			
	Total	*Demand-deficient*	*Structural*	*Frictional*	*Total*	*Demand-deficient*	*Structural*	*Frictional*
1963	35999	34200	187	1612	9529	7442	510	1577
1964	25858	22221	899	2738	7475	4568	677	2230
1965	21647	16041	1932	3674	5817	1804	1357	2656
1966	23558	18137	1698	3723	5328	1131	1902	2295
1967	39301	35735	502	3064	7548	4040	965	2543
1968	49292	45458	432	3402	7444	3750	1165	2529
1969	49967	45358	681	3928	7653	3998	1109	2546
1970	47593	42354	514	4725	7719	4368	834	2517
1971	61558	58772	136	2650	10144	7695	389	2060
1972	63978	60508	182	3288	11644	8967	409	2268

WALES

1963	17715	14135	1988	1592	5926	3768	530	1628
1964	14452	9537	2474	2441	5222	2788	561	1873
1965	16756	11011	2927	2818	5286	2072	1277	1937
1966	18710	12933	2680	3097	5205	2494	933	1778
1967	27334	23888	947	2499	7016	4689	521	1806
1968	29000	26070	411	2519	5672	3236	738	1698
1969	29853	25383	1506	2964	5838	3136	654	2048
1970	27804	23529	1198	3077	5335	3018	488	1829
1971	35204	32099	850	1547	7309	5552	210	1547
1972	36856	33895	250	2711	7907	5469	430	2008

	Males				Females			
	Total	*Demand-deficient*	*Structural*	*Frictional*	*Total*	*Demand-deficient*	*Structural*	*Frictional*
SCOTLAND								
1963	58770	55492	377	2901	21970	17158	1734	3078
1964	45513	40135	1202	4176	17991	11709	1978	4304
1965	38815	31827	2142	4846	14647	7703	2296	4648
1966	39667	32723	1564	5380	13080	6940	2088	4052
1967	56404	51389	322	4693	18046	12900	1259	3887
1968	57593	51387	715	5491	14575	7832	1871	4872
1969	59007	52510	638	5859	12917	6114	2275	4528
1970	70432	65210	373	4849	14874	9607	1556	3711
1971	98566	95732	130	2704	21129	17908	541	2680
1972	100886	97408	0	3478	24308	20471	332	3505
GREAT BRITAIN								
1963	305147	226480	16800	61867	93629	14108	24768	54753
1964	223021	98532	50846	73643	70171	0	14495	55676
1965	209401	61575	75807	72019	59612	0	8969	50643
1966	229998	97528	54894	77756	57137	0	9938	47199
1967	393284	303295	10747	79242	83490	0	27808	55682
1968	421124	325929	10728	84467	71400	0	18528	52872
1969	426742	318504	18920	89318	69409	0	18079	51330
1970	456437	352230	13534	90673	75110	0	24708	50402
1971	628536	562544	2831	63161	104412	45627	13760	45025
1972	650670	562052	3158	85470	117620	48408	16158	53054

Source: Occupational statistics of unemployment and unfilled vacancies from Department of Employment (September of each year).

6 The Determinants of Productivity Growth in the Regions of the United Kingdom: 1958–68

The purpose of this chapter is to examine regional economic growth from the supply side, using the familiar concept of the production function. In particular an attempt is made to estimate, and to assess the importance of, various determinants of productivity growth in regional manufacturing industry. In the first instance, a distinction is drawn between the effects of capital deepening on the one hand and what may loosely be called 'technical progress' on the other. In the absence of capital stock data, we incorporate and extend techniques developed by Johansen for estimating the rate of capital deepening from the neoclassical production function itself. An attempt is then made to measure the contribution of returns to scale and resource shifts to regional productivity growth.

THE NEOCLASSICAL APPROACH TO THE ANALYSIS OF PRODUCTIVITY GROWTH

The neoclassical approach to the determinants of productivity growth, which was pioneered by Solow[1] and elaborated on by others,[2] is designed to isolate two components of the growth

[1] R. M. Solow, 'Technical Change and the Aggregate Production Function', *Review of Economics and Statistics*, Aug 1957.

[2] For example, J. E. Meade, *A Neo-Classical Theory of Economic Growth* (George Allen & Unwin, 1962); M. Brown, *On the Theory and Measurement of Technological Change* (Cambridge University Press, 1968). For a survey of empirical results using the neoclassical framework see C. Kennedy and A. P. Thirlwall, 'Surveys in Applied Economics: Technical Progress', *Economic Journal*, Mar 1972.

of output per worker. The first relates to that part of the growth of labour productivity associated with an increase in capital per worker. The second relates to that part which arises from all other sources, variously called 'technical progress', 'the residual' or the 'coefficient of ignorance'.

Assume the production function is Cobb–Douglas, with constant returns to scale, and that technical progress is Hicks neutral[3] and disembodied.

Thus,
$$Y_t = A_t K_t^{\beta} L_t^{\alpha} \tag{6.1}$$

where Y is output
K is capital
L is labour
A is a measure of 'technical progress' (assumed neutral and disembodied)
β is the partial elasticity of output with respect to capital
α is the partial elasticity of output with respect to labour
and $\alpha + \beta = 1$ (constant returns)

Since $\alpha = 1 - \beta$, output per unit of labour may be written as

$$\frac{Y_t}{L_t} = \frac{A_t K_t^{\beta} L_t^{1-\beta}}{L_t} = \frac{A_t K_t^{\beta}}{L_t^{\beta}} = A_t \left(\frac{K_t}{L_t}\right)^{\beta}$$

or
$$q_t = A_t x_t^{\beta} \tag{6.2}$$

where q is output per man
and x is capital per man.

Totally differentiating equation (6.2) with respect to time and dividing both sides by q_t gives:

$$\frac{\dot{q}}{q} = \frac{\dot{A} x^{\beta}}{A x^{\beta}} + \frac{\dot{x} \beta A x^{\beta - 1}}{A x^{\beta}}$$

[3] That is, technical progress leaves the ratio of marginal products unchanged.

which simplifies to:

$$\frac{\dot{q}}{q} = \frac{\dot{A}}{A} + \beta \frac{\dot{x}}{x}$$

or

$$r = a + \beta(m) \tag{6.3}$$

where r is the rate of growth of labour productivity
m is the rate of growth of capital per worker
and a is the rate of (neutral) technical change.

The two terms on the R.H.S. of equation (6.3) show clearly the two components of productivity growth: (1) the contribution of capital deepening (βm) and (2) the contribution of 'technical progress' (a). On the perfectly competitive assumption that factors are paid the value of their marginal products, the elasticity of output with respect to capital (β) will equal capital's share of total income,[4] so that we may write (6.3) as:

$$r = a + w_k m, \tag{6.4}$$

where w_k is capital's share of output.

If data are available on labour productivity, capital per man and the share of capital in total income, the rate of (neutral) technical change (a) can be obtained as a residual.

The neoclassical approach to the analysis of productivity growth is particularly attractive because of its computational simplicity, and because it may be readily interpreted in terms of shifts in the production function and changes in technique with a given production function. As an analytical device it requires prior intellectual commitment to the concept of an aggregate production function together with the usual neoclassical assumptions with respect to factor substitutability and factor pricing.

As far as the United Kingdom economy is concerned, data on capital per worker is extremely difficult to come by. At the

[4] The proof is simple: $\beta = (\mathrm{d}Y/Y)/(\mathrm{d}K/K) = (\mathrm{d}Y.K)/(\mathrm{d}K.Y)$. If capital is paid the value of its marginal product ($\mathrm{d}Y/\mathrm{d}K$), then the expression $(\mathrm{d}Y.K)/(\mathrm{d}K.Y)$ gives the share of capital in total output (income).

regional level, the data is virtually unobtainable. If the production function is to be used for analysing regional productivity growth in the United Kingdom, therefore, we must resort to devices which allow us to overcome this serious data deficiency. One approach is that developed by Johansen,[5] which will be applied and extended here.

JOHANSEN'S APPROACH

Johansen's approach to the analysis of productivity growth on neoclassical lines obviates the need for estimates of the capital stock. While Johansen applied his method to cross-section data for individual industries, the approach is equally valid when applied to regional cross-section data. Assume that the prevailing technology in each region (r) may be approximated by a Cobb–Douglas production function (as equation (6.1)) so that regional labour productivity in any period (t) may be written:

$$q_{rt} = A_{rt} x_{rt}^{\beta rt}$$

Assuming that the exponents of the production function are constant over time, the ratio of labour productivity in the final period (q_{rt+n}) to labour productivity in the base period (q_{rt}) may be expressed as:

$$\frac{q_{rt+n}}{q_{rt}} = \frac{A_{rt+n}}{A_{rt}} \left(\frac{x_{rt+n}}{x_{rt}} \right)^{\beta r} \tag{6.5}$$

Given constant returns to scale, and that factors are paid their marginal products, we have:

$$\alpha_r = \frac{W_{rt} L_{rt}}{Y_{rt}} \quad \text{and} \quad \beta_r = \frac{R_{rt} K_{rt}}{Y_{rt}}$$

where W_r is the regional wage rate

and R_r is the regional rental per unit of capital.

[5] L. Johansen, 'A Method for Separating the Effects of Capital Accumulation and Shifts in Production Functions Upon Growth in Labour Productivity', *Economic Journal*, Dec 1961. The method is discussed in C. Kennedy and A. P. Thirlwall, op.cit., p. 30, and in G. L. Harcourt, *Some Cambridge Controversies in the Theory of Capital* (Cambridge University Press, 1972), pp. 66–9.

Rearranging the previous equation gives:

$$L_{rt} = \frac{\alpha_r Y_{rt}}{W_{rt}} \quad \text{and} \quad K_{rt} = \frac{\beta_r Y_{rt}}{R_{rt}},$$

so that capital per worker may be expressed as:

$$x_{rt} = \frac{\beta_r W_{rt}}{\alpha_r R_{rt}}$$

The ratio of final to base period capital per worker is then:

$$\frac{x_{rt+n}}{x_{rt}} = \frac{\beta_r W_{rt+n}/\alpha_r R_{rt+n}}{\beta_r W_{rt}/\alpha_r R_{rt}} = \frac{W_{rt+n}/R_{rt+n}}{W_{rt}/R_{rt}}$$

or alternatively,

$$\frac{x_{rt+n}}{x_{rt}} = \frac{W_{rt+n}/W_{rt}}{R_{rt+n}/R_{rt}} = w_r, \tag{6.6}$$

which Johansen calls the 'relative increase in wages'.[6]

Substitution of equation (6.6) into (6.5) yields:

$$\frac{q_{rt+n}}{q_{rt}} = \frac{A_{rt+n}}{A_{rt}} (w_r)^{\beta r} \tag{6.7}$$

Taking logarithms of (6.7) gives:

$$\log\left(\frac{q_{rt+n}}{q_{rt}}\right) = \log\left(\frac{A_{rt+n}}{A_{rt}}\right) + \beta_r(\log w_r) \tag{6.8}$$

Assuming that the 'relative increase in wages' (w_r) is the same for all regions, and that $\log A_{rt+n}/A_{rt}$ is uncorrelated with β_r, it is possible to estimate $\log w$ using ordinary regression analysis. $\text{Log}\, w$ is a measure of movements along the production function (i.e. increases in capital intensity), and may be substituted in equation (6.7) to obtain an estimate of the contribution of capital deepening and technical progress to the growth of labour productivity in each region. Johansen used his approach on a cross-section of twenty-eight British industries over the period 1928–50 and found that, in the aggregate, something of the order of between 26 per cent and

[6] Op. cit., p. 776.

40 per cent of the increase in labour productivity over the period could be accounted for by increases in capital per man.

Two particular comments may be made on Johansen's approach. Firstly, the discussion relating to the use of the 'relative increase in wages' as a proxy for the increase in capital per man is redundant given data deficiencies. It is equally valid to estimate the logarithmic transformation of equation (6.5) directly, which becomes:

$$\log\left(\frac{q_{rt+n}}{q_{rt}}\right) = \log\left(\frac{A_{rt+n}}{A_{rt}}\right) + \log\left(\frac{x_{rt+n}}{x_{rt}}\right)\beta_r \qquad (6.9)$$

If it is assumed that the increase in capital per worker is the same in all regions, equation (6.9) may be estimated as:

$$\log\left(\frac{q_{rt+n}}{q_{rt}}\right) = \lambda_1 + \lambda_2\beta_r + u \qquad (6.10)$$

where $\lambda_2 = \log\left(\frac{\hat{x}_{t+n}}{x_t}\right)$

and u is an error term.

In the absence of data for the 'relative increase in wages', nothing is lost by formulating the problem in this manner.

Secondly, it should be noted that it is not necessary to restrict the analysis to the case where the increase in capital per worker is assumed to be the same in all regions. The analysis can be generalised to the case where the rate of neutral technical progress is assumed to be constant, leaving the growth of capital per man free to assume any value in each region. This is easily demonstrated if we divide both sides of equation (6.9) by β_r giving:

$$\frac{1}{\beta_r}\log\frac{q_{rt+n}}{q_{rt}} = \log\frac{x_{rt+n}}{x_{rt}} + \log\frac{A_{rt+n}}{A_{rt}}\cdot\frac{1}{\beta_r} \qquad (6.11)$$

Now if it is assumed that $\log(A_{rt+n}/A_{rt})$ is the same in all regions, equation (6.11) may be estimated as:[7]

$$\frac{1}{\beta_r}\log\frac{q_{rt+n}}{q_{rt}} = \lambda_3 + \lambda_4\frac{1}{\beta_r} + u \tag{6.12}$$

where $\lambda_4 = \log\left(\frac{\hat{A}_{t+n}}{A_t}\right)$

This generalisation of Johansen's approach is interesting for two reasons. Firstly, it provides an alternative means of estimating the relative contributions of the two sources of productivity growth. Secondly, it enables an estimate to be made of the rate of capital deepening between regions. Indeed, it could be argued that keeping the rate of technical progress the same in each region is much more in keeping with the spirit of the neoclassical model, and much less of an injustice to reality, than assuming that capital deepening is the same in every region. After all, technical progress is assumed to be 'manna from heaven' and freely available, whereas capital deepening will depend on the industrial mix and relative prices, which may vary considerably from region to region.

Estimates of the Components of Productivity Growth for the Regions of the United Kingdom

It has been demonstrated that using the Cobb–Douglas production function it is possible to derive two estimating equations for analysing the determinants of productivity growth in the absence of capital data. One estimating equation assumes that each region experiences the same rate of capital deepening, leaving technical progress to vary freely: the other equation assumes that each region experiences the same rate of technical progress, allowing the rate of capital deepening to vary between regions. The two equations are:

$$\log\frac{q_{rt+n}}{q_{rt}} = \lambda_1 + \lambda_2\beta_r + u \tag{6.10}$$

[7] Since $1/\beta_r$ appears on both sides of the equation the estimated regression coefficient will be biased because of correlation between the independent variable and the error term. For the purposes at hand, this problem is not serious.

and
$$\frac{1}{\beta_r}\log\frac{q_{rt+n}}{q_{rt}} = \lambda_3 + \lambda_4\frac{1}{\beta_r} + u \tag{6.12}$$

where q_{rt} is real output per worker in region r at time t,
β_r is the elasticity of output with respect to capital in region r,
λ_2 is an estimate of $\log(x_{t+n}/x_t)$ (the rate of capital deepening),
and λ_4 is an estimate of $\log(A_{t+n}/A_t)$ (the rate of technical progress).

An attempt is made to estimate λ_2 and λ_4 using data for the total manufacturing sector of each region in the United Kingdom, for 1958 and 1968.[8]

The elasticity of output with respect to capital for each region (β_r) is assumed to be equal to the share of non-wage income in net output within each region:

i.e.
$$\beta_r = w_{kr} = 1 - (W_r/Y_r)$$

where W_r is total wage and salary payments in manufacturing industry in region r in 1963 in money terms,[9]
and Y_r is net output in manufacturing industries in each region in 1963 valued at current prices.

The increase in labour productivity in each region is calculated as the ratio between the values of net output per worker in manufacturing in 1968 and the value of net output per worker in manufacturing in 1958. Since regional price indices are not available, all the data are expressed in terms of current prices. Ideally we would wish to work in real terms, but the estimates we are interested in will not be affected provided either that the rate of inflation is the same in all regions or that there is no correlation between the rate of price increase and the share of capital in income across regions.

[8] Data and sources are presented in table 6.A1 of the appendix.
[9] 1963 was chosen as the middle year of the period over which there is comparable data on labour productivity.

When the estimating equation (6.10) was fitted to regional cross-section data for the period 1958–68, the following result was obtained:

$$\log\frac{q_{rt+n}}{q_{rt}} = \underset{}{1.068} - \underset{(1.418)}{0.755}\, w_{kr} \qquad r^2 = 0.032$$

The regression coefficient has the wrong sign. Taking antilogs of the coefficient yields an estimated value of x_{t+n}/x_t of 0.461, which in turn implies that capital per worker *declined* at the rate of 8.1 per cent per annum over the period.[10] An inspection of the scatter diagram and the residuals from the above equation, however, showed that two observations lay well above, and three well below, the hypothetical regression line. If the production function approach is accepted as a meaningful interpretation of events, we are faced with two alternative explanations of the result. First we could reject the assumption that the rate of capital deepening was the same in all regions, and accept that in two regions it was much greater, and in three regions much lower, than the average. This would involve the rejection of equation (6.10) as a valid estimating equation. Alternatively, it could be argued that the rate of growth of capital per worker was the same in all regions but that the rate of neutral technical progress differed greatly between regions. Following Johansen, we will tentatively accept the validity of equation (6.10) and assume that the poor fit is due to dissimilar rates of neutral technical progress. To cope with the 'outlying' observations, equation (6.10) was re-estimated using dummy variables. The re-estimated equation is (standard errors in brackets):

$$\log\frac{q_{rt+n}}{q_{rt}} = 0.348 + \underset{(0.392)}{0.741}\, w_{kr} - \underset{(0.023)}{0.125}\, d_1 + \underset{(0.025)}{0.211}\, d_2 \qquad r^2 = 0.950$$

where d_1 assumes the value 1 for the regions: N, YH and W, and zero otherwise

and d_2 assumes the value 1 for the regions: EM and NI and zero otherwise.

[10] Since $x_{t+n} = x_t(1+m)^n$, the rate of capital deepening (m) is calculated as: $m = \sqrt[n]{(x_{t+n}/x_t)} - 1$.

The sign of the coefficient on w_{kr} is now positive, and the estimate of $\log x_{t+n}/x_t$ $(=0.741)$ yields an estimated average annual rate of growth of capital per worker of $(+)7.7$ per cent. Given data on the rate of productivity growth in each region, and capital's share of income, the estimate of the rate of capital deepening (assumed to be the same in each region) can then be used for calculating the contribution of capital deepening and technical progress to the growth of labour productivity, using equation (6.3). Estimates of the 'deepening constant' rate of technical progress for each region are reported in table 6.1. They show the relative importance of capital accumulation as a source of regional productivity growth. For the United Kingdom as a whole the average annual rate of growth of labour productivity in manufacturing industry was 4.9 per cent, and the share of capital in income in 1963 was 0.47. Substituting these values into equation (6.3), together with the estimate of capital deepening, we find that the rate of technical progress was 1.3 per cent which accounts for 27 per cent of the measured growth of labour productivity – a figure much lower than normally found in production function studies of growth.[11] It is also apparent from table 6.1 that there is a wide variation in the rate of neutral technical progress between regions – a result somewhat at odds with the disembodied form technical progress is assumed to take. It seems that we must question the assumptions on which the analysis is based, in particular the assumption that the rate of capital deepening is the same in all regions.

An alternative procedure is to estimate equation (6.12) which assumes that the rate of neutral technical progress is the same in all regions. As we suggested earlier this seems a more reasonable assumption and certainly more in accord

[11] Matthews has estimated that technical progress accounted for 74 per cent of labour productivity growth in manufacturing industry over the period 1948 to 1962. See R. C. O. Matthews, 'Some Aspects of Post-War Growth in the British Economy in Relation to Historical Experience', *Transactions of the Manchester Statistical Society*, 1964–5. Nicholson's work for the period 1948–64 suggests a 50–50 split between the contribution of capital deepening and technical progress. See R. J. Nicholson, 'Capital Stock, Employment and Output in British Industry 1948–64', *Yorkshire Bulletin of Economic and Social Research*, Nov 1966.

TABLE 6.1 Estimates of 'capital deepening constant' rates of technical change, 1958–68

Region	r_r	m	$w_{kr}m$	a_r*
N	3.8	7.7	3.8	0.0
YH	3.9	7.7	3.5	0.4
EM	7.2	7.7	3.5	3.7
EA	5.8	7.7	3.8	2.0
SE	4.9	7.7	3.8	1.1
SW	4.6	7.7	3.3	1.3
WM	4.6	7.7	3.3	1.3
NW	5.3	7.7	3.6	1.7
W	3.7	7.7	3.8	−0.1
S	4.8	7.7	3.8	1.0
NI	7.2	7.7	3.5	3.7
UK	4.9	7.7	3.6	1.3

* $a_r = r_r - w_{kr} \,.\, m$.

with the spirit of neoclassical theory than the alternative assumption of the same rate of capital deepening. When equation (6.12) was fitted to the regional cross-section data the following result was obtained:

$$\frac{1}{w_{kr}} \log \frac{q_{rt+n}}{q_{rt}} = -0.704 + \underset{(0.660)}{1.035} \frac{1}{w_{kr}} \qquad r^2 = 0.214$$

The regression coefficient has the correct sign, but the coefficient is statistically insignificant. Moreover the implied estimate of the rate of technical progress of 10.8 per cent per annum is too high to be considered a realistic estimate. An inspection of the scatter diagram and residuals from equation (6.12), however, revealed a similar situation to that found earlier, namely five observations lying well off the hypothetical regression line. Earlier, following Johansen's lead, we investigated the implications of assuming that this was due to uneven rates of technical progress. We will now explore the possibility that the estimate of technical change is being distorted by the uneven rates of capital deepening between regions. Equation (6.12) was re-estimated with the use of dummy variables, as

TABLE 6.2 Estimates of the 'technical change constant' rates of capital deepening, 1958–68

Region	r_r	$\hat{a}$	$w_{kr}m_r$*	m_r†
N	3.8	3.5	0.3	0.6
YH	3.9	3.5	0.4	0.9
EM	7.2	3.5	3.7	8.0
EA	5.8	3.5	2.3	4.6
SE	4.9	3.5	1.4	2.9
SW	4.6	3.5	1.1	2.6
WM	4.6	3.5	1.1	2.6
NW	5.3	3.5	1.8	3.8
W	3.7	3.5	0.2	0.4
S	4.8	3.5	1.3	2.7
NI	7.2	3.5	3.7	8.0
UK	4.9	3.5	1.4	3.0

* $w_{kr}m_r = r_r - \hat{a}$.

† $m_r = \dfrac{r_r - \hat{a}}{w_{kr}}$.

before, with the following result:

$$\frac{1}{w_{kr}}\log\frac{q_{rt+n}}{q_{rt}} = 0.741 + \underset{(0.175)}{0.347}\frac{1}{w_{kr}} - \underset{(0.045)}{0.252}\,d_1 + \underset{(0.052)}{0.463}\,d_2$$

$$r^2 = 0.963$$

The estimate of the technical change parameter (antilog 0.347) now yields an implied average annual rate of technical progress of (+) 3.5 per cent. Given the actual rate of growth of labour productivity in each region, and capital's share, estimates of the rate of growth of capital per worker in each region are easily calculated using equation (6.3). Estimates of the 'technical change constant' rates of capital deepening are given in table 6.2, together with the contribution of capital deepening to growth in each region. In contrast to the results in table 6.1, they show technical progress as the main source of productivity growth. For the United Kingdom as a whole the estimated rate of technical progress in manufacturing industry is 3.0 per cent, or 72 per cent of measured productivity growth, leaving a 28 per cent contribution of capital deepening. These estimates accord much more with *a priori* expectations, and are almost identical with the relative contributions as estimated by Matthews for the period 1948–62. Some of the regional estimates of the rate of capital deepening in table 6.2 appear to be very high, but it should be borne in mind that some regions, particularly Scotland and Northern Ireland, experienced negative growth of employment. Other things being equal, this would tend to inflate the rates of growth of capital per man.

Our conclusion is that the formulation of the model which incorporates the assumption that the rate of technical progress is constant between regions seems much more reasonable than Johansen's original formulation both on theoretical and empirical grounds. This is of more than theoretical significance because it suggests that the major source of *differences* in the rate of productivity growth between regions lies not in different rates of technical progress but in differences in the rate of capital accumulation between regions.

AN ALTERNATIVE APPROACH USING THE RATE OF INCREASE IN WAGES AS A PROXY FOR THE RATE OF CAPITAL DEEPENING

An alternative approach to that of Johansen for estimating the components of productivity growth in the absence of capital data is to use the rate of increase in wages as a proxy for the rate of capital deepening, making use of the concept of the elasticity of substitution. The elasticity of substitution (σ) is defined as:

$$\sigma = \frac{d(K/L)}{(K/L)} \bigg/ \frac{d(MP_L/MP_K)}{(MP_L/MP_K)} \qquad (6.13)$$

where MP_L and MP_K are the marginal products of labour and capital respectively. Given that factors are rewarded according to the value of their marginal products this can be written as:

$$\sigma = \frac{d(K/L)}{(K/L)} \bigg/ \frac{d(W/R)}{(W/R)} \qquad (6.14)$$

The numerator of equation (6.14) is, for small changes, equal to the rate of capital deepening (m). The denominator may be expanded as $dW/W - dR/R$ so that:

$$\sigma = \frac{m}{(dW/W) - (dR/R)} \tag{6.15}$$

If the technology of the economy may be approximated by a Cobb–Douglas production function (i.e. $\sigma = 1$), equation (6.15) can be written:

$$m = \frac{dW}{W} - \frac{dR}{R} \tag{6.16}$$

Assuming that the rental per unit of capital is constant (i.e. $dR/R = 0$),[12] the rate of capital deepening may be approximated by the growth in wages per worker. Equation (6.3) then becomes:

$$r_r = a_r + w_{kr}\left(\frac{dW_r}{W_r}\right) \tag{6.17}$$

and the rate of technical progress may be calculated as:

$$a_r = r_r - w_{kr}\left(\frac{dW_r}{W_r}\right) \tag{6.18}$$

This approach has the distinct advantage over that of Johansen of allowing both the rate of capital deepening and the rate of technical progress to vary simultaneously between regions. At the aggregate level, the application of this approach leads to a similar estimate of the rate of technical progress as when Johansen's method is used assuming the rate of technical progress to be the same in each region. We take this as further evidence that it is more realistic to assume that the rate of technical progress is constant between regions than to assume that the rate of capital deepening is the same in each region. The results of applying equation (6.18) to regional data are shown in table 6.3. In every region, technical progress emerges as the major source of productivity growth. For the United Kingdom as a whole the estimated rate of technical progress is 3.2 per cent per annum, compared with an estimate of 3.0 per cent using Johansen's approach reported in table 6.2.

[12] This is not to say that rentals are fixed; rather, that the increase in rentals due to technical progress is offset by the decrease in rentals due to capital deepening.

TABLE 6.3 Rates of neutral technical progress as determined by equation (6.18); United Kingdom regions, 1958–63

Region	(1) r_r	(2) dW/W_r	(3) $w_{kr}dW/W_r$	(4) a_r*
N	3.8	2.2	1.1	2.7
YH	3.8	2.9	1.3	2.5
EM	4.2	2.5	1.1	3.1
EA	5.0	3.1	1.5	3.5
SE	5.0	3.0	1.4	3.6
SW	5.0	3.2	1.5	3.5
WM	4.4	3.2	1.3	3.1
NW	4.7	3.5	1.6	3.1
W	3.7	3.2	1.6	3.1
S	4.8	2.7	1.3	3.5
NI	6.9	3.7	1.6	5.3
UK	4.6	3.0	1.4	3.2

* $a_r = r_r - w_{kr}\left(\frac{dW_r}{W_r}\right)$.

THE CONTRIBUTION OF INTERREGIONAL RESOURCE SHIFTS TO PRODUCTIVITY GROWTH IN THE UNITED KINGDOM

Up to now the term 'technical progress' has been used to refer to the residual growth of labour productivity, after allowance has been made for the effects of capital deepening. Not all of this 'technical progress' necessarily represents shifts in the production function. For example, if factors of production are mobile, and move from one sector of the economy to another, a portion of the estimated rate of technical progress may be due to changes in the composition of output associated with a reallocation of resources. Since the aggregate residual is calculated on the basis of the total resources available to the nation (independent of their distribution between regions), a comparison between the weighted sum of the regional residuals and the national residual will give a rough estimate of the effects of interregional resource shifts.

The weights used to derive the predicted national rate of technical progress from the individual regional rates are the proportions of national output produced in each region in the base period. If the actual aggregate rate of technical progress is greater than the weighted average of the individual regions, this will be some indication of the extent to which resources have moved from relatively low to relatively high productivity regions. There are two possible sets of regional residuals to work with: those reported in table 6.1, which we feel lead to underestimates of the rate of technical progress nationally and regionally; and those reported in table 6.3. Using both sets of residuals gives remarkably similar results. From table 6.1 the estimated national rate of technical progress is 1.3 per cent per annum and the weighted average of the regional residuals is 1.4 per cent. From table 6.3 the estimated national rate of technical progress is 3.2 per cent and the weighted average of the regional residuals is 3.3 per cent. In both cases there is a negative discrepancy of 0.1 per cent, indicating that resource shifts between regions have apparently lowered the aggregate rate of productivity growth below what it might otherwise have been. While this result may be surprising at first sight, it is consistent with the finding in earlier chapters that industrial movement (between regions) appears to bear little relation to relative regional costs of location.

INCREASING RETURNS TO SCALE

Up to now it has also been assumed that production is subject to constant returns to scale. If this assumption is false, use of the constrained Cobb–Douglas production function will lead to biased estimates of the rate of technical progress. In fact, studies of the degree of returns to scale in United Kingdom manufacturing industries show that increasing returns rule in most industries and in the aggregate.[13] Increasing returns will bias the estimate of technical progress in two ways: firstly it will result in an underestimate of the

[13] M. S. Feldstein, 'Alternative Methods of Estimating a CES Production Function for Britain', *Economica*, Nov 1967; C. F. Pratten, *Economies of Scale in Manufacturing Industry* (Cambridge University Press, 1971).

effect of capital deepening since capital's share (w_k) will be an underestimate of the elasticity of output with respect to capital; secondly, it will bias upwards the residual, in that part of the residual will include the effect of increasing returns. Without estimating the production function in its unconstrained form, any adjustment to the residual to allow for increasing returns, however desirable, is likely to be subject to error. A case in point is Denison's work which for no apparent reason assumes that one-eleventh of the historical increase in output in the United States has been due to increasing returns.[14] He relates increasing returns to total output growth rather than to input expansion,[15] and he also neglects to adjust the 'weights' given to capital and labour for the existence of increasing returns. A more formal approach is clearly desirable.

Using the constrained Cobb–Douglas function, with the elasticities of output with respect to capital and labour summing to unity, the rate of technical progress is calculated (as before) as:

$$a = r - w_k(m) = g - w_k(k-l) - l \qquad (6.19)$$

where g is the rate of growth of output
k is the rate of growth of capital
and l is the rate of growth of labour.

If increasing returns prevail the income shares cannot be taken as estimates of the individual elasticities because the sum of the elasticities ($\alpha+\beta$) now exceeds unity. In this event the 'true' rate of technical progress (a^*) is:

$$a^* = g - \beta(k) - \alpha(l) \qquad (6.20)$$

or, letting $\alpha+\beta = V$ (the homogeneity parameter),

$$a^* = g - \beta(k) - (V-\beta)l, \qquad (6.21)$$

[14] E. Denison, *The Sources of Economic Growth in the United States*, Committee for Economic Development, 1962.

[15] Apparently technical progress also reaps increasing returns!

TABLE 6.4 Estimates of the contribution of returns to scale to labour productivity growth in the regions, 1958–68

Region	$CV = (V-1)l_r$ (% p.a.)
N	−0.02
YH	−0.02
EM	+0.17
EA	+0.44
SE	+0.08
SW	+0.18
WM	+0.11
NW	−0.12
W	+0.21
S	−0.02
NI	−0.02
UK	+0.03

from which it follows that,

$$a^* = g - \beta(k-l) - Vl \qquad (6.22)$$

[16]

Subtracting equation (6.19) from (6.20) yields:

$$a^* = a - (\beta - w_k)(k-l) + (1-V)l \qquad (6.23)$$

from which it is easily seen that the 'true' rate of technical progress is lower than when the production function is constrained to the extent that $\beta > w_k$ and $V > 1$. Using equation (6.23) we can adjust the estimates of the residual for the effects of increasing returns if β and V are known.

Later in the book (see appendix 1) we estimate the returns to scale in United Kingdom manufacturing in 1963 to be $(V=)\,1.13$.[17] The contribution of returns to scale (CV) to labour productivity growth may be calculated as:

$$CV_r = (V-1)l_r = 0.13l_r \qquad (6.24)$$

The estimates of the contribution of this factor to labour productivity growth in each region over the period 1958–68 are reported in table 6.4.

[16] The intuitive explanation of the scale term (V) being related to one of the factors only (in this case labour) is that scale effects accrue only to the extent that factors of production grow in proportion.

[17] Assuming that the production function is common to all regions.

Table 6.4 shows that increasing returns to scale made negative contributions to labour productivity growth in five regions; the reason being that employment fell in these regions over the period. In other words, the rate of technical progress in these regions has been biased downwards not upwards in the presence of increasing returns. In the other regions, increasing returns has contributed to productivity growth and led to upward bias in the rate of technical progress term; but the magnitude of the effect has been small.

ADJUSTMENTS TO THE ESTIMATES OF CAPITAL DEEPENING

The constrained form of the Cobb–Douglas production function will understate the contribution of capital deepening to growth in the presence of increasing returns (and overstate the residual) because the share of profits in income will understate the 'true' elasticity of output with respect to capital. In the absence of data to estimate the 'true' elasticity, how can this bias be rectified? If returns to scale are neutral in their effects between the factors, the elasticity of both factors will be raised in the same proportion. Given a unitary elasticity of substitution, and Hicks neutral technical progress, there should be a relation between income shares and output elasticities such that the 'true' elasticity is in the same proportion to the homogeneity parameter as the factor share is to unity. In other words, the 'true' elasticity of output with respect to capital may be estimated as:

$$\beta_r^* = w_{kr}(V) \tag{6.25}$$

To separate the contribution of technical progress and capital deepening to productivity growth in the presence of increasing returns (and in the absence of capital data) requires a slight reformulation of the basic Johansen approach that was used earlier. For reasons already discussed, the assumption is made that technical progress is the same in all regions, allowing the rate of capital deepening to vary.

From the production function: $Y_t = A_t K_t^\beta L_t^\alpha$, where $\alpha + \beta = V$, we may write

$$Y_t = A_t K^\beta L^{-\beta} L^V, \tag{6.26}$$

and output per unit of labour may be expressed as:

$$\frac{Y_t}{L_t} = q_t = A_t(x_t)^{\beta} L_t^{V-1} \tag{6.27}$$

The equation for labour productivity in the final period $(t+n)$ will possess exactly the same form. On the assumption that the exponents are constant over time, the ratio of final to base period productivity may be written:

$$\frac{q_{t+n}}{q_t} = \frac{A_{t+n}}{A_t}\left(\frac{x_{t+n}}{x_t}\right)^{\beta}\left(\frac{L_{t+n}}{L_t}\right)^{V-1} \tag{6.28}$$

Taking logs and rearranging gives:

$$\log\left(\frac{q_{t+n}}{q_t}\right) - (V-1)\log\left(\frac{L_{t+n}}{L_t}\right) = \log\left(\frac{A_{t+n}}{A_t}\right) + \beta\log\left(\frac{x_{t+n}}{x_t}\right) \tag{6.29}$$

Dividing both sides by β gives the new 'technical progress constant' formulation of:

$$\frac{1}{\beta_r}\log\left(\frac{q_{t+n}}{q_t}\right) - \left(\frac{V-1}{\beta_r}\right)\log\left(\frac{L_{t+n}}{L_t}\right) = \log\left(\frac{x_{t+n}}{x_t}\right) + \frac{1}{\beta_r}\log\left(\frac{A_{t+n}}{A_t}\right) \tag{6.30}$$

from which the new estimate of the rate of (constant) technical progress can be obtained using the estimating equation:

$$Z = \lambda_6 + \lambda_7\left(\frac{1}{\beta_r}\right) + u \tag{6.31}$$

where Z is the R.H.S. of equation (6.30)

and λ_7 is an estimate of $\log\left(\frac{A_{t+n}}{A_t}\right)$.

Using the new estimates of β_r from equation (6.25) and the estimate of V, equation (6.31) fitted to regional data yielded:

$$Z = 0.823 + \underset{(0.237)}{0.238}\frac{1}{\beta_r} - \underset{(0.068)}{0.232}\,d_5 + \underset{(0.058)}{0.432}\,d_6 \qquad r^2 = 0.936$$

where $d_5 = 1$ for N and W, and zero for all other regions
and $d_6 = 1$ for EM, NI, and zero for all other regions.

The estimate of the coefficient on $(1/\beta_r)$ yields an estimated rate of technical progress of $(a^* =)\,2.42$ per cent per annum. This is a 1.1 percentage points less than the earlier rate of technical progress calculated on the assumption of constant returns to scale (see equation (6.12) and table 6.2).

The contribution of capital deepening to the growth of labour productivity in each region may now be calculated as:

$$\beta_r m_r^* = r_r - a_r^* - (V-1)l \qquad (6.32)$$

These estimates are presented in table 6.5.

TABLE 6.5 Estimates of the contribution of capital deepening to productivity growth in the United Kingdom regions, 1958–68

Region	$\beta_r m_r^* = r_r - a_r^* - (V-1)l$† (% p.a.)
N	1.40
YH	1.50
EM	4.61
EA	2.94
SE	2.40
SW	2.02
WM	2.07
NW	3.02
W	1.07
S	2.40
NI	4.80
UK	2.45

† $(V-1)l$ is already estimated in table 6.4.

Now for the United Kingdom as a whole the relative contribution of capital deepening to productivity growth is approximately 50 per cent – with the remaining 50 per cent attributable to 'technical progress'.[18] The contribution of capital deepening, technical progress and increasing returns to productivity growth in each individual region (in the presence of increasing returns) is summarised in table 6.6. Since the rate of technical

[18] This is consistent with Nicholson's findings referred to earlier on p. 137.

TABLE 6.6 The components of regional productivity growth in United Kingdom regions, 1958–68

Region	a^*	$\beta_r m_r^*$ (*Residual*)	$(V-1)l_r$†	r_r
N	2.42	1.40	−0.02	3.8
YH	2.42	1.50	−0.02	3.9
EM	2.42	4.61	0.17	7.2
EA	2.42	2.94	0.44	5.8
SE	2.42	2.40	0.08	4.9
SW	2.42	2.02	0.18	4.6
WM	2.42	2.07	0.11	4.6
NW	2.42	3.02	−0.12	5.3
W	2.42	1.07	0.21	3.7
S	2.42	2.40	−0.02	4.8
NI	2.42	4.80	−0.02	7.2
UK	2.42	2.45	0.03	4.9

† Estimates from table 6.4.

progress is assumed the same in each region, and the contribution of increasing returns to productivity growth is very small, the major source of interregional differences in productivity growth must be differences in the rate of capital deepening.

The components of productivity growth reported in table 6.6 still need adjustment if some of the growth of productivity is the result of increases in the quality of factors of production which do not depend on technical change, or results from *intra*-regional resource shifts, the extent of which varies from region to region. Very little can be done about the first possibility, at least at the regional level.[19] An attempt can be made, however, to assess the contribution of resource shifts between industries within regions to each region's rate of productivity growth. Just as it was argued earlier that the residual for the nation (technical progress) will have included in it the effects

[19] At the national level (and specifically for the United States) it has been claimed by Jorgenson and Griliches that the major part of the so-called 'residual' can be accounted for by errors in the measurement of the labour and capital series, and in particular, by the failure to adjust for quality changes. See D. Jorgenson and Z. Griliches, 'The Explanation of Productivity Change', *Review of Economic Studies*, July 1967.

of interregional resource shifts, so any region's residual (in this case βm^*) will have included in it the effects of inter-industry resource shifts.

THE CONTRIBUTION OF INTRA-REGIONAL (INTER-INDUSTRY) RESOURCE SHIFTS TO REGIONAL PRODUCTIVITY GROWTH

The importance of inter-industry resource shifts as a source of productivity growth is fairly well established.[20] Some authors have attempted to explain the differing growth performance of countries and regions largely in terms of the potential for resource shifts, especially from agriculture to industry.[21] This section attempts to evaluate the importance of inter-industry resource shifts (within the manufacturing sector only) to the productivity growth of the regions over the period 1958–68.

Let the level of labour productivity in each region be the weighted sum of labour productivity in each individual industry:

i.e.
$$q_r = \sum_i q_{ir} N_{ir} \qquad (6.33)$$

where $N_{ir} = L_{ir}/L_r$ is the weight of each industry in terms of employment.

Totally differentiating equation (6.33), and dividing through by q_r, yields (for small changes) an expression for total productivity growth of:

$$\frac{dq_r}{q_r} = \sum_i \frac{dq_{ir} N_{ir}}{q_r} + \sum_i \frac{q_{ir} dN_{ir}}{q_r} \qquad (6.34)$$

The last term on the R.H.S. is an estimate of the contribution of intra-regional resource shifts (CRS) to regional productivity

[20] For the American economy, Massell has estimated that 30 per cent of the technical progress term is accountable for in terms of shifts in the composition of output. There are no corresponding studies for Britain. See B. F. Massell, 'A Disaggregated View of Technical Change', *Journal of Political Economy*, Dec 1961.

[21] G. H. Borts and J. L. Stein, *Economic Growth in a Free Market* (Columbia University Press, 1964); E. F. Denison, *Why Growth Rates Differ: Post-War Experience in Nine Western Countries* (Brookings Institution, 1967).

growth, and is identical to the measure expressed by Denison.[22] Estimates of the contribution of resource shifts to regional productivity growth, calculated on this basis, are given in table 6.7 using provisional estimates of the allocation of the regional manufacturing workforce in 1968.[23]

TABLE 6.7 Estimates of the contribution of intra-regional resource shifts to the aggregate rate of productivity growth in the regions, 1958–68

Region	*CRS** (% p.a.)
N	−0.6
YH	−0.1
EM	+0.5
EA	+1.4
SE	+0.2
SW	−0.1
WM	+0.1
NW	+0.4
W	+0.1
S	+0.6
NI	+0.5
UK	+0.1

* Calculated as: $\sqrt[n]{\dfrac{q_r + \sum_i q_{ir} dN_{ir}}{q_r}} - 1$

The results in table 6.7 show that in three regions resources were reallocated between industries such that productivity growth was impaired. In all other regions, and in the aggregate, however, the resource shifts were such as to increase the rate of productivity growth – in one or two regions by a fairly substantial amount. East Anglia stands out as the region where

[22] See E. Denison, *The Sources of Economic Growth in the United States* (Committee for Economic Development, 1962), p. 225.

[23] These data are reported in Board of Trade, 'Area Analyses of the Provisional Results of the Census of Production for 1968', *Board of Trade Journal*, vol. 199, 1970, pp. 488–96.

TABLE 6.8 Components of productivity growth in the manufacturing sector of United Kingdom regions 1958–68

Region	*Rate of labour productivity growth (% p.a.)*	*Capital deepening*	*Contribution of: Increasing returns*	*Resource shifts*	*Technical progress*
	(r_r)	$(\beta_r m_r)^{**}$	$(V-1)l_r$	CRS	a^*
N	3.8	2.00	−0.02	−0.60	2.42
YH	3.9	1.60	−0.02	−0.10	2.42
EM	7.2	4.11	0.17	0.50	2.42
EA	5.8	1.54	0.44	1.40	2.42
SE	4.9	2.20	0.08	0.20	2.42
SW	4.6	2.12	0.18	−0.10	2.42
WM	4.6	1.97	0.11	0.10	2.42
NW	5.3	2.62	−0.12	0.40	2.42
W	3.7	0.97	0.21	0.10	2.42
S	4.8	1.80	−0.02	0.60	2.42
NI	7.2	4.30	−0.02	0.50	2.42
UK	4.9	2.35	0.03	0.10	2.42

resource shifts contributed most to the increase in labour productivity over the period, for which expansion of the region's workforce in vehicles was largely responsible. The high estimate for Scotland is mainly attributable to the expansion of metal manufacture over the period. No single explanation can be cited as responsible for the negative impact of resource shifts in the North, although there is an apparent decline in chemicals and shipbuilding.

The estimates of intra-regional resource shifts reported in table 6.7 are a measure of the aggregation problem in estimating the components of productivity growth, and must be subtracted from the estimates of the residual in table 6.6 to obtain a more accurate measure of the contribution of capital deepening (βm^{**}). Table 6.8 reports the revised estimates of the components of productivity growth after allowance has been made for intra-regional resource shifts, and brings together all the components of total productivity growth that we have been analysing.

The contribution of each of the components to the *differences* in productivity growth rates between regions may be assessed using an evaluation of inner products (a technique for analysing the sources of interregional differences described in chapter 1). The total variation in regional productivity growth rates (expressed as squared deviations from the national rate) may be expressed as:

$$\sum_r \Delta r^2 = \sum_r a^{*2} + \sum_r \Delta(\beta m^{**})^2 + \sum_r \Delta((V-1)l)^2 + \sum_r \Delta(\text{CRS})^2 + R \quad (6.35)$$

where Δ represents the difference between the regional value of each component and the corresponding national value

and *R* represents all interaction terms.

Table 6.9 reports the magnitudes of the sums of squares of the above equation, and the proportional contribution of each element to the total variation in regional productivity growth rates. It is clear that the largest source of differences in the rate of productivity growth between regions, even after adjustment for returns to scale and resource shifts, remains the rate of capital deepening.

TABLE 6.9 Decomposition of the 'inner product' of productivity growth in the regions 1958–68

Source of variation	*Sum of squares*	*Proportion of total sum of squares (%)*
$\sum_r \Delta a^{*2}$	0	0
$\sum_r \Delta(\beta m^{**})^2$	12.38	80.4
$\sum_r \Delta((V-1)l)^2$	0.28	1.8
$\sum_r \Delta\text{CRS}^2$	2.93	19.0
Residual (interaction)	−0.20	−1.2
$\sum_r \Delta r^2$	15.39	100

The main conclusions of this chapter may now be briefly summarised as follows:

(1) In the absence of capital data, the 'technical change constant' variant of Johansen's model appears to provide the basis for making reasonable estimates of the components of regional productivity growth in the manufacturing sector; and for obtaining estimates of the rate of capital deepening in each region. This implies that the major source of differences in the rate of productivity growth between regions will be differences in the rate of capital deepening.

(2) A useful alternative approach to the above may be simply to use the rate of growth of wages in a region as a proxy for capital deepening.

(3) An analysis of intra-regional resource shifts revealed that while, on average, they contributed little to productivity growth in any one region, they are an important source of *interregional* differences in productivity growth rates.

(4) An analysis of increasing returns, on the other hand, showed that interregional differences in returns to scale are not a major contributor to interregional differences in productivity growth.

(5) Technical progress remains a major determinant of the *level* of productivity growth within regions even after adjustment for increasing returns. This finding is consistent with studies at the national level, but the estimates are almost certainly biased upwards because no allowance has been made for improvements in the quality of factor inputs and the fact that a good deal of technical progress must be embodied in capital. Acceptance of the embodiment hypothesis[24] would enhance the contribution of capital deepening to the *level* of regional productivity growth and diminish somewhat the contribution of technical progress. The relative importance of the sources of interregional *differences* in productivity growth would not necessarily be affected however.

[24] For a discussion of the hypothesis and the models based on them see C. Kennedy and A. P. Thirlwall, 'Surveys in Applied Economics: Technical Progress', *Economic Journal*, Mar 1972.

TABLE 6.A1 Data used in the study of productivity growth in the manufacturing sector of the regions: 1958–68[1]

Region	$q_r 68/q_r 58$[2]	w_{kr}[3]	$r_r m$[4]	r_r[5]	l[6]
N	1.80	0.50	6.0	3.8	−0.1
YH	1.81	0.46	6.1	3.9	−0.1
EM	2.46	0.46	9.4	7.2	1.3
EA	2.16	0.50	8.0	5.8	3.4
SE	1.99	0.49	7.1	4.9	0.6
SW	1.93	0.43	6.8	4.6	1.4
WM	1.93	0.43	6.8	4.6	0.8
NW	2.06	0.47	7.5	5.3	−0.9
W	1.77	0.50	5.9	3.7	1.6
S	1.97	0.49	7.0	4.8	−0.2
NI	2.46	0.46	9.4	7.2	−0.1
UK	2.03	0.47	7.1	4.9	0.3

(1) *Source:* Board of Trade, *Report on the Census of Production 1963* (London: HMSO, 1970), part 133; 'Area analyses of the provisional results of the Census of Production for 1968', *Board of Trade Journal*, vol. 199, 1970, pp. 488–96.

(2) Value of net output per employee in 1968, expressed as a proportion of the value of net output per employee in 1958.

(3) w_{kr} equals unity minus the share of wages and salaries in net output (i.e. $w_{kr} = 1-(W_r/Y_r)$) in 1963.

(4) Average annual rate of growth of the *value* of output per employee, 1958–68.

(5) Estimated rate of growth of *real* output per employee ($r_r = r_r m - p_r$ where p = average annual rate of growth of wholesale prices of all manufacturing products over the period 1958–68 – for the United Kingdom as a whole = 2.2% p.a.).
Source of price data: London and Cambridge Economic Service, *The British Economy Key Statistics 1900–1970* (London: Times Newspapers Ltd, 1972), p. 8.

(6) Average annual rate of growth of employment (% p.a.).

7 Interregional Differences in 'Efficiency': 1958 and 1963

In the previous chapter we were interested in the determinants of labour productivity growth in the regions, and in the major sources of interregional differences in productivity growth over time. In this chapter an attempt is made to examine the sources of interregional differences in productivity at a point in time. In particular, we shall be interested in estimating regional 'efficiency' parameters[1] using the Constant Elasticity of Substitution (CES) production function.

The CES production function

Assuming constant returns to scale, the CES production function may be specified as:[2]

$$Y = \gamma[\delta K^{-\rho} + (1-\delta)L^{-\rho}]^{-1/\rho} \tag{7.1}$$

where γ is the (neutral) efficiency parameter
δ is the distribution parameter
ρ is the substitution parameter

[1] The 'efficiency parameter' of the CES production function is similar to the 'technological parameter' (A) in the Cobb–Douglas function. Changes in the 'efficiency parameter' give rise to an equiproportional increase in output for any given quantity of inputs. See D. F. Heathfield, *Production Functions* (Macmillan, 1971), and M. Brown, *On the Theory and Measurement of Technological Change* (Cambridge University Press, 1968).

[2] Original derivations of the CES production function can be found in K. J. Arrow, H. B. Chenery, B. S. Minhas and R. M. Solow, 'Capital-Labour Substitution and Economic Efficiency', *Review of Economics and Statistics*, Aug 1961, and in M. Brown and J. de Cani, 'Technological Change and the Distribution of Income', *International Economic Review*, Sep 1963.

The side relation used to estimate the elasticity of substitution may be written as:[3]

$$\log\left(\frac{Y}{L}\right)=\frac{1}{1+\rho}\log\left[\gamma^{\rho}(1-\delta)^{-1}\right]+\frac{1}{1+\rho}\log w \qquad (7.2)$$

where w is the wage rate

and $\frac{1}{1+\rho}$ is the elasticity of substitution, σ.

Equation (7.2) provides an estimating equation:

$$\log\left(\frac{Y}{L}\right)=a_1+b_1(\log w) \qquad (7.3)$$

where a_1 is an estimate of $\sigma\log\left[\gamma^{\rho}(1-\delta)^{-1}\right]$
and b_1 is an estimate of σ.

Equations (7.2) and (7.3) provide the basis for estimating interregional differences in the efficiency parameter, γ.

Assuming that the distribution parameter δ, and the substitution parameter ρ, are the same in each region, the logarithm of output per worker in any region r may be written (from equation (7.2)) as:

$$\log\left(\frac{Y}{L}\right)_r=\sigma\log\left[\gamma_r^{\rho}(1-\delta)^{-1}\right]+\sigma\log\left(\frac{W}{L}\right)_r \qquad (7.4)$$

Rearranging to obtain an expression for the efficiency parameter gives:

$$\log(\gamma_r)=\frac{\log(Y/L)_r-\sigma\log(W/L)_r+\sigma\log(1-\delta)}{\sigma\rho} \qquad (7.5)$$

Data for output per worker (Y/L) and earnings per worker (W/L) are available for the regions from the Census of Production. Estimates of the elasticity of substitution, and by

[3] For the derivation of this side relation see C. E. Ferguson, 'Time Series Production Functions and Technological Progress in American Manufacturing Industry', *Journal of Political Economy*, Apr 1965; J. M. Katz, *Production Functions, Foreign Investment and Growth* (North-Holland, 1969).

implication the substitution parameter, are made in appendix 1 of the book. But without data on the distribution parameter there are still two unknowns (γ and δ) in equation (7.5). If the distribution parameter is assumed to be the same in each region, however, it is possible to obtain a solution for the efficiency parameter, comparing each region's efficiency parameter *relative* to the average (i.e. to the United Kingdom).

Since $\sigma = 1/(1+\rho)$, and $\sigma\rho = 1-\sigma$, equation (7.5) may be rewritten as:

$$\log(\gamma_r) = \frac{\log(Y/L)_r - \sigma\log(W/L)_r}{1-\sigma} + \frac{\log(1-\delta)}{\rho} \qquad (7.6)$$

and similarly for the United Kingdom:

$$\log(\gamma_{UK}) = \frac{\log(Y/L)_{UK} - \sigma\log(W/L)_{UK}}{1-\sigma} + \frac{\log(1-\delta)}{\rho} \qquad (7.7)$$

Subtracting equation (7.7) from (7.6) gives:

$$\log\left(\frac{\gamma_r}{\gamma_{UK}}\right) = \frac{\Delta\log(Y/L) - \sigma\Delta\log(W/L)}{1-\sigma} \qquad (7.8)$$

where Δ represents the difference between a region and the United Kingdom.

Making use of the assumption that δ is the same in all regions, therefore, enables an estimate to be made of the 'relative efficiency parameter' (γ_r/γ_{UK}), given data on σ, (Y/L) and (W/L) alone. The relative efficiency parameter for each region is the anti-logarithm of the estimate obtained in equation (7.8). Since the CES production function is usually restricted to examining the sources of productivity differences over time, it is particularly interesting to demonstrate its use for evaluating the sources of interregional differences in efficiency at a point in time. There is no reason in principle why models of economic growth should not be applied in a cross-section context, especially as 'time' neither shapes the analysis nor determines the form of the model.

Estimates of the relative efficiency parameter for regional manufacturing, 1958 and 1963

Data on output per worker and average earnings are available for 1958 and 1963 and are reported in table 7.A1 of the appendix to the chapter. The estimates of the elasticity of substitution derived in appendix 1 of the book are 1.317 for 1958 and 1.089 for 1963. Table 7.1 reports estimates of the relative efficiency parameter for each region obtained by applying equation (7.8) to regional data for 1958 and 1963, together with indices of labour productivity in the manufacturing sector of the regions in the same years for comparison (UK = 1.000).

Discrepancies between the rankings of the efficiency parameter estimates and the rankings of the labour productivity indices are a reflection of differences in the level and/or effectiveness of the capital stock. Wales is perhaps the most interesting region with labour productivity well above average in both years, but with an efficiency parameter well below

TABLE 7.1 Estimates of the relative efficiency parameter and indices of labour productivity in the regions, 1958 and 1963

Region	*Estimates of the relative efficiency parameter in manufacturing**		*Indices of labour productivity in manufacturing†*	
	1958	*1963*	*1958*	*1963*
N	0.937	0.668	1.090	1.050
YH	0.939	1.180	0.945	0.915
EM	1.600	1.120	0.928	0.912
EA	0.863	0.540	0.975	0.992
SE	1.080	0.817	1.079	1.105
SW	1.010	0.885	1.000	1.022
WM	1.270	2.340	0.970	0.960
NW	0.922	1.030	0.943	0.963
W	0.786	0.632	1.182	1.135
S	0.942	0.668	0.965	0.978
NI	1.030	0.935	0.678	0.760
UK	1.000	1.000	1.000	1.000

Sources: * Calculated using equation (7.8) from data in table 7.A1.
† Calculated from data in table 7.A1.

average. This implies that the level, and/or effectiveness, of the capital stock is relatively high in this region.[4] The reverse appears to be the case for the West Midlands region which has an efficiency parameter for both years well above average, but labour productivity below average. It appears that whilst there are significant differences in the magnitude of the efficiency parameter between regions, differences in this parameter are being offset by differences in the level and effectiveness of capital per worker.[5]

To ascertain the relative contribution of the efficiency parameter and capital per worker to the level of labour productivity between regions, equation (7.1) can be transformed, by dividing by L and taking logarithms, to yield:

$$\log(Y/L)_r = \log\gamma_r - \frac{1}{\rho}\log[\delta(K/L)_r^{-\rho} + (1-\delta)] \qquad (7.9)$$

Similarly for the nation:

$$\log(Y/L)_{UK} = \log\gamma_{UK} - \frac{1}{\rho}\log[\delta(K/L)_{UK}^{-\rho} + (1-\delta)] \qquad (7.10)$$

Subtracting equation (7.10) from (7.9) gives:

$$\Delta\log(Y/L) = \Delta\log\gamma + \Delta\log(\phi(K/L) \qquad (7.11)^6$$

where $\Delta\log\gamma = \log\gamma_r - \log\gamma_{UK}$

and $$\Delta\log(\phi(K/L)) = -\frac{1}{\rho}\log[\delta(K/L)_r^{-\rho} + (1-\delta)] + \frac{1}{\rho}\log[\delta(K/L)_{UK}^{-\rho} + (1-\delta)]$$

[4] Support for this hypothesis may be found in E. Nevin, A. R. Roe and J. I. Round, *The Structure of the Welsh Economy* (University of Wales Press, 1966), pp. 2–6.

[5] The coefficient of rank correlation between the relative efficiency parameter and the indices of labour productivity is negative for both years.

[6] ϕ is a composite of distribution and substitution effects. Since the substitution and distribution parameters are assumed to be the same in each region, however, the source of differences in the last term on the R.H.S. of equation (7.11) will be that of variations in the capital–labour ratio itself.

The last term on the R.H.S. of equation (7.11) expresses the relative importance of differences in the capital-labour ratio between regions as a source of regional differences in labour productivity. Since we have estimates of $\Delta \log(Y/L)$ and $\Delta \log \gamma$, reported in table 7.1, the last term on the R.H.S. of equation (7.11) may be calculated as:

$$\Delta \log[\phi(K/L)] = \Delta \log(Y/L) - \Delta \log \gamma \qquad (7.12)$$

We can then determine explicitly the importance of the terms on the R.H.S. of equation (7.11) in determining differences in labour productivity between regions. Squaring both sides of equation (7.11) and summing over regions yields an expression for the inner product of productivity differences in terms of its sources:

$$\sum_r [\Delta \log(Y/L)]^2 = \sum_r (\Delta \log \gamma)^2 + \sum_r \{\Delta \log[\phi(K/L)]\}^2 + R \qquad (7.13)$$

where R represents interaction terms.

From the total sum of squares accounted for by differences in capital per man on the one hand and differences in the efficiency parameter on the other, we find that in both years, differences in capital per worker were the major source of differences in levels of labour productivity between regions.

It must be emphasised that these results depend crucially on the assumption that the efficiency parameter does not vary systematically with the wage rate, which is the assumption necessary to use the side relation in equation (7.2) to measure the elasticity of substitution. If the assumption is not valid, a part of the contribution of the efficiency parameter to labour productivity will be reflected in the magnitude of the estimated elasticity of substitution and thus included in the contribution of capital deepening. In other words, to the extent that higher 'efficiency' is reflected in higher wages, the above analysis is likely to underestimate the contribution of efficiency differences to productivity differences.

An additional defect of the above analysis is that constant returns is assumed. We now relax this assumption.

THE CES PRODUCTION FUNCTION WITH ALLOWANCE FOR INCREASING RETURNS

To allow for increasing returns the CES production function takes the form:

$$Y=\gamma[\delta K^{-\rho}+(1-\delta)L^{-\rho}]^{-v/\rho} \tag{7.14}$$

where v is the homogeneity parameter. The side relation in the presence of increasing returns, equivalent to equation (7.2), may be derived as follows. Differentiate equation (7.14) with respect to L to obtain an expression for the marginal product of labour (assumed equal to the wage rate):

$$w=\frac{\partial Y}{\partial L}=v\gamma(1-\delta)L^{-\rho-1}[\delta K^{-\rho}+(1-\delta)L^{-\rho}]^{-(v/\rho)-1} \tag{7.15}$$

Substituting equation (7.14) into (7.15) yields:

$$w=v(1-\delta)L^{-\rho-1}Y[\delta K^{-\rho}+(1-\delta)L^{-\rho}]^{-1} \tag{7.16}$$

From equation (7.14) we also find that:

$$Y^{\rho/v}\gamma^{-\rho/v}=[\delta K^{-\rho}+(1-\delta)L^{-\rho}]^{-1} \tag{7.17}$$

Equation (7.16) may therefore be rewritten as:

$$w=v\gamma^{-\rho/v}(1-\delta)L^{-\rho-1}\,Y\,Y^{\rho/v} \tag{7.18}$$

Multiplying both sides by (Y^{ρ}) gives:

$$Y^{\rho}w=v\gamma^{-\rho/v}(1-\delta)L^{-(1+\rho)}Y^{1+\rho}\,Y^{\rho/v} \tag{7.19}$$

Rearranging and dividing through by Y^{ρ} yields:

$$w=v^{-\rho/v}(1-\delta)(Y/L)^{1+\rho}\,Y^{(\rho/v)-\rho} \tag{7.20}$$

It follows that:

$$(Y/L)^{1+\rho}=\gamma^{\rho/v}v^{-1}(1-\delta)^{-1}wY^{\rho-(\rho/v)} \tag{7.21}$$

Now:

$$\rho-(\rho/v)=\rho\left(1-\frac{1}{v}\right)=\rho\left(\frac{v-1}{v}\right)$$

Taking logarithms of (7.21) and dividing through by $(1+\rho)$ gives:

$$\log(Y/L) = \frac{1}{1+\rho}\log[\gamma^{\rho/v}(1-\delta)^{-1}v^{-1}] + \frac{1}{1+\rho}\log w + \left(\frac{\rho}{1+\rho}\right)\left(\frac{v-1}{v}\right)\log Y \quad (7.22)$$

Since $1/(1+\rho)$ is equal to the elasticity of substitution σ, equation (7.22) may be written:

$$\log(Y/L) = \sigma \log[\gamma^{\rho/v}(1-\delta)^{-1}v^{-1}] + \sigma \log w + (1-\sigma) \times \left(\frac{v-1}{v}\right)\log Y \quad (7.23)$$

Equation (7.23) is in the same form as equation (7.2), but now with an allowance for scale (in the form of the additional variable log Y). The efficiency parameter for any region γ_r, assuming that the distribution, substitution and homogeneity parameters do not differ between regions, may therefore be expressed as:

$$\log \gamma_r = \frac{\log(Y/L)_r - \sigma \log w_r - \dfrac{(1-\sigma)(v-1)}{v}\log Y_r}{\sigma\dfrac{\rho}{v}} + \frac{\log v + \log(1-\delta)}{\rho/v} \quad (7.24)$$

In the case of constant returns to scale the relative efficiency parameter was calculated by taking the expression for the regional efficiency parameter and subtracting the equivalent national expression from it (see equation (7.8)). This approach cannot reasonably be adopted in the present case owing to the appearance of the scale term, log Y_r, in equation (7.24). If the national scale term Y_{UK} was taken as the base, the scale deflator would be

$$\left[\frac{(1-\sigma)(v-1)}{v}\right](\log Y_r - \log Y_{UK})$$

which would result in a huge negative term, and thus

TABLE 7.2 Estimates of the relative efficiency parameter in each region with adjustment for returns to scale: 1958 and 1963*

Region	*1958*	*1963*
N	0.991	0.931
YH	0.934	1.040
EM	1.050	1.060
EA	0.969	0.895
SE	1.010	0.828
SW	1.050	1.070
WM	1.180	1.470
NW	0.913	0.946
W	0.907	0.970
S	0.943	0.832
NI	1.040	1.040

* The rank correlation between the estimates and the estimates of the relative efficiency parameter in table 7.1 is 0.985 for 1958 and 0.970 for 1963.

extremely high values of the relative efficiency parameter for all regions. A way round this problem is to take the mean of all regions as the relevant benchmark for comparison. Subtraction of the 'mean efficiency parameter' from the efficiency parameter for each region yields:

$$\log\left(\frac{\gamma_r}{\gamma_x}\right) = \frac{\Delta\log(Y/L) - \sigma\Delta\log(W/L)}{\left(\dfrac{1-\sigma}{v}\right)} - (v-1)\Delta\log Y \qquad (7.25)$$

where Δ represents the difference between a region and the mean for all regions (where x denotes mean). Note that equation (7.25) reduces to equation (7.8) under constant returns to scale (i.e. $v = 1$). Revised estimates for the elasticity of substitution in the presence of increasing returns, and the estimates for returns to scale (calculated in appendix 1 of the book) are as follows: 1958 $\sigma = 1.439$, $v = 1.060$; 1963 $\sigma = 1.221$, $v = 1.125$. Table 7.2 gives the new estimates of the relative efficiency parameter calculated from equation (7.25). Again there is little association between the estimates of the efficiency parameters and labour productivity in each of the years (see table 7.1).

The model indicates two possible explanations for this: (i) differences in the amount and effectiveness of capital per worker are offsetting 'efficiency' differences and/or (ii) scale effects. As before, the contribution of the different sources of productivity to interregional differences in the level of productivity can be estimated by transforming the production function (equation (7.14)) and taking the deviation of the logarithm of labour productivity in any region from the mean of all regions,[7] that is:

$$\Delta \log(Y/L) = \Delta \log \gamma + \Delta \log[\phi(K/L)] + \Delta g \log(Y) \qquad (7.26)$$

where $g = \dfrac{(1-\sigma)(v-1)}{v}$ = elasticity of labour productivity with respect to output.

Squaring both sides of equation (7.26) and summing over all regions yields an expression for the total sum of squares of labour productivity:

$$\sum_r [\Delta \log(Y/L)]^2 = \sum_r (\Delta \log \gamma)^2 + \sum_r \{\Delta \log[\phi(K/L)]\}^2 + \sum_r [\Delta g \log(Y)]^2 + R \qquad (7.27)$$

where R stands for interaction terms. From the calculation of the components of the total sum of squares in equation (7.27), it is apparent that differences in capital intensity between regions remain the major single source of differences in labour productivity between regions. Differences in the scale of output account for a very small part of the differences in labour productivity between regions.

Regional Efficiency Parameters and the Doctrine of General Locational Disadvantage

Other things remaining the same, we can see from the form of the CES production function that interregional differences in the efficiency parameter will result in interregional

[7] Estimates of $\Delta \log[\phi(K/L)]$ are obtained as a residual from equation (7.26) with knowledge of all other terms.

differences in labour productivity. Dividing equation (7.1) through by L gives:

$$Y/L = \gamma[\delta(K/L)^{-\rho} + (1-\delta)]^{-1/\rho} \qquad (7.28)$$

There is some evidence from tables 7.1 and 7.2 that the 'peripheral' regions of the north, Wales and Scotland have efficiency parameters below that for the average of the country as a whole. The notion that the 'efficiency' of production is relatively lower in the peripheral regions, and that this in turn reflects locational disadvantages specific to that region, will be referred to as the doctrine of 'inherent, or locational, disadvantage.'[8] A great deal of regional policy seems to reflect, at least in part, this notion.[9] Specific reference to the doctrine of locational disadvantage is usually found, however, not in studies of the production function type that we have employed, but in shift and share analyses.[10] For example, it is often claimed that '... the generally poorer industry-by-industry performance of the development areas in comparison with the country as a whole reflects general locational disadvantages....'[11]

Locational disadvantage will reflect the general environment of production in the region, including such factors as climate, transport costs, labour quality, managerial ability, the age and quality of capital equipment, and many other factors.[12] Provided that these factors do not vary systematically with the wage rate between regions (wages being more

[8] For a discussion of this concept see G. McCrone, *Regional Policy in Britain*, George Allen & Unwin, 1969, pp. 169–80, and 'The Location of Economic Activity in the United Kingdom', *Urban Studies*, Oct 1972.

[9] See Dept of Economic Affairs and H.M. Treasury, *The Development Areas: A Proposal for a Regional Employment Premium* (HMSO, 1967); N. Kaldor, 'The Case for Regional Policies', *Scottish Journal of Political Economy*, Nov 1970.

[10] For example, T. W. Buck, 'Shift and Share Analysis – a Guide to Regional Policy?', *Regional Studies*, Dec 1970; F. J. B. Stillwell, 'Further Thoughts on the Shift and Share Approach', *Regional Studies*, Dec 1970.

[11] A. J. Brown *et al.*, 'The "Green Paper" on the Development Areas', *National Institute Economic Review*, no. 40, 1967.

[12] See P. Hart and A. I. MacBean, 'Regional Differences in Productivity, Profitability and Growth: A Pilot Study', *Scottish Journal of Political Economy*, Feb 1961.

or less institutionally determined) the estimates of the efficiency parameters derived previously should reflect the operation of these factors within the regions. As noted earlier, the 'problem' regions of the North, North West, Scotland and Wales all seem to exhibit relatively low efficiency parameters with and without adjustment for increasing returns. It is also of interest to consider the regions in which the 'intermediate areas' are situated: Yorkshire and Humberside, the North West and the South West.[13] In general, there is not much to distinguish the regions scheduled as Development Areas from those including the Intermediate Areas, using the criterion of the efficiency parameter. Taken together, both sets of regions tend to exhibit low efficiency parameters relative to the average. By contrast, the Midlands regions in particular exhibit consistently high efficiency parameters relative to the nation.

It is also of some interest to examine the relationship between the 'differential growth' component[14] of shift-share studies and the relative levels of the efficiency parameter for each region. To the extent that the sign and magnitude of the growth component reflects general locational factors, we would expect to find some association between the values of the growth component between regions and the corresponding values of the regional efficiency parameters. For the period 1958–63, the regions of the North, North West, and Scotland, with lower than average efficiency parameters, all had negative growth components in the manufacturing sector (see chapter 8). These three regions plus Wales, also a region with a below average efficiency parameter, also had negative growth components in all activities taken together (i.e. including primary and tertiary industries).[15] While the rank correlation between the relative efficiency parameter and the magnitude of the differential growth component is statistically insignificant, it appears that no region with a negative differential

[13] See Department of Economic Affairs, *The Intermediate Areas*, Cmnd. 3998 (HMSO, 1969).

[14] See chapters 3 and 8 for a discussion of this concept.

[15] See A. P. Thirlwall, 'A Measure of the "Proper Distribution of Industry"', *Oxford Economic Papers*, Mar 1967, appendix 2, p. 57.

growth component had an efficiency parameter above average. To this extent at least general locational disadvantage appears to be associated with a negative growth component in shift-share analysis.

We now turn to consider in more detail the determinants of employment growth in the regions, first using the standardisation procedures outlined in chapter 1 and touched on in chapter 3, followed by an analysis concentrating directly on explanatory relationships derived from the mainstream of economic theory.

TABLE 7.A1 Output per worker and average earnings in the manufacturing sector of United Kingdom regions: 1958 and 1963 (£'s)

	*Net output per worker**		*Average earnings†*	
Region	*1958*	*1963*	*1958*	*1963*
N	1095	1425	597	725
YH	955	1245	538	670
EM	937	1240	546	665
EA	985	1345	540	675
SE	1090	1495	615	770
SW	1010	1390	571	725
WM	980	1305	590	741
NW	953	1310	540	695
W	1195	1540	615	775
S	975	1350	547	680
NI	685	1035	427	556
UK	1010	1362	573	718

* Net output in each region divided by total employment.
† Total wages and salaries divided by total employment.

Source: Board of Trade, *Report on the Census of Production 1963* (London, HMSO, 1970), part 133, p. 6f.

8 The Determinants of Employment Growth in Regional Manufacturing Industry

Interregional differences in the rate of growth of employment in manufacturing industry were highlighted in chapter 1. An analysis of the determinants of regional employment growth is interesting and important because employment growth in relation to workforce growth has a direct bearing on the percentage level of unemployment. If the rate of growth of labour supply was the same in all regions, regional differences in the percentage level of unemployment would be directly related to regional variations in labour demand (employment growth). In practice, of course, the growth of the workforce is not the same in all regions. Through the process of migration, workforce growth tends to adjust to demand conditions preventing interregional differences in the percentage level of unemployment from widening continuously.

This chapter is divided into two sections. The first section uses standardisation procedures (or shift-share analysis) to consider the extent to which interregional differences in employment growth in manufacturing can be attributed to regional differences in industrial structure as opposed to differences in the growth of demand for labour within industries between regions. The use of shift-share analysis, however, is no more than a classificatory device; it provides no economic explanations of why the strength of demand for labour may differ within industries between regions – if that is the major source of the problem. The second section of the chapter therefore adopts a traditional macroeconomic approach, concentrating on the proximate economic determinants of employment growth in a growth framework.

SHIFT-SHARE ANALYSIS OF EMPLOYMENT GROWTH

Shift-share analysis of employment growth attempts to isolate at least two components of regional growth rate differences – differences due to structural divergencies on the one hand, and differences due to the differential growth of industries between regions on the other. How much of the slow growth of employment in the high unemployment regions, for example, has been the result of the regional structure being heavily weighted with industries which nationally have been expanding very slowly (or even declining), and how much has been the result of industries in these regions growing more slowly than elsewhere? This is the type of question that shift-share analysis attempts to answer. These two sources of growth differences are sometimes called the 'composition' and 'growth' effects. Using the standardisation procedures outlined in chapter 1, which take the nation as the standard for regional comparison, the two components or 'difference' terms are easy to define. Letting $(\mathrm{d}L_r/L_r)$ be the rate of employment growth in the region, then:

$$\frac{\mathrm{d}L_r}{L_r} = \sum_i \left(\frac{\mathrm{d}L_{ir}}{L_{ir}}\right)\frac{L_{ir}}{L_r} \tag{8.1}$$

where L_{ir} is employment in industry i in region r
and L_r is total regional employment.

Similarly, letting $\mathrm{d}L/L$ be the rate of employment growth in the nation, then:

$$\frac{\mathrm{d}L}{L} = \sum_i \left(\frac{\mathrm{d}L_i}{L_i}\right)\frac{L_i}{L} \tag{8.2}$$

where L_i is employment in industry i in the nation
and L is total national employment.

The 'difference' terms are then $[(\mathrm{d}L_{ir}/L_{ir})-(\mathrm{d}L_i/L_i)]$ and $[(L_{ir}/L_r)-(L_i/L)]$. The first 'difference' term is the 'growth' difference and the second 'difference' term is the 'composition' difference. The contribution of these differences to the total difference between $\mathrm{d}L_r/L_r$ and $\mathrm{d}L/L$ depends on the weights applied to the difference terms. Let us first outline the possibilities and then discuss what would seem to be the most reasonable procedure to adopt, especially in the light of the criticism of shift-share analysis that it fails to consider the dependence of the growth effect on structure and therefore underestimates the contribution of structure to regional performance.

Applying regional weights to one of the difference terms and national weights to the other gives:

$$\frac{\mathrm{d}L_r}{L_r} - \frac{\mathrm{d}L}{L} = \sum_i \frac{\mathrm{d}L_{ir}}{L_{ir}}\left(\frac{L_{ir}}{L_r} - \frac{L_i}{L}\right) + \sum_i \frac{L_i}{L}\left(\frac{\mathrm{d}L_{ir}}{L_{ir}} - \frac{\mathrm{d}L_i}{L_i}\right) \quad (8.3)$$

or

$$\frac{\mathrm{d}L_r}{L_r} - \frac{\mathrm{d}L}{L} = \sum_i \frac{\mathrm{d}L_i}{L_i}\left(\frac{L_{ir}}{L_r} - \frac{L_i}{L}\right) + \sum_i \frac{L_{ir}}{L_r}\left(\frac{\mathrm{d}L_{ir}}{L_{ir}} - \frac{\mathrm{d}L_i}{L_i}\right) \quad (8.4)$$

Applying *either* regional *or* national weights to both difference terms gives:

$$\frac{\mathrm{d}L_r}{L_r} - \frac{\mathrm{d}L}{L} = \sum_i \frac{\mathrm{d}L_{ir}}{L_{ir}}\left(\frac{L_{ir}}{L_r} - \frac{L_i}{L}\right) + \sum_i \frac{L_{ir}}{L_r}\left(\frac{\mathrm{d}L_{ir}}{L_{ir}} - \frac{\mathrm{d}L_i}{L_i}\right) + \sum_i \left[\left(\frac{L_{ir}}{L_r} - \frac{L_i}{L}\right)\left(\frac{\mathrm{d}L_i}{L_i} - \frac{\mathrm{d}L_{ir}}{L_{ir}}\right)\right] \quad (8.5)$$

or

$$\frac{\mathrm{d}L_r}{L_r} - \frac{\mathrm{d}L}{L} = \sum_i \frac{\mathrm{d}L_i}{L_i}\left(\frac{L_{ir}}{L_r} - \frac{L_i}{L}\right) + \sum_i \frac{L_i}{L}\left(\frac{\mathrm{d}L_{ir}}{L_{ir}} - \frac{\mathrm{d}L_i}{L_i}\right) + \sum_i \left[\left(\frac{L_i}{L} - \frac{L_{ir}}{L_r}\right)\left(\frac{\mathrm{d}L_i}{L_i} - \frac{\mathrm{d}L_{ir}}{L_{ir}}\right)\right] \quad (8.6)$$

The last term on the R.H.S. of equation (8.5) and (8.6) is an interaction term which we will say more about later.

Applying the mean of the national and regional weights to both difference terms gives:

$$\frac{\mathrm{d}L_r}{L_r} - \frac{\mathrm{d}L}{L} = \sum_i \tfrac{1}{2}\left(\frac{\mathrm{d}L_{ir}}{L_{ir}} + \frac{\mathrm{d}L_i}{L_i}\right)\left[\frac{L_{ir}}{L_r} - \frac{L_i}{L}\right] + \sum_i \tfrac{1}{2}\left(\frac{L_i}{L} + \frac{L_{ir}}{L_r}\right) \times \left[\frac{\mathrm{d}L_{ir}}{L_{ir}} - \frac{\mathrm{d}L_i}{L_i}\right] \quad (8.7)$$

In each equation the 'growth' (g) and 'composition' (c) components are given by:

In equation (8.3): $g = \sum_i \left(\frac{L_i}{L}\right)\left(\frac{dL_{ir}}{L_{ir}}\right) - \frac{dL}{L}$

$$c = \frac{dL_r}{L_r} - \sum_i \left(\frac{dL_{ir}}{L_{ir}}\right)\left(\frac{L_i}{L}\right)$$

In equation (8.4): $g = \frac{dL_r}{L_r} - \sum_i \left(\frac{L_{ir}}{L_r}\right)\left(\frac{dL_i}{L_i}\right)$

$$c = \sum_i \left(\frac{dL_i}{L_i}\right)\left(\frac{L_{ir}}{L_r}\right) - \frac{dL}{L}$$

In equation (8.5): $g = \frac{dL_r}{L_r} - \sum_i \left(\frac{dL_i}{L_i}\right)\left(\frac{L_{ir}}{L_r}\right)$

$$c = \frac{dL_r}{L_r} - \sum_i \left(\frac{dL_{ir}}{L_{ir}}\right)\left(\frac{L_i}{L}\right)$$

In equation (8.6): $g = \sum_i \left(\frac{dL_{ir}}{L_{ir}}\right)\left(\frac{L_i}{L}\right) - \frac{dL}{L}$

$$c = \sum_i \left(\frac{dL_i}{L_i}\right)\left(\frac{L_{ir}}{L_i}\right) - \frac{dL}{L}$$

In equation (8.7) the 'growth' and 'composition' effects are given directly.

It is obvious from the above schema that the estimated contribution of 'composition' and 'growth' differences to interregional differences in employment growth will depend on the particular weighting system adopted. The usual way to estimate the effect of regional structure on a region's relative employment growth rate, which also has some basis in economic theory (see chapter 3, pp. 51–2), is to consider what a region's growth rate would be if all industries in the region grew at the same rate as in the nation (thus abstracting from any differential growth differences within industries), and to ascribe any difference between this hypothetical regional rate and the national rate to the fact that the region must be structurally different. This is shown in

TABLE 8.1 Estimates of the composition and growth effects using equation (8.4) for the period 1958–63

Region	*'Composition' effect*	*'Growth' effect*	*Total difference between region's growth of employment and growth in the UK*
N	−0.53	−0.57	−1.10
YH	−0.66	0.26	−0.40
EM	−0.23	0.33	0.10
EA	1.14	2.26	3.40
SE	0.19	0.21	0.40
SW	0.05	0.05	0.10
WM	0.50	—	0.50
NW	−0.20	−0.70	−0.90
W	0.38	0.72	1.10
S	−0.46	−1.14	−1.60
NI	−1.85	0.95	−0.90

equations (8.4) and (8.6) where structural differences are weighted by the national rate of growth of employment in each industry. Equation (8.4) has been used extensively by various investigators[1] with the result that composition does not appear to account for the major part of the lagging growth of the depressed regions or for the faster growth of the more prosperous regions. The major part of inter-regional differences in employment growth rates appears to arise from individual industries growing much slower in the depressed regions and much faster in the prosperous regions. The results of applying equation (8.4) to calculate composition effects for the short period 1958 to 1963 support this general conclusion. The results are given in table 8.1.

Of the five regions with growth rates below the average, the composition effect accounted for the major part of the negative differential in only two – Yorkshire and Humberside, and Northern Ireland. Of the six regions with growth rates

[1] For example, M. Hemming, 'The Regional Problem', *National Institute Economic Review*, Aug 1963; A. P. Thirlwall, 'A Measure of the Proper Distribution of Industry', *Oxford Economic Papers*, Mar 1967.

above the average, the composition effect accounted for the major part of the positive differential in three of the regions. Overall, an evaluation of inner products shows that 47.5 per cent of the total sum of squares of interregional differences can be accounted for by the growth effect and 33 per cent by the composition effect, leaving a positive covariance term between composition and growth effects of 19.5 per cent.

The general conclusion that seems to emerge from shift-share analysis that the structure of regions is of relatively minor importance in explaining their comparative growth performance has been questioned by some,[2] on the grounds that the structural characteristics of a region will influence the magnitude of the growth effect so that the results from the traditional use of standardisation procedures almost certainly underestimates the role of structural differences in accounting for interregional employment growth rate differences.[3] It is argued in particular that standardisation procedures take no account of income multiplier effects or input-output relationships between industries; that is, the shift-share technique implicitly assumes that each industry is independent when, in fact, industries may be extremely interdependent. Thus the decline in employment in some industries can affect adversely the growth of others because a decline in employment means a decline in local demand, and probably a decline in demand for inputs from other activities in the region. In short, a part of any negative growth effect in a lagging region could be traced back to its industrial structure, in the sense that a

[2] Notably by D. I. MacKay, 'Industrial Structure and Regional Growth: A Methodological Problem', *Scottish Journal of Political Economy*, June 1968.

[3] It is also sometimes argued that the composition effect is found to be unimportant because of the high level of industry aggregation used in analysis. It is true that because of aggregation, the growth effect will contain within it some sub-sector composition effect. But since the sub-sector composition effect may be positive or negative for small changes in the level of aggregation, it cannot be said with certainty that moving from a high level of aggregation to a lower level will enhance the importance of the composition effect and diminish the importance of the growth effect, although, of course, in the limit the growth effect would disappear entirely if each region concentrated on a separate industry!

region which has a below average representation of industries which are performing well nationally might be expected to perform relatively poorly in industries supplying intermediate products used in those sectors. Furthermore an above average representation of declining industries might have depressive effects on aggregate demand affecting the prospects and performance of local service industries. The only form of interdependence between structure and growth that standardisation procedures can take account of is that arising from the possibility that the growth of industries may be higher than average in regions which are relatively specialised in those activities, because of acquired advantages and lower costs, etc. The possibility of measuring this interdependence can be seen from the interaction terms in equations (8.5) and (8.6). A negative sign for the interaction term in equation (8.5) and a positive sign for the interaction term in equation (8.6) would indicate a positive relationship between specialisation of the industry in the region and the differential growth of the industry concerned. A positive sign in equation (8.5) and a negative sign in (8.6) would indicate the opposite – that employment grew slower in industries in which the region specialised, tending to make its industrial structure more diverse. It is fairly clear that the sign or magnitude of the interaction term could not be an indication of the interdependence between structure and growth referred to by the critics of shift-share analysis. For example, if a high proportion of employment in rapidly expanding industries (nationally) caused faster than average growth in *all* industries in the region, the interaction between composition differences and growth differences could be positive for some industries and negative for others and the magnitude and sign of the total interaction term would be meaningless.

To meet the criticism that the neglect of the interdependence between composition and growth effects understates the contribution of structural differences to interregional growth rate differences, one possibility is to take the sign and magnitude of the covariance term between the composition and growth effects in an evaluation of inner products as a measure of interdependence, and attribute it to structure. The covariance between the composition and growth effects in table 8.1, reported earlier, is positive and accounts for 19.5 per cent of the total sum of squares of interregional differences in employment growth. If this is added to the total sum of squares accounted for by composition effects, the influence of structure becomes the major determinant of interregional growth rate differences.

Although we may wish to concede the argument of the critics of shift-share analysis, it should also be emphasised that the alleged bias in shift-share analysis against structural explanations of relative employment growth performance does not always manifest itself in an insignificant composition component. It often depends on the weighting system employed. To illustrate the point, if we keep the growth component the same as in table 8.1 and add the interaction component of equation (8.6) to the composition component already calculated (that is, if we estimate the 'composition' and 'growth' components as in equation (8.5)) a different

TABLE 8.2 Alternative estimates of the composition effect and measures of interaction

Region	*Alternative 'Composition effect'**	*'Growth' effect*	*Interaction component (minus)*	*Total difference*
N	−1.33	−0.57	−0.80	−1.10
YH	−0.34	0.26	0.32	−0.40
EM	−0.83	0.33	−0.60	0.10
EA	−4.08	2.26	−5.22	3.40
SE	0.06	0.21	−0.13	0.40
SW	−0.35	0.05	−0.40	0.10
WM	−0.56	0.00	−1.06	0.50
NW	−0.95	−0.70	−0.75	−0.90
W	−0.60	0.72	−0.98	1.10
S	−0.50	−1.14	−0.04	−1.60
NI	−2.24	0.95	−0.39	−0.90

* As defined in equation (8.5) which is equal to the original composition effect plus the interaction term from equation (8.6). Since the signs of the interaction terms in equation (8.5) will be the opposite of those in (8.6), the interaction term in the above table must be subtracted from the other components to sum to the total difference.

pattern of results emerge from that in table 8.1. The estimates of the composition and growth effects, and of the interaction term, from applying equation (8.5) to data for the period 1958–63 are shown in table 8.2. An evaluation of inner products reveals that the composition effect now accounts for 138 per cent of the total sum of squares of interregional differences in employment growth compared to the growth effect which accounts for 47.5 per cent.[4]

It will be noticed from table 8.2 that the composition effect for all regions except one is negative. Compared with the results in table 8.1, this arises from the fact that the interaction terms that were added to the original composition effects are negative (except for the Yorkshire and Humberside region). Given the earlier discussion of the interpretation of the signs attaching to the interaction terms, it must be concluded that over the period all regions except Yorkshire and Humberside were tending to expand fastest in industries in which they were least specialised, producing a tendency towards the convergence of regional industrial structures. This bears out what we found in chapter 2 using changes in the coefficient of regional specialisation as the test of convergence (see table 2.1), and is also a tendency discernible over the longer time period 1948–63.[5] It is interesting to consider why there has been this convergence. Convergence will occur if industries undergoing secular decline are more geographically concentrated than are growth industries, which is likely if the former have a raw material base. Convergence might also be the result of the implementation of policies to influence industrial location and to diversify regional economies.

Given that the estimates of the growth and composition effects depend on the weighting system employed, and to which component the interaction term is assigned, all of which is arbitrary, the most sensible solution in work of this nature would seem to be to dispense with the problem by applying the mean of regional and national weights to both difference

[4] The proportions sum to more than 100 per cent because of a large negative covariance term.

[5] See A. P. Thirlwall, 'Weighting Systems and Regional Analysis: A Reply to Mr. Cunningham', *Oxford Economic Papers*, Mar 1969.

TABLE 8.3 Estimates of the composition and growth effects using the mean of regional and national weights (equation (8.7)), 1958–63

Region	*Growth effect*	*Composition effect*	*Total difference*
N	−0.17	−0.93	−1.10
YH	0.10	−0.50	−0.40
EM	0.63	−0.53	0.10
EA	4.87	−1.47	3.40
SE	0.28	0.12	0.40
SW	0.25	−0.15	0.10
WM	0.53	−0.03	0.50
NW	−0.33	−0.57	−0.90
W	1.21	−0.11	1.10
S	−1.12	−0.48	−1.60
NI	1.14	−2.04	−0.90

terms, as in equation (8.7). When this is done, the results in table 8.3 were obtained for the period 1958–63.

The results show an interesting pattern. In the regions of lagging growth, structure seems mainly responsible, whereas in the regions of more rapid growth, the growth effect seems to be mainly responsible. Moreover, there is a negative relation between the growth and composition effects. Differences in the growth effect are the major source of interregional differences in the growth of employment accounting for 150 per cent of the total sum of squares compared with differences in the composition effect which accounts for only 47 per cent of the total sum of squares. We end, therefore, with the broad conclusion that we began with, that while structural differences between regions are not unimportant in accounting for differences in employment growth between regions they are probably not the most important factor. The evidence on whether favourable composition raises the growth effect is hard to come by and what there is is equivocal.

A MACROECONOMIC VIEW OF EMPLOYMENT GROWTH

The major shortcoming of the shift-share analysis of employment growth is that it does not consider causal explanations of differential employment growth between regions derived from the main body of economic theory. It is essentially a classificatory device designed to show up the extent to which a region's position relative to all other regions can be ascribed to factors specific to the region. The purpose now is to consider the economic determinants of employment growth in the regions using (i) the labour requirements approach, which makes employment growth a function of output growth and productivity growth, and (ii) the labour manning approach which makes employment growth a function of the rate of capital accumulation.

THE LABOUR REQUIREMENTS APPROACH

The labour requirements approach to employment growth might well be called the Keynesian approach. The rate of growth of output is determined by the rate of growth of demand, and the rate of growth of employment depends on the rate of growth of output, given the rate of growth of labour productivity. An increase in labour productivity using this approach necessarily reduces labour requirements, and to prevent a decline in employment the demand for labour (i.e. the growth of output) would have to increase. This is most easily seen using the identity

$$L_r = \left(\frac{L}{O}\right)_r O_r = \frac{1}{(O/L)_r} O_r \qquad (8.8)$$

where L_r is regional employment
O_r is regional output
and $(O/L)_r$ is labour productivity in the region.

Totally differentiating equation (8.8) and dividing through by L_r gives an expression for the rate of growth of employment of:

$$\left(\frac{\mathrm{d}L}{L}\right)_r = \left(\frac{\mathrm{d}O}{O}\right)_r - \left(\frac{\mathrm{d}(O/L)}{(O/L)}\right)_r$$

or

$$l_r = g_r - r_r \qquad (8.9)$$

TABLE 8.4 Average annual growth rates of employment, output and labour productivity in the manufacturing sector of the regions: 1958–68

Region	l_r	g_r	r_r
N	−0.1	3.7	3.8
YH	−0.1	3.8	3.9
EM	1.3	8.5	7.2
EA	3.4	9.2	5.8
SE	0.6	5.5	4.9
SW	1.4	6.0	4.6
WM	0.8	5.4	4.6
NW	−0.9	4.4	5.3
W	1.6	5.3	3.7
S	−0.2	4.6	4.8
NI	−0.1	7.1	7.2
UK	0.3	5.2	4.9

Source: Board of Trade, *Report on the Census of Production 1963* (London, HMSO, 1970), part 133.
Board of Trade, 'Area Analyses of the Provisional Results of the Census of Production for 1968', *Board of Trade Journal*, vol. 199, 1970, pp. 488–96.

where l is the rate of growth of employment
g is the rate of growth of output
r is the rate of growth of labour productivity.

Clearly an increase in r will reduce employment growth unless g rises to compensate. Given r, employment growth is determined by output growth.[6]

Table 8.4 reports rates of growth of output, employment and labour saving in the manufacturing sector of United Kingdom regions over the period 1958 to 1968. The original data, expressed in money prices, has been deflated by the national rate of increase in the wholesale price of all manu-

[6] In terms of the production function $O_r = R_r L_r^{\alpha}$, the growth of employment is given by $l_r = 1/\alpha(g_r - r_r)$. With constant returns ($\alpha = 1$), this expression is the same as equation (8.9).

In terms of the more general Cobb–Douglas production function including capital as a factor of production, $O_r = A_r L_r^{\alpha} K_r^{\beta}$, the growth of employment is given by: $l_r = (g_r - \beta . k_r - a_r)/\alpha$, where k is the rate of growth of capital and a is the rate of growth of total productivity.

factured goods. In five regions over the period, the rate of labour saving (i.e. the rate of productivity growth) exceeded the rate of growth of output, giving rise to a decline in the absolute numbers employed. Two of these regions, Northern Ireland and the North West, experienced productivity growth in excess of the rate for the United Kingdom; and Scotland's rate was close to the average. These regions are also amongst those with the highest unemployment. As McCrone has remarked, 'It is in many ways ironic to find that, during a period when the United Kingdom as a whole was suffering from labour shortage so that the growth of output has very largely to come from productivity increases, the regions with surplus labour resources actually achieved faster productivity growth.'[7]

It does not follow from what we have said above, however, that the major source of interregional differences in employment growth lies in differences in the rate of labour saving, or that high rates of labour saving are incompatible with high rates of employment growth. Some insight into these questions can be obtained by an evaluation of inner products. Let $\Delta l_r = \Delta g_r - \Delta r_r$ be the deviation of a region's employment growth rate from the national rate. Squaring both sides of the expression and summing over regions yields an expression for the total sum of squares of regional employment growth:

$$\sum_r (\Delta l_r)^2 = \sum_r (\Delta g_r)^2 + \sum_r (\Delta r_r)^2 - 2\sum_r [(\Delta g_r)(\Delta r_r)] \quad (8.10)$$

The covariance term gives the interaction between output growth and productivity growth, which is interesting in its own right. Table 8.5 gives the magnitudes of the components of the total sum of squares using the data in table 8.4. The most important single source of interregional differences in employment growth is differences in the rate of growth of output. The interaction between output growth and productivity growth served to reduce differences in employment growth between regions. This implies that output growth and

[7] G. McCrone, op.cit., p. 160.

productivity growth are positively related.[8] The positive association between output growth and productivity growth is frequently referred to as Verdoorn's law.[9]

TABLE 8.5 Sources of interregional differences in employment growth

Source of variation	*Sum of squares*	*Proportion of total sum of squares* (%)
$\sum_r (\Delta g_r)^2$	36.41	237.5
$\sum_r (\Delta r_r)^2$	15.40	96.7
$-2\sum_r [(\Delta g_r)(\Delta r_r)]$	−35.86	−234.2
$\sum_r (\Delta l)^2$	15.95	100

The importance of the 'Verdoorn effect' for employment growth depends, of course, not upon the mere existence of a relationship between r and g, as found above, but on the precise magnitude of the relationship. To show this, let the Verdoorn relationship be specified as:

$$r_r = r_{ar} + \lambda g_r \tag{8.11}$$

where r_{ar} is the rate of autonomous productivity growth in the region

and λ is the Verdoorn coefficient, assumed to be the same in all regions.

Substituting equation (8.11) into (8.9) gives an expression for the rate of growth of employment of:

$$l_r = g_r(1-\lambda) - r_{ar} \tag{8.12}$$

The level of employment will increase or decrease according to whether $g_r(1-\lambda) - r_{ar} \gtrless 0$. The importance of the magnitude of the Verdoorn effect is easily seen if we assume $r_{ar} = 0$. In that case $l_r \lesseqgtr 0$ according to whether $\lambda \lesseqgtr 1$. If the Verdoorn

[8] That is, the negative sign of the interaction term indicates that the terms inside the square brackets of equation (8.10) are positively correlated.

[9] P. J. Verdoorn, 'Fattori che Regolano lo Sviluppo della Produttività del Lavoro', *L'Industria*, 1949. An English translation by G. and A. P. Thirlwall is available on request from the authors.

coefficient is greater than unity, output growth will induce declines in employment. Between zero and unity, employment growth will vary inversely with the size of λ.

It is also interesting to examine here the relationship between the Verdoorn coefficient and the degree of returns to scale in the Cobb–Douglas production function. It was shown in chapter 6 that, if the production function is not homogenous of degree one, the rate of growth of output may be specified as:

$$g_r = a_r + \beta_r(k-l) + vl \tag{8.13}$$

where a_r is the rate of neutral technical progress
v is the degree of returns to scale.

To obtain a relationship between λ and v assume that autonomous productivity growth in equation (8.12) is equal to the rate of technical progress plus the effects of capital deepening in equation (8.13) and set both equal to zero. From (8.12) we get $l_r = g_r(1-\lambda)$, and from (8.13) we get $l_r = (1/v)g_r$, which gives a relation between λ and v of:

$$\lambda = 1-(1/v)$$

If technical progress and capital deepening were strictly autonomous, and there was constant returns to scale ($v = 1$), the Verdoorn coefficient would be zero. λ would be unity if the degree of returns to scale was infinitely large or if a part of technical progress and capital deepening were induced. Most empirical studies (including Verdoorn's own study) of the Verdoorn coefficient yield estimates of between 0.4 and 0.6.[10] For this to be solely due to the influence of increasing returns to scale, the homogeneity parameter (v) would have to assume a value of between 1.66 and 2.50. Such values are unrealistic. It follows that the Verdoorn coefficient cannot be interpreted simply as returns to scale as measured by the

[10] P. J. Verdoorn, op.cit. See also N. Kaldor, *Causes of the Slow Rate of Economic Growth of the United Kingdom* (Cambridge University Press, 1966); W. Beckerman, *The British Economy in 1975* (Cambridge University Press, 1966); K. A. Kennedy, *Productivity and Industrial Growth* (Clarendon Press, 1971).

homogeneity parameter but must also include the effects of induced technical progress and capital deepening.[11]

We noted earlier from equation (8.12) that if autonomous productivity growth is constant, and output is increasing, employment will increase or decrease according to whether $(g-r_a) \gtrless \lambda g$. Kaldor has estimated for the manufacturing sectors of twelve OECD countries that $r_a = 1.04$ and $\lambda = 0.48$.[12] This implies that the average rate of growth of output necessary to prevent employment from falling (i.e. setting $l = 0$) is 2.0 per cent. The actual growth rate of output for the United Kingdom over the period considered by Kaldor was 3.2 per cent per annum. Using regional data for the United Kingdom[13] our estimate of equation (8.11) is (standard error in brackets):

$$r_r = 2.116 + \underset{(0.147)}{0.512} g_r: \qquad r^2 = 0.573$$

The estimated equation shows a Verdoorn coefficient which is significantly different from zero and unity at the 99 per cent confidence level, and a high rate of autonomous productivity growth. In fact, given the national rate of productivity growth in manufacturing over the period of 4.9 per cent per annum, approximately one-half appears to be attributable to autonomous factors; the remaining half induced by the growth of output itself. In chapter 6 we estimated the components of national productivity growth as: $r = a^* + \beta m^{**} + (v-1)l + (v-1)l + \text{CRS}$, where $a^* = 2.42$; $\beta m^{**} = 2.35$; $(v-1)l = 0.03$, and $\text{CRS} = 0.10$. Since increasing returns is clearly an induced part of productivity growth, the autonomous component of productivity growth must be concealed in the joint effects of technical progress (a^*), capital deepening (βm^{**}) and the contribution of resource shifts (CRS). These three terms account for 4.87 percentage points of the productivity growth, which implies that just under one-half of the rate of technical pro-

[11] This is the interpretation adopted by Kaldor. See N. Kaldor, op.cit., and his paper 'The Irrelevance of Equilibrium Economics', *Economic Journal*, Dec 1972. See also chapter 10, pp. 213–14.

[12] N. Kaldor, op.cit.

[13] Table 8.4.

gress and capital deepening combined must be autonomous, and just over one-half induced by the growth of output. This suggests that the contribution of interregional differences in the rate of growth of output is likely to be more important as a source of interregional differences in the rate of employment growth than the calculations of table 8.5 would suggest. This is because part of the variation in productivity growth which is treated as a separate component in the earlier analysis should be attributed to variations in output growth. To take account of this distinction between the effects of autonomous and induced productivity growth on employment growth, we redefine employment growth in each region as equal to:

$$l_r = g_r - r_{ar} - \lambda g_r \qquad (8.15)$$

or

$$l_r = g_r(1-\lambda) - r_{ar}$$

Correspondingly for the nation we have:

$$l_{\text{UK}} = g_{\text{UK}}(1-\lambda) - r_{a\text{UK}} \qquad (8.16)$$

Subtracting equation (8.16) from (8.15) yields an expression for deviations of regional employment growth from the national rate of:

$$\Delta l_r = \Delta g_r(1-\lambda) - \Delta r_{ar} \qquad (8.17)$$

Squaring both sides of equation (8.17) and summing over all regions yields an expression for the total sum of squares of:

$$\sum_r (\Delta l_r)^2 = \sum_r (\Delta g_r(1-\lambda))^2 - \sum_r (\Delta r_{ar})^2 + R \qquad (8.18)$$

The results from an evaluation of inner products are not directly comparable with the results in table 8.5 because the interaction term (R) is now zero, as expected (i.e. having 'removed' the dependence of productivity growth on output growth). The results still show, however, that output growth rate differences are the main source of employment growth rate differences.[14] To the extent that output growth is deter-

[14] Differences in output growth between regions contribute 60 per cent, and differences in autonomous productivity growth 40 per cent, to the variation in employment growth between regions.

mined by demand, and employment growth affects the level of unemployment, the results here support the analysis in chapter 5 which attributes unemployment rate differences between regions mainly to differences in the pressure of demand.

THE 'MANNING RATIO' APPROACH TO THE DEMAND FOR LABOUR

Using this approach, employment is viewed as the use of labour to operate, or 'man', capital equipment. The demand for labour is then determined by the capital stock in use and the 'manning ratio', i.e.

$$L = \frac{L}{K_a} . K_a \tag{8.19}$$

where K_a is the actual capital stock in use.

Or, in terms of growth rates,

$$l = k_a - m \tag{8.20}$$

where m is the rate of growth of the capital–labour ratio.

In chapter 6 we derived estimates of the rate of capital deepening in each region using the 'progress constant' formulation of Johansen's technique for estimating the contribution of technical progress and capital deepening to growth in the absence of capital data. Since the estimates were derived from observations of actual (as opposed to potential) output the estimated rates of capital deepening refer to the actual rate of growth of capital per worker *in use* (as opposed to the rate of increase in capital in *existence*). And it is, of course, capital in use (not capital in existence) which is relevant to the determination of employment. Given these estimates of the rate of capital deepening for each region (m_r), together with the rates of growth of employment, the rates of growth of the active capital stock may be calculated for each region as:

$$k_{ar} = m_r + l_r \tag{8.21}$$

These estimates are presented in table 8.6. The estimated national rate of growth in the active capital stock is 5.3 per

TABLE 8.6 Estimated rates of capital deepening, growth in the active capital stock and employment 1958–68

Region	m_r*	k_{ar}†	l_r
N	4.0	3.9	−0.1
YH	3.5	3.4	−0.1
EM	8.9	10.2	1.3
EA	3.1	6.5	3.4
SE	4.5	5.1	0.6
SW	4.9	6.3	1.4
WM	4.6	5.4	0.8
NW	5.6	4.7	−0.9
W	1.9	3.5	1.6
S	3.7	3.5	−0.2
NI	9.4	9.3	−0.1
UK	5.0	5.3	0.3

* Obtained from chapter 6, table 6.8.
† $k_{ar} = m_r + l_r$.

cent per annum, which is approximately 2 per cent greater than the estimates of the growth of the capital stock in manufacturing industry made by others over roughly the same period. The 'Blue Book' estimates of the value of the capital stock (at constant 1963 prices) in manufacturing in the United Kingdom give an average annual rate of growth of 3.2 per cent per annum over the period 1958–68.[15] Matthews gives a figure for the average annual rate of growth of the capital stock in manufacturing 1948–62 of 3.1 per cent.[16] And Feinstein's data indicates that the capital stock in manufacturing and construction increased at the rate of 3.3 per cent per annum over the period 1955–65.[17] On this evidence, our method of estimating the rates of capital deepening and of the active capital stock appears to overestimate the national rate.

[15] See, *British Economy: Key Statistics 1900–1970* (Times Newspapers, 1972), p. 12.
[16] R. C. O. Matthews, op.cit., p. 91.
[17] C. H. Feinstein, *National Income Expenditure and Output of the United Kingdom 1855–1965* (Cambridge University Press, 1972).

There is still the question, however, of whether the estimates provide a reasonable approximation to the relative ranking of regions according to their rates of capital accumulation, since it is the relative rates of growth which are relevant to the explanation of differences in employment growth between regions. One test of this would be to examine the ranking in relation to the ranking of the best available 'proxy' for the utilisation of capital. The best surrogate for the utilised capital stock is probably electricity consumption by industrial users. Unfortunately the Electricity Board regions do not exactly coincide with the Standard Regions, but in spite of this the rank correlation between the regional estimates of the growth of the capital stock and the regional estimates of the growth of electricity supplied to industrial users is statistically significant at the 90 per cent confidence level. In the absence of published data on regional capital stocks, our estimates might be said to provide a reasonable approximation to the relative growth rates of regional capital stocks.

What the results in table 8.6 show is that while the growth in the active capital stock was positive in all regions over the period, employment none the less declined in five regions out of eleven. In the North West, the employment decline was particularly severe. In terms of the manning ratio approach to the determinants of employment growth, we are left with the conclusion that falls in the manning ratio (i.e. increases in capital intensity) must have more than offset the employment creating effects of increases in the active capital stock. Compared with the rate of decline in the manning ratio for the United Kingdom as a whole, however, only two of the five regions of employment decline experienced a fall in the manning ratio greater than average (the North West and Northern Ireland). In other words, there is not much evidence that the employment problems of the traditionally depressed regions have been aggravated by the attraction of more capital intensive industries compared to other regions.[18] This is not to say, however, that the rate of employment decline could not have been eased if industries in these regions were

[18] Through the operation of regional policy, for example, which subsidises the cost of capital in depressed regions.

less capital intensive. If the capital–labour ratio had not risen in these regions, employment growth may well have been positive.

The relative importance of differences in the rate of change in the manning ratio and in the active capital stock as sources of interregional differences in the rate of employment can be ascertained by an evaluation of inner products using equation (8.20) for each region and subtracting the national equation from each giving:

$$\Delta l_r = \Delta k_{ar} - \Delta m_r \qquad (8.22)$$

Squaring both sides of equation (8.22) and summing over all regions gives:

$$\sum_r (\Delta l_r)^2 = \sum_r (\Delta k_{ar})^2 + \sum_r (\Delta m_r)^2 - 2[(\Delta k_{ar})(\Delta m_r)] \qquad (8.23)$$

Using data in table 8.6 we find that differences in the rate of growth in the active capital stock and in the manning ratio both served to make for considerable differences in the rate of employment growth between regions, but differences in the growth of capital are slightly more important in terms of the proportion of the total sum of squares 'explained'. The single most important source of variation, however, seems to be the interaction component which has served to reduce differences in employment growth. The interaction term is positive implying that relatively high rates of capital accumulation were associated with relatively high rates of capital deepening and vice versa. Apparently, capital accumulation was undertaken primarily as a substitute for, rather than as a complement to, employment growth. As a result, the expansion of employment in regions accumulating capital rapidly was lower than might otherwise have been the case, with the opposite the case in regions accumulating capital more slowly.

We have demonstrated in this chapter that interregional differences in employment growth have resulted primarily from differences in the rate of growth of output on the one hand and from differences in the rate of growth of capital on the other. These findings are not inconsistent; indeed, they support each other. As we should expect they imply a close relationship between the rate of growth of output and the rate of capital accumulation. This relationship is examined more closely in the next chapter.

9 The Growth Experience of the Regions: A Harrodian Interpretation

The purpose of this chapter is to attempt to analyse the growth and employment experience of the regions in terms of the Harrod-Domar model of economic growth.[1] Harrod's theory is concerned with the relationships between three different rates of growth and the implications of divergencies between them: (1) the rate of growth consistent with the full employment of labour (g_n); (2) the rate of growth consistent with full utilisation of the capital stock (g_w); and (3) the actual rate of growth (g). To understand the relationship between the supply and demand for labour over time it is necessary to examine the precise relationships between these three rates of growth: the 'natural rate' (g_n); the 'warranted rate' (g_w) and the actual rate (g). Harrod contends that there is no mechanism in the private sector which ensures that all these growth rates will coincide: 'I am confident that the theory that the "warranted" equilibrium growth rate of laissez-faire capitalism without management or interference, is unstable, stands firm; and that this is the fundamental explanation of the business cycle.'[2] A large part of growth theory has been concerned with this claim and with attempts to examine mechanisms which may equalise at least two of the growth rates mentioned. The theories that have stemmed from Harrod may be broadly characterised as neoclassical on the one hand and Keynesian

[1] R. F. Harrod, 'An Essay in Dynamic Theory', *Economic Journal*, Mar 1939. R. F. Harrod, *Towards a Dynamic Economics* (Macmillan, 1948); R. F. Harrod, *Economic Dynamics* (Macmillan, 1973); E. Domar, 'Capital Expansion, Rate of Growth and Employment', *Econometrica*, Apr 1946.

[2] *Economic Dynamics*, p. 45.

on the other.[3] Neoclassical models are primarily concerned with the relationship between the warranted and natural rates of growth.[4] In these models equality between the warranted and natural rates of growth comes about through changes in the capital-output ratio resulting from variations in the rate of interest and the wage rate. Keynesian (or Cambridge) models on the other hand are more concerned with the relationship between the actual and the warranted rates of growth.[5] Professor Robinson believes that 'when a steady rate of growth is actually going on, the "share" of savings adapts to it'.[6] In contrast to neoclassical models on the other hand, Professor Robinson also argues that '... even if all the other conditions are fulfilled, growth at the natural rate will not be realised if firms lack the energy to carry it out. There is no law of nature that the natural rate of growth should prevail.'[7] The models also differ in their explanation of the source and behaviour of unemployment over time. In a neoclassical model unemployment must be explained either in terms of frictions which prevent adjustment mechanisms operating, or in terms of the slow speed of adjustment. Taking a Cambridge view of the world, the behaviour of unemployment must be explained in terms of decisions to accumulate subject to the constraints imposed by the supply of labour and the real wage rate.

[3] For surveys see: F. H. Hahn and R. C. O. Matthews, 'The Theory of Economic Growth: A Survey', *Economic Journal*, Dec 1964; A. K. Sen (ed.), *Growth Economics* (Penguin, 1970).

[4] T. W. Swan, 'Economic Growth and Capital Accumulation', *Economic Record*, Nov 1956; R. M. Solow, 'A Contribution to the Theory of Economic Growth', *Quarterly Journal of Economics*, Feb 1956; J. E. Meade, *A Neoclassical Theory of Economic Growth* (George Allen & Unwin, 1962); R. M. Solow, *Growth Theory: An Exposition* (Clarendon Press, 1971).

[5] N. Kaldor, 'Alternative Theories of Distribution', *Review of Economic Studies*, no. 2, 1955–6; J. Robinson, *Essays in the Theory of Economic Growth* (Macmillan, 1972); J. Robinson, *Economic Heresies* (Macmillan, 1971).

[6] J. Robinson, 'A Reply [to Harrod]', *Economic Journal*, Sep 1970.

[7] J. Robinson, *Economic Heresies* (Macmillan, 1971), p. 118.

THE RELATION BETWEEN THE ACTUAL AND NATURAL GROWTH RATES

We begin the study by describing the unemployment experience of the regions in terms of relative rates of growth of employment and the workforce, as indicative of divergencies between the actual and natural rates of growth, and in terms of the initial conditions of the regions. Table 9.1 gives some measure of the excess supply of labour in the regions over the period, together with the relative rates of growth of employment and the workforce and the implied relationship between g and g_n for each region. Strictly speaking the concept of a 'full employment' or 'natural' rate of growth in regional manufacturing should include induced labour migration and also the possibility of absorbing unemployed labour from other sectors into manufacturing. We have not been able

TABLE 9.1 Estimates of the excess supply of labour and the relative growth rates of employment (l) and the workforce (n) 1958–68

Region	*Excess supply of labour*[1] *(as % of the workforce)*	$(l_r - n_r)$	$g : g_n$
N	1.3	−0.2	$g < g_n$
YH[2]	−0.3	0	$g = g_n$
EM[3]	−0.5	0.1	$g > g_n$
EA, SE	−0.2	0	$g = g_n$
SW	0	0	$g = g_n$
WM[4]	−0.4	−0.1	$g < g_n$
NW	0.5	0.2	$g > g_n$
W	1.5	0.1	$g > g_n$
S	1.6	0	$g = g_n$
NI	—	0.1	$g > g_n$

Key: 1 Estimates from A. P. Thirlwall, 'Types of Unemployment with Special Reference to Non Demand-deficient Unemployment in Great Britain', *Scottish Journal of Political Economy*, Feb 1969. Estimates cover all industries; and negative sign indicates excess labour demand.

2 Data in first column refers to old Standard Region, E and WR.

3 Data in first column refers to old Standard Region, NM.

4 Data in first column refers to old Standard Region, M.

to take these endogenous effects into account. It should be remembered, therefore, that throughout the chapter the term natural rate of growth refers to the recorded growth of the manufacturing workforce only.

It is apparent from table 9.1 that the regions may be divided into three groups depending on the behaviour of unemployment over time. Firstly there are those regions where employment is increasing faster than the workforce. With the exception of the East Midlands region, these were all regions with an initial reserve of unemployed labour. Mrs Robinson has called this situation a 'limping golden age'.[8] $g > g_n$ can only be a transient phase, however; ultimately the rate of growth of the workforce will become an effective constraint on g. Secondly, there are those regions in which employment and workforce growth are roughly equal. The southern half of the country falls into this category which can be said to have experienced a 'golden age'[9] by maintaining a low and stable unemployment rate over time. Scotland also falls into this category with employment and the workforce falling roughly at the same rate. Its high initial unemployment and labour reserves, however, make its situation more akin to a limping golden age. Thirdly, there are those regions where $g < g_n$ and unemployment is rising over time. There are two regions in this category, the West Midlands and the North. The North, with initial excess labour supply, is an example of a 'leaden age',[10] while the West Midlands where excess demand for labour is slowly giving way to excess supply is another example of a limping golden age.

THE RELATION BETWEEN THE ACTUAL AND WARRANTED GROWTH RATES

While the unemployment experience of the regions may be described in the way we have done, it cannot be *explained* solely in terms of the relationship between the actual and natural rates of growth. As we have already noted, both

[8] J. Robinson, *Essays*, op. cit., p. 53.
[9] Ibid., p. 52.
[10] Ibid., p. 54.

empirically and theoretically, the decision to accumulate capital is also of crucial importance. This is where Harrod's concept of the warranted (or desired) rate of growth becomes important. Harrod defines the warranted rate of growth (g_w) as '... that overall rate of advance which, if executed, will leave entrepreneurs in a state of mind in which they are prepared to carry on a similar advance'.[11] In short, it is that rate of growth which maintains equality between the growth of capacity and the growth of demand. To find this rate, let the investment demand function be written:

$$I = v_r(\Delta Y) \tag{9.1}$$

where I is current investment demand
ΔY is the change in output
v_r is the desired incremental capital-output ratio,

and write the net withdrawals function as

$$S-(X-M) = (s-b)Y \tag{9.2}$$

where S is current savings
X is exports
M is imports
s is the propensity to save
b is the net balance of payments expressed as a proportion of output
and Y is output.

Equilibrium between planned investment and planned 'saving' gives:

$$v_r(\Delta Y) = (s-b)Y \tag{9.3}$$

and the equilibrium (warranted) growth rate of output is therefore:

$$\frac{\Delta Y}{Y} = g_w = \frac{(s-b)}{v_r} \tag{9.4}$$

The actual growth rate (g) may be expressed as:

$$g = \frac{(s-b)}{v} \tag{9.5}$$

[11] R. F. Harrod, *Towards a Dynamic Economics* (Macmillan, 1948), p. 81.

where v is the actual incremental capital-output ratio. The relationship between the actual and desired capital-output ratio may be expressed as:

$$v_r = \theta v \tag{9.6}$$

where θ is a measure of capacity utilisation. If there is excess capacity, and $v > v_r$, then $\theta < 1$. If there is deficient capacity, and $v < v_r$, then $\theta > 1$. Using equation (9.6) and substituting for v in equation (9.5), we obtain a relationship between g and g_w:

$$g = \theta \frac{(s-b)}{v_r} = \theta g_w \tag{9.7}$$

If the actual growth rate exceeds the rate warranted by thriftiness and technical conditions, capacity will be deficient ($\theta > 1$). Manufacturers' expectations will be revised upwards, the rate of capital accumulation will tend to increase, and the actual growth rate will rise further above g_w. On the other hand, if the actual growth rate falls short of the warranted rate, excess capacity will build up ($\theta < 1$). Expectations will be revised downwards, reducing g still further below g_w.

The deviations between g and g_w are likely to be amplified by the influence of the degree of capacity utilisation (θ) on investment demand. There is a large body of empirical evidence[12] to support a theory of investment demand which embodies a flexible accelerator. If capacity is deficient, not only will expectations of output growth be revised upwards but the desired level of investment demand (relative to any expected rise in output) will also increase. This introduces more instability into the system.[13] When g_w exceeds g the presence of excess capacity will tend to result in a reduction in the desired level of new investment over and above the reduction arising from a downward revision of expectations.

[12] A. D. Knox, 'The Acceleration Principle and the Theory of Investment: A Survey', *Economica*, Aug 1952; D. Smyth, 'Empirical Evidence on the Acceleration Principle', *Review of Economic Studies*, June 1964; M. K. Evans, *Macroeconomic Activity: Theory, Forecasting and Control* (Harper & Row, 1969).

[13] R. C. O. Matthews, *The Trade Cycle* (Cambridge University Press, 1959).

As far as the regions of the United Kingdom are concerned, we have no direct information on the warranted rate of growth. We must infer the relationship between g_w and g either from indirect evidence or through the judicious use of assumptions. It could be assumed that the warranted and actual rates are equal. The Cambridge school have argued that any steady rate of growth will, after a time, become warranted, but this presupposes adjustment mechanisms which should themselves be subjected to test. Another possibility would be to assume that g_w equals g_n. But again this would be 'unwarranted' without resort to empirical verification. Alternatively it may be hypothesised that in the event of a divergence between g and g_w some observable phenomena are affected in a predictable way or that some adjustment mechanism comes into play. Evidence on the affected variable, or on the adjustment mechanism itself, could then be used to deduce the implied relationship between g_w and g. There are two possible sources of evidence both based on Harrod's proposition that a divergence between g_w and g will be reflected in variations in the degree of capacity utilisation. One relates to differences between the growth of the capital stock in use and in existence; the other relates to movements in the capital-output ratio directly.

In terms of the distinction between the capital stock in use (K_a) and the capital stock in existence (K_e), an inequality between g_w and g implies an inequality between the growth of the 'active' capital stock (k_a) and the growth of the existing stock (k_e). If g exceeds g_w, then k_a will exceed k_e (assuming some margin of excess capacity to start with)–and if g_w exceeds g, then k_e will exceed k_a. If investment behaviour is determined by the capital stock adjustment principle, where the accelerator is flexible, a discrepancy between g and g_w reflected in the difference between k_a and k_e should be quite marked. In the last chapter we argued that our estimates of the rate of increase in the capital stock in the regions were estimates of the capital stock in use. The question is, can these estimates be adjusted to give some idea of the growth in the actual capital stock? An approach commonly adopted is to assume that capital is unemployed in the same proportion as the labour force so that:

$$\theta = (1-u) \tag{9.8}$$

The rate of growth of the existing capital stock could then be measured as:

$$k_e = k_a - \frac{\Delta(1-u)}{(1-u)} = k_a - (l-n) \tag{9.9}$$

It is easily seen, however, that this is tantamount to assuming that the warranted rate of growth is equal to the natural rate, so that the implied relationship between g and g_w is the same as between g and g_n. When $l = n$, the growth of the actual capital stock is equal to the active capital stock which implies that $g = g_w$; but if $l = n$, $g = g_n$. If $l \gtrless n$, $k_a \gtrless k_e$ and $g \gtrless g_w$; but also if $l \gtrless n$, $g \gtrless g_n$. This approach adds very little, therefore, to what we already know.

There is a second source of evidence on divergencies between g and g_w, however, and that is movements in the capital-output ratio. If the theory of divergent growth is accepted, deviations of g from g_w will be reflected, via the utilisation coefficient, in variations in the capital-output ratio. If capacity is deficient ($g > g_w$), the actual capital-output ratio should be observed to be falling relative to its predicted level. If there is excess capacity ($g < g_w$) the actual capital-output ratio should be observed to be rising relative to its predicted level. There is no problem in estimating the rate of change in the capital-output ratio (d); it is simply:

$$d = k_a - g \tag{9.10}$$

The difficulty is choosing a benchmark against which to measure high or low values of d. One possibility would be to compare d in the regions with the national rate of change of d. This would assume, however, that the warranted growth rate was the same in all regions, and would ignore factors specific to each region which determine the required capital-output ratio, e.g. different rates of technical progress and variations in production techniques. A second possibility, which is adopted here, is to use the notion of the technical progress function and to take regional deviations of actual growth from growth predicted by the technical progress function as a measure of regional discrepancies between g and g_w.

THE TECHNICAL PROGRESS FUNCTION

The technical progress function, originated by Kaldor,[14] establishes a relationship between the rate of growth of output and the rate of capital accumulation. Increases in the rate of growth of output are associated with increases in the rate of growth of capital, but at a diminishing rate. The function is depicted graphically in figure 9.1.

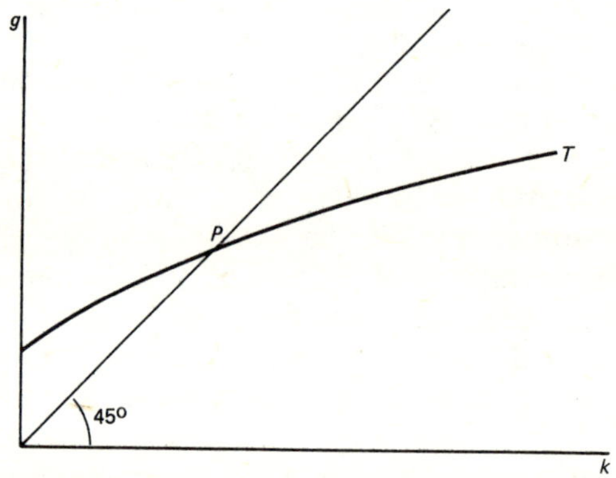

FIGURE 9.1

At some growth rate the capital-output ratio is constant, satisfying Harrod's requirement for steady growth, i.e. v_r is constant. This will be the point of long run equilibrium: point P in the diagram. At any other point on the curve the economy will be in short run equilibrium since the capital stock is fully employed, but there will be a tendency for the capital-output ratio to change. There may also be short run deviations from the function due to lags in the adjustment of the capital stock. For example, Kaldor indicates '...periods of accelerating

[14] N. Kaldor, 'A Model of Economic Growth', *Economic Journal*, Dec 1957.

growth are likely to be periods when the capital-output ratio is falling, and periods of decelerating growth are those in which the capital-output ratio is rising'.[15] In other words, if g exceeds g_w (accelerating growth) the output-capital ratio is likely to be greater than that predicted by the technical progress function. If g_w exceeds g (decelerating growth) the reverse will be the case.

If the technical progress function for each region could be observed, the actual rate of growth of output could be compared with the rate predicted by the function. This would enable us to infer the relationship between g_w and g. If output growth in any region was higher than predicted this could be interpreted as $g > g_w$. Similarly, if output growth was less than predicted on the basis of the prevailing rate of capital accumulation, this could be interpreted as $g_w > g$. Unfortunately, because of insufficient data we cannot observe a technical progress function for each region. If, however, we assume that the technical progress function is the same in all regions, thus retaining the spirit of the analysis in chapter 6, it could then be argued that each region 'selects' a position on the common technical progress function in the light of its own factor supplies, quality of entrepreneurship, etc. This would enable us to estimate the technical progress function from regional cross section data, and to take regional deviations from the function as indicative of discrepancies between g and g_w. Using this approach, the technical progress function was estimated, in linear and non-linear form, for the period 1958–68. The difference in results between the linear and non-linear forms is not substantial. The estimated linear function is (standard errors in brackets):[16]

$$g = 2.278 + \underset{(0.157)}{0.622}(k) \quad r^2 = 0.633$$

It has been argued that values of output growth (g) in

[15] Ibid., p. 623n.

[16] The non-linear form exhibited a slight, though insignificant, trace of diminishing returns as indicated by a negative sign on the quadratic term. Data on k were obtained from Table 8.6.

TABLE 9.2 The relationship between g and g_w and between g and g_n

Region	Deviations of actual g from predicted g	$g : g_w$	$g : g_n$
N	−1.0	$g < g_w$	$g < g_n$
YH	−0.6	$g < g_w$	$g = g_n$
EM	−0.1	$g < g_w$	$g > g_n$
EA	+2.9	$g > g_w$	$g = g_n$
SE	0.0	$g = g_w$	$g = g_n$
SW	−0.2	$g < g_w$	$g = g_n$
WM	−0.2	$g < g_w$	$g < g_n$
NW	−0.8	$g < g_w$	$g > g_n$
W	+0.8	$g > g_w$	$g > g_n$
S	+0.1	$g > g_w$	$g = g_n$
NI	−1.0	$g < g_w$	$g > g_n$

excess of those predicted by the function reflect rising profit rates as capacity is more heavily utilised and thus an excess of g over g_w. Growth rates of output less than those predicted by the function imply $g_w > g$. In table 9.2 the deviations of actual g from predicted g are given, together with the implied discrepancies between g and g_w (and the relationship between g and g_n reported in table 9.1). Table 9.2 reveals a wide variety of growth experience. The South East has apparently experienced relatively steady growth with the actual, warranted and natural rates equal and with minimum unemployment on average. The South West and Yorkshire and Humberside have apparently experienced equality between the actual and natural rates, but with the warranted rate in excess of this. This is suggestive that growth is constrained by labour supply. The East Midlands, North West and Northern Ireland have desired and actual growth rates in excess of the natural rate. This could not be lasting, for either 'animal spirits' will be dimmed before full employment is reached, or the constraint of full employment will reduce the actual rate of growth. Scotland and East Anglia appear to have experienced growth at the natural rate but with the actual rate of growth in excess of the desired rate. This is consistent with the simultaneous existence of surplus labour and capital shortage. Scotland has a chronic surplus of labour as indicated by the high level of registered unemployment. In East Anglia the labour surplus is disguised in agriculture. Only Wales appears to have grown faster than the natural rate and also faster than the rate warranted by thriftiness and technical conditions. This is evidence of a very dynamic region, but in which growth will ultimately be constrained by labour supply. In the North and West Midlands, growth has proceeded at less than the warranted rate and also at a rate less than sufficient to maintain the workforce fully employed.

The above analysis not only provides an interpretation of the growth experience of any single region but also enables us to establish some brief points about regional economic growth in general. First, steady growth in the sense of a constant capital-output ratio does not appear to have prevailed in any region; although one region, the South East, appears to operate in conditions approaching short run producers equilibrium ($g = g_w$). Secondly, it appears that in some regions the rate of capital accumulation has effectively determined the rate of growth of output, not the operation of bottlenecks associated with labour supply. If any single conclusion can be drawn it is that the regions exhibit a wide range of growth postures. In particular, the contrast between the North and West Midlands on the one hand and the southern regions on the other must be noted. It should also be borne in mind that the picture might look somewhat different if migration flows between regions had been taken into account and the workforce figures in manufacturing adjusted accordingly. The equality between g and g_n in the South East and Scotland, for example, is almost certainly the result of large inflows of labour into the South East and large outflows of labour from Scotland. Without this adjustment mechanism unemployment may well have been higher in Scotland and lower in the South East unless the view is taken that growth itself is positively related to workforce growth so that the growth of output and employment would have been higher in Scotland had there not been net emigration, and growth would have been slower in the South East had there not been net immigration. This type of argument is the essence of models of circular cumulative causation.

In the next chapter a model of cumulative causation is developed which has at its heart the Verdoorn effect which works through the expansion of output and factor supplies and which gives rise, in turn, to increasing returns and induced technical progress, as discussed in chapter 8.

10 An Export Demand Model of Interregional Growth Rate Differences

In recent years, many economists, notably Myrdal[1] and Kaldor,[2] have attacked the predictions of neoclassical theory that regional growth rate differences will tend to narrow with trade and the free mobility of the factors of production. On the contrary, it is argued, regions which obtain an initial growth advantage will tend to sustain it through attracting growth-inducing forces, and by exerting backwash effects on the other regions. Myrdal has called the persistence and widening of regional disparities the process of circular and cumulative causation. Kaldor contends that: 'The principle of cumulative causation – which explains the unequal incidence of industrial development by endogenous factors resulting from the process of historical development itself rather than by exogenous differences in resource endowment – is an essential one for the understanding of the diverse trends of development as between different regions.'[3]

The purpose of this chapter is to develop a model which makes regional growth a function of the rate of growth of exports, and which incorporates the process of circular cumulative causation through the Verdoorn effect which we discussed in chapter 8. The model will then be used to consider such questions as: the role of regional structure in determining regional growth; whether regional *growth rate differences* will tend to narrow or diverge through time, and

[1] G. Myrdal, *Economic Theory and Underdeveloped Regions* (Methuen, 1963).

[2] N. Kaldor, 'The Case for Regional Policies', *Scottish Journal of Political Economy*, Nov 1970.

[3] Ibid., p. 343.

whether policies of regional 'devaluation' can raise a region's growth rate.

Consider initially two regions that do not trade with each other, and which are growing at equal rates. Then assume that trade opens up and one of the regions obtains an initial growth advantage. According to the principle of circular cumulative causation, competition between the two regions, and free factor mobility, could lead to increasing divergence in the growth rates of the two regions and could even turn the growth rate of one of the two regions negative. The question is, what are the conditions for divergence to take place, and are they likely to be satisfied? If we take a two region model, a necessary condition for the growth rates of two regions to diverge is that the growth rate of one of the regions diverges from its own equilibrium rate. It is also a sufficient condition if the growth rate of the other region is stable or diverges from equilibrium in the opposite direction. If we first examine the determinants of equilibrium growth in one region, the assumptions implicit in the hypothesis that regional growth may diverge can then be readily seen.

THE MODEL

The main thrust of the model to be developed is Hicks's[4] view that it is the growth of autonomous demand which governs the long run rate of growth of output. In a regional context, Kaldor has argued that the main autonomous demand factor will be demand emanating from outside the region; that is to say, the demand for a region's exports. According to Kaldor, a region's growth is fundamentally determined by the growth of demand for its exports to which the rate of growth of investment and consumption adjust. Regions which gain an initial competitive advantage find that the operation of the Verdoorn effect increases their competitive advantage still further. If differences in labour productivity between regions are not offset by differences in wage rates, the initial competitive advantage is continually reinforced.

[4] J. Hicks, *The Trade Cycle* (Oxford University Press, 1950).

Regions at a competitive disadvantage find it difficult to alter their industrial structure to produce the goods which give the favoured region its growth advantage, so that growth differences persist. Moreover, individual regions do not possess mechanisms for exchange rate adjustment to make their goods more competitive. The regional equivalent to devaluation of the national currency would be a perpetual wage subsidy.[5]

Now let us specify the model. First, let

$$g_t = \gamma(x_t) \qquad (10.1)^{6,7}$$

where g_t is the rate of growth of output in time t
x_t is the rate of growth of exports in time t
and γ is the (constant) elasticity of output growth with respect to export growth (=1 if exports are a constant proportion of output).

[5] Kaldor, it will be remembered, has been credited with the invention of the Regional Employment Premium which since 1967 has given a flat rate subsidy per unit of labour employed to employers in manufacturing industry in Development Areas. It should be stressed, however, that local 'devaluation' can only raise permanently a region's *growth rate* if the export demand function is additive rather than multiplicative; that is, if the demand function is such that the rate of growth of exports is based on absolute price differences between domestic suppliers and competitors as opposed to the differences in the rate of growth of prices between domestic and competitive suppliers. If the rate of growth of exports is the dependent variable, a multiplicative export demand function is much easier to handle, but, as we shall see, if it is employed, a flat rate subsidy to labour, combined with 'markup' pricing, cannot raise the equilibrium growth rate permanently. The same is true of the effect of currency devaluation at the national level. For a fuller discussion, see later.

[6] Apart from the theoretical considerations underlying this specification there are a number of practical considerations that make export demand for highly specialised regions (or countries) extremely important. In most industries in a region, local demand is likely to be trivial compared with the optimum production capacity of the industries. The viability of regional enterprise must largely depend on the strength of demand from outside the region. There are also a number of important reasons why export demand may be a more potent growth-inducing force than other elements of demand, especially in open, backward areas – either regions or countries. The first is that exports allow regional specialisation which may bring dynamic as well as static gains. Secondly, exports permit imports and imports may be important in developing areas which lack the capacity to produce development goods

Note that all the growth variables throughout the model are measured in discrete time. Let the export demand function in turn be written as:

$$X_t = P_{dt}^{\eta} P_{ft}^{\delta} Z_t^{\varepsilon} \tag{10.2}$$

so that we can write the rate of growth of exports as approximately:[8]

$$x_t = \eta(p_{dt}) + \delta(p_{ft}) + \varepsilon(z_t) \tag{10.3}$$

where X_t is the quantity of exports in time t
P_{dt} is the domestic (export) price in time t
P_{ft} is the competitor's price in time t
Z_t is the level of 'world' income in time t
η is the price elasticity of demand for exports
δ is the cross elasticity of demand for exports
ε is the income elasticity of demand for exports
and lower case letters represent discrete rates of growth of the variables.

The rates of growth of income outside the region ('world' income) and competitors' prices are taken as exogenous to the region. The rate of change of domestic (export) prices can be derived from the markup pricing equation:[9]

$$P_{dt} = \left(\frac{W}{R_t}\right)(T_t) \tag{10.4}$$

where W_t is the level of money wages in time t
R_t is the average product of labour (in the export sector) in time t
and T_t is $1+\%$ markup on unit labour costs in time t.

themselves. Thirdly, if the exchange of information and technical knowledge is linked to trade, exporting facilitates the flow of technical knowledge which can improve the growth rate.

[7] In the short term, autonomous investment (e.g. originating from government) may compensate for poor export performance. As far as the model to be developed is concerned, however, the inclusion of two autonomous demand components leads to complications in deriving the equilibrium and dynamic solutions to the model since the weights attached to the two components will vary with the growth rate. This, coupled with the fact that the export component will ultimately dominate the other component if export growth is faster than autonomous investment growth, has led us, like Kaldor, to

From equation (10.4) we can write (approximately):

$$p_{dt} = w_t - r_t + \tau_t \tag{10.5}$$

where the lower case letters stand for rates of growth of the variables. In other words, the rate of change of domestic prices is equal to the growth of unit labour costs plus the rate of change of 'markup' on costs; and the rate of growth of unit labour costs is the difference between the growth of money wages and the growth of labour productivity.

To close the model, in the sense of providing a link between growth and exports via prices and providing the possibility of self-sustaining growth, we have the Verdoorn relationship:

$$r_t = r_a + \lambda(g_t) \qquad (10.6)^{10}$$

where r_a is the rate of autonomous productivity growth
and λ is the Verdoorn coefficient.

Combining equations (10.1), (10.3), (10.5) and (10.6) we can derive an expression for the equilibrium growth rate:

$$g = \frac{\gamma[\eta(w - r_a + \tau) + \varepsilon(z) + \delta(p_f)]}{1 + \gamma\eta\lambda} \tag{10.7}$$

Since $\eta < 0$, the Verdoorn coefficient (λ) affects the growth rate positively and will magnify regional growth rate differences if there are initial differences in the other parameters of the model. As far as the other variables and parameters are concerned, the growth rate varies positively with r_a, z, ε, δ and p_f, and negatively with w and τ. The effect of η is ambiguous since it appears in both the numerator

ignore autonomous investment demand in the model. All investment is induced.

[8] That is, excluding interaction terms.

[9] The markup is assumed to be on unit labour costs, not on total prime costs (which include raw material costs). Any change in 'imported' raw material costs will affect the level of the markup term.

[10] Relating productivity growth in the export sector to the rate of growth of total output, as opposed to the rate of growth of exports, is to treat the economy as if it were a single fully integrated firm in which it is impossible to distinguish between production runs for export and production runs for domestic consumption. On the assumption that $g = x$ the equilibrium growth rate is unaffected.

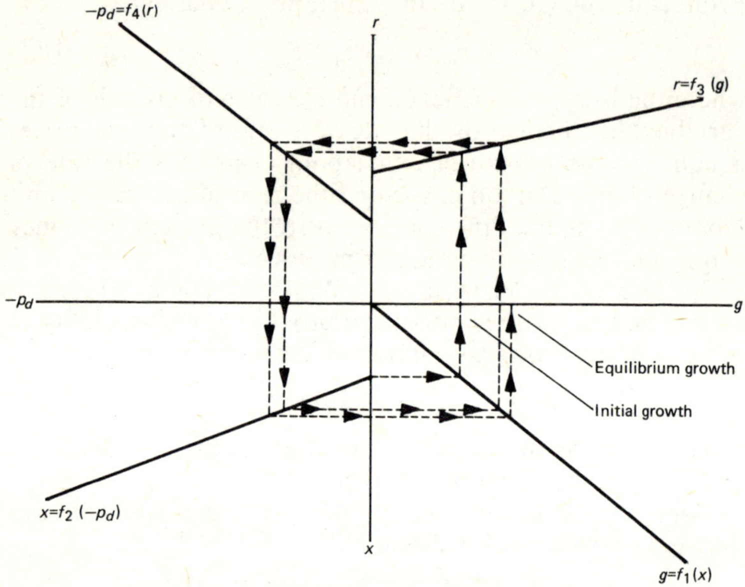

FIGURE 10.1

and the denominator of the equation. Whether growth varies positively or negatively with the absolute size of η depends on the values of the other variables and parameters. The most likely terms for which initial differences may exist are r_a, η, δ and ε. The sustaining role of the Verdoorn effect is perhaps most clearly seen in the case of a region obtaining an advantage in activities producing goods with favourable income elasticities of demand in which increasing returns prevail. The region will obtain a competitive advantage in these activities compared with other regions and then maintain that advantage through the existence of the Verdoorn relation. In models of cumulative causation this is the essence of the theory of divergence between 'centre' and 'periphery' and between industrial and agricultural regions. It is interesting to note, however, that the mere existence of the Verdoorn relation cannot cause regional growth rates to differ (if the determinants of regional growth are the same in each region) unless the Verdoorn *coefficient* differs between regions.

In other words, an autonomous shock which raises a region's output is not enough for its growth advantage to be maintained through the Verdoorn effect except to the extent that the autonomous shock affects favourably the parameters of the model.

The dependence of the equilibrium growth rate on the parameters of the model, and the sustaining role of the Verdoorn effect, is illustrated in figure 10.1 opposite. For illustration, but without discussion for the moment, the growth rate is shown converging to its equilibrium rate. The disequilibrium behaviour of the model is considered explicitly in the text section.

The distance of the curves from the origin reflects factors affecting each variable other than the variable specified in the functional relation. The relationship between productivity growth and output growth in the top right hand quadrant of the diagram makes clear the sustaining influence of the Verdoorn effect. Other things being equal the steeper the slope of the Verdoorn relation, the higher the equilibrium growth rate will be and the greater the difference between regional growth rates for given differences between regions in other variables and parameters.

Divergent or convergent growth?

Under what circumstances, however, will regional growth rates diverge? We argued earlier that a necessary condition for the growth rates of two regions to diverge is that the growth rate of one of the regions diverges from its own equilibrium rate. It is also a sufficient condition if the growth rate of the other region is stable or diverges from equilibrium in the opposite direction. Whether divergence will take place is essentially an empirical issue depending on the stability conditions of the model in disequilibrium. None of the cumulative causation school are clear as to what the stability conditions are in their various models. In order to consider the growth rate in disequilibrium a variety of lag structures could be introduced into the equations which constitute the model. If, for simplicity, we confine ourselves to a first-order system, inspection of the model shows that, since the model is 'circular', a one-period lag in any of the equations gives the same stability conditions, namely that convergence to or divergence from equilibrium growth depends on whether $|\gamma\eta\lambda| \lesseqgtr 1$, as illustrated in figure 10.1.[11] To consider the growth rate in disequilibrium it would not be unreasonable on economic grounds to specify exports in time t as a lagged function of its determinants. It can take time for exporters and/or foreign buyers to adjust to changes in prices and income. Thus we could write $X_t = P^{\eta}_{dt-1} P^{\delta}_{ft-1} Z^{\varepsilon}_{t-1}$, giving for discrete changes, the approximation:

$$x_t = \eta(p_{dt-1}) + \delta(p_{ft-1}) + \varepsilon(z_{t-1}) \qquad (10.8)$$

where lower case letters are rates of growth as before. Using equation (10.8) instead of (10.3) and combining with (10.1), (10.5) and (10.6), and assuming the rate of growth of the exogenous variables to be constant, gives the first order difference equation:

$$g_t = \gamma[\eta(w_{t-1} - r_a + \tau_{t-1}) + \delta(p_{ft-1}) + \varepsilon(z_{t-1})] - \gamma\eta\lambda(g_{t-1}) \qquad (10.9)$$

the general solution to which is:

$$g_t = A(-\gamma\eta\lambda)^t + \frac{\gamma[\eta(w_{t-1} - r_a + \tau_{t-1}) + \varepsilon(z_{t-1}) + \delta(p_{ft-1})]}{1 + \gamma\eta\lambda} \qquad (10.10)$$

where A is the initial condition.

The time path of g depends on the value of $\gamma\eta\lambda$. Since $\eta < 0$, $(-\gamma\eta\lambda)$ will be > 0. The condition for cumulative divergence from equilibrium is that $(-\gamma\eta\lambda) > 1$. This seems unlikely because: $\gamma = 1$ if exports are a constant proportion of output; the price elasticity of demand for exports (η) rarely exceeds $|2|$, and the Verdoorn coefficient (λ) rarely exceeds 0.5. In short, taking reasonable parameter values for the model,

[11] A one-period lag in two of the equations, giving a second-order system, yields two real roots $\pm\sqrt{(-\gamma\eta\lambda)}$. The stability conditions are therefore the same as in the first order system. This is true however that many equations are lagged. This fact considerably enhances the generality of our result.

regional growth divergence is unlikely to occur. It follows that to explain why growth rates differ between regions, we must explain why the equilibrium growth rates differ between regions.

The second term on the R.H.S. of equation (10.10) (i.e. the particular solution to the first-order difference equation) shows that the equilibrium growth rate depends on seven main economic parameters and variables that may vary from region to region – η, w, r_a, τ, ε, δ and λ. If it is assumed that the percentage markup on unit labour costs is the same in each region, and that for institutional reasons w is fairly uniform from region to region,[12] we are left with differences in η, δ, r_a, ε and λ as explanations of differences in regional growth rates. The price and income elasticities of demand for regional exports will depend on the nature of the products produced. The rate of autonomous productivity growth, r_a, and the Verdoorn coefficient, λ, will depend on the technical dynamism of productive agents in the region and the extent to which capital accumulation is induced by growth and embodies technical progress. The determinants of r_a and λ are closely related to the determinants of the position and shape of Kaldor's technical progress function, discussed in chapter 9. The technical progress function in linear form may be specified as:

$$r = d + \pi(m) \qquad (10.11)$$

where r is the rate of growth of output per man
m is the rate of growth of capital per man
d is the rate of disembodied technical progress.

Now let m and d be functions of the rate of growth of output so that:

$$d = \alpha_1 + \beta_1(g) \qquad (10.12)$$

and

$$m = \alpha_2 + \beta_2(g) \qquad (10.13)$$

[12] For evidence on this point see A. P. Thirlwall, 'Regional Phillips Curves', *Bulletin of the Oxford Institute of Economics and Statistics*, Feb 1970.

Substituting (10.12) and (10.13) into (10.11) gives:

$$r = (\alpha_1 + \pi\alpha_2) + (\beta_1 + \pi\beta_2)(g) \qquad (10.14)$$

Hence:

$$r = r_a + \lambda(g)$$

where $r_a = (\alpha_1 + \pi\alpha_2)$
and $\lambda = (\beta_1 + \pi\beta_2)$.

The autonomous rate of growth of productivity, r_a, is determined by the autonomous rate of disembodied progress, the autonomous rate of capital accumulation per worker and the extent to which technical progress is embodied in capital accumulation. The Verdoorn coefficient, λ, is determined by the rate of induced disembodied technical progress, the degree to which capital accumulation is induced by growth and the extent to which technical progress is embodied in capital accumulation. To the extent that the determinants of r_a and λ vary between industries, r_a and λ may also vary between regions depending on the industrial composition of the regions. From this analysis it would appear that raising a region's growth rate is fundamentally a question of making regions more 'competitive' and/or altering the industrial structure so that goods are produced with higher income elasticities of demand and higher Verdoorn coefficients attached to them.

Regional 'competitiveness'

To make regions more 'competitive' a policy of wage subsidies to manufacturers in lagging growth regions is sometimes advocated, to achieve the same effect regionally as a policy of currency devaluation nationally. The argument needs to be treated with some caution, however. It is easy to show that a wage subsidy in a regional context is equivalent to a devaluation of the currency in a national context, but the argument that wage subsidies can raise a region's growth rate *permanently* is less convincing. To show the equivalence of wage subsidies and currency devaluation, let the price of domestic exports in terms of the overseas currency equal P_o. Then $P_{ot} = P_{dt} \times$ exchange rate, or:

$$p_{ot} = \theta_t + p_{dt} \tag{10.15}$$

where p_{ot} is the rate of growth of home prices expressed in overseas currency in time t

θ_t is the rate of change in the exchange rate in time t

and p_{dt} is the rate of growth of prices in domestic currency in time t.

Expressing the domestic price in the same units as the overseas currency, equation (10.3) becomes:

$$x_t = \eta(\theta_t + p_{dt}) + \varepsilon(z_t) + \delta(p_{ft}) \tag{10.16}$$

and the equilibrium growth rate is:

$$g_t = \frac{\gamma[\eta(w_t - r_a + \tau_t + \theta_t) + \varepsilon(z_t) + \delta(p_{ft})]}{1 + \gamma\eta\lambda} \tag{10.17}$$

Partially differentiating (10.17) with respect to θ gives:

$$\frac{\partial g}{\partial \theta} = \frac{\gamma\eta}{1 + \gamma\eta\lambda}$$

and with respect to w gives:

$$\frac{\partial g}{\partial w} = \frac{\gamma\eta}{1 + \gamma\eta\lambda}$$

Hence

$$\frac{\partial g}{\partial \theta} = \frac{\partial g}{\partial w}$$

But neither a once-for-all devaluation, nor a continual flat rate wage subsidy, can have a permanent effect on the rate of change of the price level, only on the level of prices. Unless the export demand function is additive, the effect of devaluation, or the introduction of flat rate wage subsidies, on the growth rate cannot therefore be permanent. θ and w become zero in the periods after wage subsidies have been introduced or devaluation has taken place. As far as an additive export demand function is concerned, it is not at all clear what theory of demand would generate the argument that the *rate of growth* of exports is related to the absolute difference between domestic and foreign prices.[13] We believe it is much more satisfactory to regard the level of exports as determined by relative prices in a multiplicative demand function than by the absolute difference between domestic and foreign prices in an additive demand function. If this argument is accepted wage subsidies at the regional level are equivalent at the most to an autonomous shock which, as we argued earlier, could only affect the growth rate permanently if the structural parameters of the growth model were thereby affected favourably.

If anything, however, policies of 'devaluation' tend to ossify the industrial structure, inhibiting structural change, as developing economies have belatedly discovered. Export promotion and import substitution properly directed offer a much more hopeful solution to lagging growth by altering the industrial structure of regions so that they produce goods with 'favourable' price and income elasticities of demand. At the regional level, this policy conclusion points to the need to relate regional taxes and subsidies to activities with particular structural characteristics rather than to particular factors of production, either capital or labour. We believe the income elasticity of demand for exports to be a particularly important parameter at both the national and regional level. Regional policy for stimulating regional growth could usefully direct its attention to identifying activities with a high income elasticity of demand and encouraging these to locate in depressed regions by policies of capital incentives and labour subsidies.

While the effect of regional wage subsidies on regional growth is unlikely to be permanent, regional 'devaluation' could have a permanent effect on the percentage level of unemployment. The initial effect of 'devaluation' will be to lower unemployment. Since changes in the percentage level of unemployment are the outcome of the difference between the growth of labour demand and supply, and the growth of

[13] Beckerman, who has used an additive function in a national context is not clear on this point. See W. Beckerman, 'Projecting Europe's Growth', *Economic Journal*, Dec 1962.

demand is unaffected by devaluation, there can be a lower level of unemployment than would otherwise be the case. If the percentage level of unemployment was stable before 'devaluation', the stable level of unemployment will now be lower. If the percentage level of unemployment was rising before 'devaluation', wage subsidies will reduce the (rising) unemployment level below what it would otherwise have been. Interpreted as a weapon to reduce unemployment, therefore, regional devaluation may have some merit. As a means of stimulating regional growth, however, its value is doubtful. The Regional Employment Premium, payable to manufacturing industry in Development Areas, was a policy of regional devaluation and must be interpreted as a policy for reducing the level of unemployment rather than as a policy for stimulating growth.[14]

PRODUCTIVITY GROWTH

An alternative, more permanent, strategy for raising a region's growth rate would be to encourage the growth of autonomous and induced labour productivity. This is easily seen from the model. Measures to raise r_a and λ, however, will increase the rate of labour saving, reduce the rate of employment growth and raise the level of unemployment compared with alternative strategies. This is a familiar conflict between output growth and employment growth if the strategy to stimulate output growth involves rapid productivity growth. National policies to promote growth through increased productivity must tread with great care if regional unemployment disparities are not to worsen. At the minimum, the policies must be accompanied by measures of demand stimulation in the regions of high unemployment. The spread of technical progress from central to peripheral areas presents a similar sort of problem in the absence of demand expansion in the peripheral areas. *The spread of technical progress merely serves to 'export' unemployment.*

[14] Kaldor, however, clearly envisaged the policy as a means of stimulating growth as well. See N. Kaldor, 'The Case for Regional Policies', *Scottish Journal of Political Economy*, Nov 1970.

Government investment

Government investment as a component of autonomous demand has not been incorporated in our formal model for the reasons mentioned earlier. But its role should not be overlooked. On the one hand it is a policy variable that can be operated on to raise the growth rate directly. It is a substitute for policies of export demand expansion which rely on influencing wages and labour productivity. Secondly, and at the same time, government investment can influence the industrial and export structure of regions by the establishment of activities producing goods with 'favourable' price and income elasticities of demand. In the depressed regions of Britain there has been heavy reliance on public investment as a direct stimulus to demand and growth; there has been less emphasis on the role of government investment to improve the export performance of lagging regions. To use government investment policy for this latter purpose would require, of course, much more careful scrutiny of the investment projects in the light of the goods to be produced. This is perhaps a luxury that cannot be afforded, but if export demand is a major component of regional demand, the implications of regional policies for the export performance of regions needs some consideration if the long run growth prospects of lagging regions are to be improved and continual government investment is not to be required to bail the regions out of difficulty.

Conclusion

The model we have described contains a number of insights into the determinants of regional growth and suggests a number of policy prescriptions. The major assumption underlying the model is that growth is demand-led and is not constrained by factor supplies. It is a variant of models sometimes known as 'export-base' models and is open to the well-known criticisms of these models such as that the growth process should be viewed in terms of factor supplies rather than in terms of demand considerations and that exports are not the sole, or even the major, autonomous demand component of regional demand.[15] Both criticisms are weak. The former criticism is particularly weak in the context of open regional economies where factors flow freely between regions. In rapidly expanding regions, demand tends to create its own supply and whether growth is viewed from the side of demand or supply is not particularly important. Demand and supply move together. In lagging, depressed regions, the view that economic growth is constrained by factor supplies is clearly not applicable. These areas are characterised by an excess supply of labour and, in general, by excess productive capacity. This is certainly true of the depressed regions of the United Kingdom. The notion that a demand-constrained model is relevant to the depressed regions of the United Kingdom is supported by our analysis of regional unemployment rate differences in chapters 4 and 5, and by the work of Brown at the National Institute of Economic and Social Research who concludes that to understand the regional problem 'differences in the pressure of demand are of key importance'.[16] Unemployment is high in certain regions '... basically, and predominantly, because these regions suffer from a deficiency of effective demand, which is persistent rather than periodic'.[17] For these regions, a model which emphasises the growth rate of demand, rather than factor supplies, is the most relevant.

[15] For a critique of 'export base' models see C. M. Tiebout, 'Exports and Regional Economic Growth', *Journal of Political Economy*, Apr 1956. The factor supplies approach to regional growth is implicit in G. Borts and J. L. Stein, *Economic Growth in a Free Market* (Columbia University Press, 1964), and in H. Siebert, *Regional Economic Growth: Theory and Policy* (International Textbook Co., 1969).

[16] A. J. Brown, *et alia*, 'Regional Problems and Regional Policy', *National Institute Economic Review*, Nov 1968, p. 42.

[17] Ibid., p. 45.

11 Summary and Conclusions

It is difficult to summarise the preceding chapters at all concisely, but some attempt at reiteration of certain points may assist the reader. We shall concentrate on mentioning particular techniques of analysis introduced in the different chapters, together with some of the most important observations made and conclusions drawn.

The introductory chapter deals with the conceptual and empirical background to the study. It emphasises the need for a dynamic approach to the analysis of regional performance, in particular the need to see unemployment as determined by the relative growth rates of the workforce, output and labour productivity. The theme of regional variety is also introduced, and two techniques (the evaluation of inner products and shift-share analysis) are discussed for analysing the extent and sources of interregional differences with respect to various indices of regional 'welfare'. Heavy stress is laid on the importance of regional industrial structure and demand pressure as determinants of regional economic performance. Indeed one of the dominant themes throughout the book is the emphasis on the differential pattern of aggregate demand, determined in part by interregional differences in industrial structure, as the main explanation of the so-called regional problem. This echoes the conclusion of Professor Brown's major study[1] that to understand the regional problem 'differences in the pressure of demand are of key importance'. In a dynamic economy differences in the strength of demand between regions have three important sources. One lies in the nature of the demand characteristics of the products produced by different regions; the second has to do with differences in the propensity to invest, and the third lies in the pattern of

[1] A. J. Brown, *The Framework for Regional Economics in the United Kingdom* (Cambridge University Press, 1973).

interregional demand and linkages whereby some regions rely much more heavily than others on imported inputs. Hence for a given expansion of aggregate demand, the multiplier effects are stronger in some regions than others. All these factors are related to the structure and openness of regional economies.

Interest in the structure of regions leads in chapter 2 to a consideration of the pattern and determinants of regional specialisation and industrial localisation. Measures of the degree of regional specialisation and the localisation of industry are presented and discussed and the tendency is found for both regional specialisation and industrial localisation to have declined over time. An attempt is then made to 'explain' the observed patterns of regional specialisation with reference to the Heckscher–Ohlin theorem, but with disappointing results. Classical hypotheses of the basis of trade, involving the consideration of comparative labour productivities and efficiency wages, are also considered. None of the hypotheses is strongly supported by the evidence, which leads us to question the proposition (basic to much regional analysis) that relative prices serve to explain the 'quantity composition' of trade.

Chapter 3 examines *changes* in the pattern of specialisation and some evidence is found that such changes are related to regional comparative advantage. An examination of the pattern of changes in the concentration of industries also revealed changes consistent with the evidence. Patterns of industrial movement, however, appear to be unrelated to differences in absolute labour costs between regions. This finding is not inconsistent with finding a relation between changes in the pattern of localisation and unit labour costs, because changes in localisation are determined not only by the movement of firms but also by the differential growth of industries within regions. We also argue here that it may be possible to interpret the 'differential growth component' of a shift-share analysis as being related to regional competitiveness (locational advantage).

In chapter 4 an attempt is made to identify cyclical and non-cyclical components of regional unemployment and to measure the differing sensitivity of regions to changes in national unemployment. Interregional differences in the cyclical component of unemployment do not appear to be a major source of differences in regional unemployment rates. On the other hand we find significant differences between regions in their sensitivity to changes in the national rate of unemployment and that these differences account for a significant proportion of the total variation in unemployment rates between regions. Disaggregating these sensitivity coefficients for each region, it is found that the major source of differences lies not in dissimilar industrial structures but in the tendency of industries to fluctuate more in some regions (normally the depressed regions) than in others.

Chapter 5 continues the analysis of unemployment using the quantity and characteristics of vacancies by occupation to classify and measure 'types' of unemployment. First a distinction is made between demand-deficient and non demand-deficient unemployment, and then an attempt is made to apportion non demand-deficient unemployment into structural and frictional components. An important finding is that there appears to be very little difference between regions in the extent of non demand-deficient unemployment. This implies in turn that the major source of interregional differences in the level of unemployment must be differences in demand-deficient unemployment. It is also found that the magnitude of structural unemployment does not differ markedly between regions for any given pressure of demand in the regions. This indicates that if the pressure of demand was equalised between regions, skill mismatches and labour market bottlenecks would be no more severe in one part of the country than another. Our analysis also indicates that occupational immobility is probably a more important cause of structural unemployment than geographic immobility, and we conclude from this, as well as on the basis of more general considerations, that policies to reduce structural unemployment should be orientated more towards improving occupational mobility than towards fostering geographic mobility from regions with surplus labour to regions short of labour.

Finally, in considering the pressure of demand as measured by vacancy rates which would be required to equalise regional unemployment rates, we find that the pattern of demand would have to be substantially different from the pattern that has prevailed over the post-war years. Indeed, the rank ordering of the required vacancy rates is almost the reverse of the ordering that has prevailed.

In chapter 6 production functions are used to examine the determinants of productivity growth within regions, and to analyse interregional differences in productivity growth. A good deal of attention is given to the Johansen technique for estimating the neoclassical production function in the absence of capital data. The technique requires that either the rate of capital deepening or technical progress be assumed the same in all regions. We argue that it is probably more realistic to assume that the rate of (disembodied) technical progress is the same in all regions. As such, the effects of capital deepening are obtained as a residual. Two other sources of growth, returns to scale, and resource reallocation, are also estimated and subtracted from the residual. Returns to scale are estimated as a negative source of productivity growth in some regions because employment has declined, but differences in returns to scale are not found to be a major source of interregional productivity growth rate differences. Resource reallocation is also estimated to have made a negative contribution to productivity growth in some regions, and differences in the extent and effectiveness of resource reallocation appear to have been an important source of interregional productivity growth rate differences. Allowing for returns to scale and resource reallocation, however, differences in the rate of capital deepening turn out to be the major source of interregional differences in productivity growth, and the rate of capital deepening is estimated to be of roughly equal importance to technical progress in determining the level of productivity growth within regions.

In chapter 7, the Constant Elasticity of Substitution (CES) production function is used (with an allowance for returns to scale) to examine the sources of interregional differences in the level of labour productivity in the years 1958 and 1963. Three sources of variation are distinguished: differences in the efficiency parameter of the CES function; differences arising from variations in the capital-labour ratio; and differences due to the influence of returns to scale. Variations in capital intensity appear to be the main source of interregional differences in the level of labour productivity. We note, however, that both the Development Areas and Intermediate Areas of the United Kingdom tend to exhibit relatively low efficiency parameters compared to the nation. On the other hand, there appears to be no significant relationship between the differential growth component of shift-share analysis and regional efficiency parameters.

Chapter 8 analyses the determinants of employment growth in the regions. First the classificatory device of shift-share analysis is adopted which attempts to analyse growth rate differences in terms of differences in the industrial structure of regions and the differential growth of industries between regions. Secondly, the demand for labour is examined in terms of labour requirements per unit of output and the demand for labour to 'man' capital. It is concluded from shift-share analysis that interregional employment growth rate differences are more related to the performance of individual industries within regions than to differences in regional industrial structure, although the point made by critics of shift-share analysis, that the effects of structure on growth are not adequately taken account of in the formal analysis, is well taken. It is concluded from the labour requirements approach to the demand for labour that variations in output growth have been a major determinant of variations in employment growth, and that there exists a strong Verdoorn relation between productivity growth and output growth which has served to reduce differences in regional rates of employment growth. Taking the labour manning approach to the demand for labour it is concluded that differences in the growth rates of capital are slightly more important than differences in the rate of capital deepening in accounting for interregional differences in employment growth. The conclusions from using the labour requirements approach and the labour manning approach imply a strong association between relative rates of output growth and capital accumulation across regions.

Chapter 9 attempts to characterise the growth experience

of regions in terms of the relationship between the actual, warranted and natural rates of growth. The relationship between the actual and warranted rates of growth is investigated with the aid of Kaldor's technical progress function. The main conclusion is that the regions exhibit a wide variety of growth experience.

In the final chapter a model of regional growth is developed based on Kaldor's view that the rate of output growth in a regional economy is fundamentally determined by the rate of growth of export demand. The model also incorporates the notion of 'circular and cumulative causation' by the specification of a Verdoorn relationship linking productivity growth to output growth. The model developed provides a number of insights into the determinants of interregional growth rate differences, and the conditions under which interregional growth rate differences will continue to persist or diverge.

The price and income elasticities of demand for regional exports are identified as important growth determinants, and in this sense we argue that the industrial structure of the regional economy assumes great importance. The model also shows how the Verdoorn effect can sustain regional growth rate differences once they emerge through differences in the variables and parameters that determine the growth rate. Using the model it is also shown that policies of regional devaluation (e.g. through wage subsidies) are probably irrelevant for raising the growth rate permanently although they may have merit in reducing the level of unemployment below what it would otherwise have been.

Appendix 1

The Elasticity of Substitution and Returns to Scale in United Kingdom Manufacturing Industry, 1958 and 1963

At various stages throughout the book we have used estimates of the elasticity of substitution and the degree of returns to scale in UK manufacturing industry. In this appendix we discuss the derivation of these estimates. Previous estimates by Feldstein were based on inter-industry data for the years 1954, 1957 and 1960.[1] Our estimates are based on intra-industry data from the Regional Tables of the 1963 Census of Production and allow us to estimate not only the elasticity of substitution and returns to scale in manufacturing as a whole, but in individual industries as well. At the end of the appendix we discuss the validity of the estimates in the light of the recent paper by Fisher which questions the propriety of econometric estimation of production function parameters.[2]

The elasticity of substitution

There are two concepts of the elasticity of substitution: one is the technical elasticity of substitution (σ_t); the other is the

[1] M. S. Feldstein, 'Alternative Methods of Estimating a CES Production Function for Britain', *Economica*, Nov 1967.

[2] F. M. Fisher, 'Aggregate Production Functions and the Explanation of Wages: A Simulation Experiment', *Review of Economics and Statistics*, Nov 1971.

price elasticity of substitution (σ_p).[3] The technical elasticity of substitution is a technological parameter which expresses the configuration of the production surface, and may be defined as:

$$\sigma_t = \frac{d(K/L)}{(K/L)} \Big/ \frac{dR}{R} \tag{A1.1}$$

where R is the ratio of the marginal products of the two factors, labour (L) and capital (K).

The price elasticity of substitution is an 'economic' parameter which expresses the relationship between a proportionate change in relative factor prices and the proportionate change in relative factor quantities utilised in the production process, and may be defined as:

$$\sigma_p = \frac{d(K/L)}{(K/L)} \Big/ \frac{d(w/r)}{(w/r)} \tag{A1.2}$$

where w is the wage rate
and r is the rental per unit of capital.

If factors of production are rewarded according to the value of their marginal products, σ_t and σ_p would be the same and it would be possible to infer the value of the (unobservable) technical elasticity of substitution from the estimate of the price elasticity of substitution. This is not possible here because the necessary capital and rental data are not available. An indirect method is required in the absence of capital data.

Arrow, Chenery, Minhas and Solow presented an alternative procedure in their pioneer article on the CES production function.[4] Their method makes use of an 'equivalence relation', derived earlier by R. G. D. Allen,[5] whereby the value of the elasticity of substitution is shown to be equal to the ratio of

[3] Joan Robinson refers to the former as the more fundamental of the two. See J. Robinson, *The Economics of Imperfect Competition*, 2nd edition (Macmillan, 1969), p. 257.

[4] K. J. Arrow, H. B. Chenery, B. S. Minhas and R. M. Solow, 'Capital-Labour Substitution and Economic Efficiency', *Review of Economics and Statistics*, Aug 1961.

[5] R. G. D. Allen, *Mathematical Analysis for Economists* (Macmillan, 1938).

the proportionate change in output per employee (average product) to the proportionate change in the wage rate (marginal product). This relation, and the conditions under which it will hold, may be demonstrated as follows (all variables are measured in real terms):

Let $Y = wL + rK$ be the distribution or cost function.

Dividing both sides by L gives:

$$\frac{Y}{L} = w + r\left(\frac{K}{L}\right)$$

or

$$q = w + rx \qquad \text{(A1.3)}$$

Expressing the total differential of (A1.3) as:

$$\mathrm{d}q = \mathrm{d}w + \mathrm{d}r \,.\, x + \mathrm{d}x \,.\, r,$$

it follows that:

$$\frac{\mathrm{d}q}{\mathrm{d}x} = \frac{\mathrm{d}w}{\mathrm{d}x} + \frac{\mathrm{d}r}{\mathrm{d}x} \,.\, x + r \qquad \text{(A1.4)}$$

If factors are rewarded according to their marginal products, it follows from (A1.4) that:

$$\frac{\mathrm{d}q}{\mathrm{d}x} - r = \frac{\mathrm{d}w}{\mathrm{d}x} + \frac{\mathrm{d}r}{\mathrm{d}x} \,.\, x = 0,$$

and thus

$$\frac{\mathrm{d}w}{\mathrm{d}x} = -\frac{\mathrm{d}r}{\mathrm{d}x} \,.\, x \qquad \text{(A1.5)}$$

or

$$\frac{\mathrm{d}w}{\mathrm{d}r} = -x \qquad \text{(A1.6)}$$

Taken together equations (A1.3) and (A1.6) imply that the factor price frontier[6] for each technique is a straight line. While this is a reasonable 'parable' in a world of 'jelly' capital, the conditions under which the above equations will hold in a world of heterogenous capital goods are quite special – specifically, only if each activity has the same organic composition

[6] As expressed in P. A. Samuelson, 'Parable and Realism in Capital Theory: The Surrogate Production Function', *Review of Economic Studies*, June 1962.

of capital.[7] With the above, together with the assumption that there are enough different techniques to generate a smooth factor price envelope, we can now derive the 'equivalence relation' for the elasticity of substitution.

Assuming that the price and technical elasticities of substitution are equal in value, the elasticity of substitution may be written as:

$$\sigma = \frac{\mathrm{d}x}{x} \bigg/ \frac{\mathrm{d}(w/r)}{(w/r)} \tag{A1.7}$$

The denominator of (A1.7) may be expanded so that:

$$\sigma = \frac{\mathrm{d}x}{x} \cdot \frac{1}{\dfrac{\mathrm{d}w}{w} - \dfrac{\mathrm{d}r}{r}} = \frac{\mathrm{d}x}{x} \cdot \frac{1}{\dfrac{r\mathrm{d}w - w\mathrm{d}r}{rw}}$$

and hence:

$$\sigma = \frac{\mathrm{d}x \,.\, w \,.\, r}{x \,.\, r \,.\, \mathrm{d}w - x \,.\, w \,.\, \mathrm{d}r} = \frac{w \,.\, r}{x \,.\, r \,.\, \dfrac{\mathrm{d}w}{\mathrm{d}x} - x \,.\, \dfrac{\mathrm{d}r}{\mathrm{d}x} \,.\, w} \tag{A1.8}$$

Substitution of (A1.5) into the denominator of (A1.8) yields:

$$\sigma = \frac{w \,.\, r}{x \,.\, r \,.\, \dfrac{\mathrm{d}w}{\mathrm{d}x} + \dfrac{\mathrm{d}w}{\mathrm{d}x} \,.\, w} = \frac{w \,.\, r}{(x \,.\, r + w)\dfrac{\mathrm{d}w}{\mathrm{d}x}} \tag{A1.9}$$

Substitution of (A1.3) into (A1.9) gives:

$$\sigma = \frac{w \,.\, r}{q\left(\dfrac{\mathrm{d}w}{\mathrm{d}x}\right)} \tag{A1.10}$$

Since by assumption $r = \mathrm{d}q/\mathrm{d}x$, the above expression may be rewritten as:

$$\sigma = \frac{w \,.\, \mathrm{d}q}{q \,.\, \mathrm{d}w} = \frac{\mathrm{d}q}{q} \bigg/ \frac{\mathrm{d}w}{w}$$

[7] See G. C. Harcourt, *Some Cambridge Controversies in the Theory of Capital* (Cambridge University Press, 1972), pp. 131–76.

or $$\sigma = \frac{d \log q}{d \log w} \qquad \text{(A1.11)}$$

Equation (A1.11) says that one measure of the elasticity of substitution is the elasticity of output per head with respect to the wage rate, i.e. the regression coefficient in an estimating equation of the form:

$$\log q = \log a + b \log w + \varepsilon \qquad \text{(A1.12)}$$

where ε is an error term.

It has been demonstrated by Arrow *et alia* that the relationship in equation (A1.12) can be derived, under the assumptions stated above, from a production function of the following form:

$$Y = \gamma[\delta K^{-\rho} + (1-\delta)L^{-\rho}]^{-1/\rho} \qquad \text{(A1.13)}$$

That is, a production function of the form (A1.13) may be derived by integration, under neoclassical assumptions, from the estimating equation (A1.12). Equation (A1.13) is the CES production function.

The estimating equation (A1.12) has the particular advantage of not requiring estimates of the capital stock, and is easily computed. In the next section, estimates of the elasticity of substitution for the UK manufacturing sector are presented applying equation (A1.12) to regional cross-section data.

Estimation with constant returns to scale

Before presenting the results, however, the assumptions underlying the use of equation (A1.12) for estimating the elasticity of substitution must be made clear. First, it must be assumed that the observations within any industry represent different points on the same 'representative' isoquant which entails, in turn, the assumption that the observations, as points on different isoquants, can be 'collapsed' on to a representative isoquant exhibiting a constant elasticity of substitution. Also entailed is the assumption that the observations of average product and the wage are generated by firms using optimal input combinations given ruling factor prices. This implies that firms conform to neoclassical assumptions with respect to marginal productivity factor pricing, perfect competition, profit maximisation, etc. To treat the observations 'as if' they come from the same isoquant itself requires that two conditions be met: firstly, that the production function exhibits constant returns to scale so that the average product of labour depends solely on the capital-labour ratio;[8] secondly, that the observations are taken from different points on the same production surface – in other words, that the choice of techniques facing firms in the same industry in different regions is identical. Only if all the above assumptions hold is it possible to conceive of, and measure, the elasticity of substitution using the method proposed.[9] It must be stressed, however, that the existence (or significance) of this relationship embodied in equation (A1.12) cannot itself be construed as evidence for the existence of a production function, or that such a function is common to all regions. Nor can it be taken as evidence for the fulfilment of any of the assumptions of the neoclassical model.[10]

There are two further problems to note before presenting the results. Throughout the theoretical discussion and the derivation of the estimating equation, all the variables were expressed in real terms, and yet our regional data is in money terms because there are no regional price indices. It can be shown that if the price index is identical for all regions no bias in the estimates will result. If, however, the wage rate and the price index are positively correlated, then the elasticity of substitution will be biased towards unity. We proceed on the assumption that the price index is uniform across regions. A second problem arises if factor rewards are not equal to their marginal products. Estimation techniques appropriate to this

[8] The consequences of dropping this assumption will be discussed later.

[9] These are in addition, of course, to the econometric requirements that the wage rate is exogenous and that the wage rate does not vary systematically with differences in the efficiency parameter.

[10] K. J. Arrow, *et alia*, op. cit., p. 232. We will return to this point later.

situation have been discussed by Dhrymes,[11] Feldstein[12] and Katz.[13] Since the data necessary to perform the appropriate tests are not available, the matter will not be pursued further. The analysis will proceed on the assumption that the 'degree of imperfection' is the same in all regions.

When equation (A1.12) was fitted to aggregate manufacturing data for the years 1958 and 1963 using ordinary least squares, the following results were obtained (standard errors in brackets):[14]

$$1958: \quad \log q = 0.756 + \underset{(0.126)}{1.317} \log w \qquad r^2 = 0.924$$

$$1963: \quad \log q = 0.679 + \underset{(0.132)}{1.089} \log w \qquad r^2 = 0.883$$

The estimates of the elasticity of substitution in both years are significantly different from zero, and for 1958 the estimate is significantly different from unity also. The 1963 estimate, however, suggests that the prevailing technology may be Cobb–Douglas. The coefficient of determination (r^2) indicates that approximately 90 per cent of variations in labour productivity between regions are associated with regional variations in the wage rate. If the assumptions of the model are accepted, this result implies that approximately 90 per cent of the differences in labour productivity between regions may be accounted for by differences in the capital-labour ratio.[15]

Estimates of the elasticity of substitution for separate SIC Orders are presented in table A1.1. Rather surprisingly, ship-

[11] P. Dhrymes, 'Some Extensions and Tests for the CES Class of Production Functions', *Review of Economics and Statistics*, Nov 1965; P. Dhrymes and P. Zarembka, 'Elasticities of Substitution for Two-Digit Manufacturing Industries: A Correction', *Review of Economics and Statistics*, Feb 1970.

[12] M. S. Feldstein, op. cit., p. 388.

[13] J. M. Katz, *Production Functions, Foreign Investment and Growth* (North Holland, 1969).

[14] Data used are regional cross-section data from the Regional tables of the Census of Production. See Board of Trade, *Report on the Census of Production 1963* (London: HMSO, 1970), part 133.

[15] See also the discussion in chapter 9.

TABLE A1.1 Estimates of the elasticity of substitution (*b*) in United Kingdom manufacturing industries: 1958 and 1963 (SIC order level)

	1958			1963		
SIC no.	b_1	s.e.b_1	R^2	b_1	s.e.b_1	R^2
III	1.4252	0.4210	0.560	0.7244	0.4364	0.234
IV	0.5004	0.2599	0.292	1.7160	0.5822	0.491
V	0.9594	0.3728	0.495	0.6539	0.2227	0.489
VI	1.1972	0.3185	0.611	0.5867	0.4469	0.161
VII	2.7070	1.2626	0.396	1.1421	0.4748	0.452
VIII	2.1165	0.1583	0.962	1.2263	0.6762	0.320
IX	0.5926	0.2247	0.436	1.0285	0.3296	0.520
X	1.4376	0.2399	0.800	1.9164	0.3541	0.765
XI	0.8416	0.4194	0.309	1.2937	0.4063	0.530
XII	1.0000	0.1682	0.797	1.0157	0.1942	0.752
XIII	0.8150	0.2009	0.647	1.1944	0.6650	0.839
XIV	0.2952	0.2424	0.142	0.9894	0.1830	0.765
XV	0.7694	0.0817	0.908	1.0919	0.2034	0.762
XVI	1.0082	0.1732	0.790	1.2393	0.1940	0.819
Total man.	1.3172	0.1258	0.924	1.0886	0.1318	0.883

TABLE A1.2 Significance tests on the estimates of σ: 1958 and 1963*

	1958		1963		Total	
Value of	No.	%	No.	%	No.	%
$\sigma = 0$	1	7	0	0	1	4
$\sigma = 1$	9	65	10	71	19	69
$\sigma > 1$	2	14	1	7	3	10
$0 < \sigma < 1$	2	14	0	0	2	7
ambiguous	0	0	3	22	3	10
	14	100	14	100	28	100

* The 5 per cent significance level is used throughout.

building and marine engineering (VII) and vehicles (VIII) appear to have a very high elasticity of substitution.[16] Most of the other estimates are grouped around unity – the Cobb–Douglas case. Table A1.2 presents a breakdown of the estimates according to whether the elasticity of substitution is unambiguously significantly different from zero, or unity.[17] Out of twenty-eight cases (fourteen in each year) four are not significantly different from zero, and twenty-two are not significantly different from unity. Four industries show elasticities of substitution significantly different from zero and unity: paper, printing and publishing (XV in 1958); vehicles (VIII in 1958); textiles (X in 1958 and 1963); and chemicals and allied industries (IV in 1958).

An unfortunate feature of the results is the instability of the estimates. The rank correlation coefficient between the estimates for 1958 and those for 1963 is not statistically significant from zero. The diversity of results, however, is in accord with the findings of other workers in the field.[18]

It is also clear from table A1.2 that it cannot be assumed that the elasticity of substitution is identical in all activities. In the context of the Heckscher-Ohlin theorem, this means that factor reversals are likely to occur.[19]

NON-CONSTANT RETURNS TO SCALE

If returns to scale are not constant, output per unit of labour is not only dependent on the capital-labour ratio but also on the level of output. The side relation for estimating the elasticity of substitution then becomes:

$$\log q = \log a + b_2 \log w + b_3 \log Y \qquad \text{(A1.14)}$$

where Y is the level of output.

[16] This may be due to the aggregative nature of the data used.

[17] For an application to US data, see C. F. Ferguson, 'Cross Sectional Production Functions and the Elasticity of Substitution in American Manufacturing', *Review of Economics and Statistics*, Aug 1963.

[18] See M. Nerlove, 'Recent Empirical Studies of the CES and Related Production Functions', in M. Brown (ed.), *The Theory and Empirical Analysis of Production* (Columbia University Press, 1967).

[19] See discussion in chapter 2.

It has been demonstrated by Katz[20] that, given a production function of the form $Y = \gamma[K^{-\rho} + (1-\delta)L^{-\rho}]^{-v/\rho}$, the coefficient b_3 in equation (A1.14) may be written as:

$$b_3 = \frac{(1-\sigma)(v-1)}{v}$$

where $\sigma = b_2$ is the elasticity of substitution
v is the homogeneity parameter.

Given the assumptions of the model, and that prices are constant between regions, the degree of returns to scale (v) can be calculated as:

$$v = \frac{1-b_2}{1-b_2-b_3}$$

To make calculation of v slightly easier, it is possible to estimate a transformation of equation (A1.14) by subtracting $\log Y$ from both sides of the equation, giving:

$$\log L = -\log a - b_2 \log w + (1-b_3)\log Y \qquad \text{(A1.15)}$$

Denoting the estimate of $(1-b_3)$ as b_4, v can be calculated as:

$$v = \frac{1-\sigma}{b_4-\sigma}$$

Fitting equation (A1.15) to regional cross section data for total manufacturing industry in the United Kingdom for the years 1958 and 1963 gave the following results (standard errors in brackets):

$$1958{:}\quad \log L = -0.982 - \underset{(0.138)}{1.439}\log w + \underset{(0.015)}{1.025}\log Y : r^2 = 0.999$$

$$1963{:}\quad \log L = -0.888 - \underset{(0.148)}{1.221}\log w + \underset{(0.016)}{1.025}\log Y : r^2 = 0.999$$

The estimated values of v are: 1.060 in 1958 and 1.125 in 1963. There is thus some evidence of increasing returns to scale in the aggregate. The allowance for returns to scale increases slightly the estimates of the elasticity of substitution for both years.

[20] Op. cit.

Individual industry estimates of the elasticity of substitution and returns to scale are reported in table A1.3. The homogeneity parameter was calculated by two different methods. In cases where both coefficients of equation (A1.15) are significant, v was calculated as described earlier in the text. In cases where the elasticity of substitution was not statistically significant, v was calculated as the elasticity of output with respect to labour with log w removed from the estimating equation. Significant returns to scale appear to rule in most industries, although in one or two cases there seems to be considerable instability in the estimates from one year to the next. There are no industries showing decreasing returns in both years.

TABLE A1.3 Estimates of the elasticity of substitution and returns to scale in United Kingdom manufacturing industries 1958 and 1963

	1963		*1958*	
SIC order	*Elasticity of substitution* (σ)	*Returns to scale* (v)	*Elasticity of substitution* (σ)	*Returns to scale* (v)
III	0.545 (0.527)	1.039	1.036 (0.525)	1.097
IV	1.711 (0.619)	0.996	−0.215 (0.312)	1.075
V	0.626 (0.315)	1.019	0.045 (0.226)	1.138
VI	0.644 (0.813)	1.020	1.559 (0.597)	1.042
VII	1.378 (0.338)	1.219	2.959 (0.945)	1.027
VIII	0.689 (1.564)	1.074	2.128 (0.181)	0.995
IX	1.670 (0.324)	1.069	0.699 (0.225)	0.913
X	1.872 (0.343)	1.068	1.433 (0.253)	1.022
XI	1.088 (0.393)	0.570	0.889 (0.374)	2.473
XII	1.119 (0.249)	1.254	0.912 (0.182)	1.450
XIII	1.194 (0.187)	1.000	0.790 (0.216)	1.071
XIV	0.783 (0.281)	1.083	−0.405 (0.338)	1.064
XV	1.375 (0.337)	1.088	0.963 (0.160)	0.619
XVI	1.176 (0.366)	0.956	1.431 (0.396)	1.196
Total man.	1.221 (0.148)	1.125	1.439 (0.138)	1.060

Note: Bracketed terms are standard errors.

Table A1.4 presents the results of significance tests on the estimated values of the elasticity of substitution. As before, most industries appear to approximate to the Cobb–Douglas case.

TABLE A1.4 Significance tests on the estimates of σ in Table A1.3 1958 and 1963*

	1958		*1963*		*Total*	
Value of	*No.*	%	*No.*	%	*No.*	%
$\sigma = 0$	2	14	0	0	2	7
$\sigma = 1$	9	65	9	64	18	65
$\sigma > 1$	2	14	2	14	4	14
$0 < \sigma < 1$	0	0	0	0	0	0
ambiguous	1	7	3	22	4	14
	14	100	14	100	28	100

* The 5 per cent significance level is used throughout.

INTERPRETATION OF THE RESULTS: A CRITIQUE

While many economists have long held the view that the concept of an aggregate production function cannot be carried over to real world situations, its use has continued to be justified by the apparent ability of the aggregate Cobb–Douglas function to account for the 'constancy' of labour's share of national income. This success has often been cited as the only evidence in favour of the marginal productivity theory of wage determination. In a recent paper, however, Fisher[21] demonstrates some interesting propositions relating to the fitting of aggregate production functions to national (time series) data. In particular, he attempts to show using simulation experiments that an aggregate Cobb–Douglas function *only* works well as long as labour's share is roughly constant. According to Fisher: 'the suggestion [of the simulation experiments] is clear, however, that labour's share is not roughly constant because the diverse technical relationships of modern economies are truly representable by an aggregate Cobb–Douglas, but rather that such relationships appear to be representable by an aggregate Cobb–Douglas because labour's share happens to be roughly constant.'[22] Fisher indicates

[21] F. M. Fisher, 'Aggregate Production Functions and the Explanation of Wages: A Simulation Experiment', *Review of Economics and Statistics*, Nov 1971.

[22] Ibid., p. 325.

that these conclusions may be extended to apply to the CES production function.

There are two logically distinct, but related, issues here. One concerns the validity of interpreting reduced equations (side relations) as estimating, or as evidence for the existence of, a production function and its associated parameters. If we accept the side-relation coefficients as production function parameters, the second issue is concerned with explaining why, given that labour's share is roughly constant, such estimates appear to indicate that the production function is Cobb–Douglas in form.

Let us take the latter issue first, and illustrate using the CES side relation which we have already used to estimate the elasticity of substitution: $\log q = \log a + b \log(w)$, where q is output per man (Y/L), w is the wage rate (W/L) and b is the elasticity of substitution. We note first that for the wage share to be constant $\mathrm{d}W/W = \mathrm{d}Y/Y$ or, subtracting $\mathrm{d}L/L$ from both sides:

$$\frac{\mathrm{d}Y}{Y} - \frac{\mathrm{d}L}{L} = \frac{\mathrm{d}W}{W} - \frac{\mathrm{d}L}{L} \qquad \text{(A1.16)}$$

We also note that the elasticity of substitution can be written as:

$$b = \frac{(\mathrm{d}Y/Y) - (\mathrm{d}L/L)}{(\mathrm{d}W/W) - (\mathrm{d}L/L)} \qquad \text{(A1.17)}$$

It therefore follows that, if labour's share is constant, the numerator and denominator of equation (A1.17) will be the same and b will be unity. If shares are not constant, the numerator and denominator of (A1.17) are not equal and $b \neq 1$. In terms of this formulation of the problem, Fisher is correct that the value of the elasticity of substitution, and hence assumptions about the form of the production function, depend on the observed constancy, or otherwise, of labour's share of income. This conclusion can be generalised to the CES class of production functions.[23]

[23] Our discussion also means that tests of the CES estimates, based on a comparison between observed and predicted wage shares (e.g. Ferguson's 'largely independent' test), are hardly valid. See C. E. Ferguson, op. cit., p. 309.

The other issue raised by Fisher is whether the coefficients in equations such as (A1.12) and (A1.15) can be interpreted as production function parameters. There are a number of reasons for believing that they cannot, which relate to the assumptions of the model and the problem of identification. Firstly, even if all neoclassical behavioural assumptions were satisfied, it is unlikely that the observations used reflect a production surface; nor is it likely that the observations within each industry come from the same production surface. Thus the two basic assumptions on which the model is based may be questioned. It is also highly unlikely that the observations are generated by firms using optimal input combinations given the ruling factor prices. Secondly, the assumption that the wage rate is exogenous is also likely to be violated. Given the widespread use of payments by results, in addition to more general productivity agreements, the CES side relation is incapable of separating out the effects of changes in the wage rate (and thus technique) on average product from the effects of changes in average product on the wage rate. Thirdly, there is the question of identification in the sense that the equations used, containing wage and productivity variables, are consistent with alternative behavioural relations. For example, the CES side relation, assuming the elasticity of substitution is unity, is consistent with a productivity based theory of wage determination or a full-cost theory of pricing behaviour.

To show the side relation as a wage equation, we can write the untransformed version of equation (A1.12) as:

$$Y/L = a(W/L)^b \tag{A1.18}$$

If $b = 1$, the Cobb–Douglas case, and Y/L is assumed exogenous, equation (A1.18) may be written as:

$$W/L = \frac{1}{a}(Y/L) \tag{A1.19}$$

which is an expression for wage determination based on productivity. Kuh found some evidence for the existence of such a relationship in the United States.[24] The finding from the side relation (equation (A1.12)) that the b coefficient approximates to unity may indicate that the observations are being generated, not by production function relations, but by a linear wage determination model based on productivity.

Alternativelv we can derive the relation from a pricing theory based on prime costs plus margins.[25] Price per unit of output (p) is made up of the unit wage costs plus unit materials costs plus unit profits, i.e.

$$p = w\frac{L}{O} + m\frac{M}{O} + \pi \qquad \text{(A1.20)}$$

where w is the wage rate
O is output
m is price per unit of raw materials
and M is quantity of raw materials.

Let profit per unit (π) equal wage cost per unit times some mark-up (τ) for overheads and earnings,

$$\pi = w\frac{L}{O}(\tau) \qquad \text{(A1.21)}$$

From equations (A1.20) and (A1.21) the value of gross output (pO) is equal to:

$$pO = wL(1+\tau)+mM$$

Value added is $pO-mM = Y = wL(1+\tau)$. Dividing both sides by L gives:

$$Y/L = (1+\tau)\frac{W}{L} \qquad \text{(A1.22)}$$

This pricing, or distribution, equation is also consistent with the form of the CES estimating equation.

[24] E. Kuh, 'A Productivity Theory of Wage Levels – an Alternative to the Phillips Curve', *Review of Economic Studies*, Oct 1967.

[25] The margins are assumed to be calculated on a 'wage-cost plus' basis rather than on a 'full prime-cost' basis.

While we have used the estimates of equation (A1.12) as measures of the elasticity of substitution, it must be remembered that the results of estimating the CES side relation cannot by themselves be automatically interpreted as production function parameters. Interpreted as production function parameters, however, the estimates may form a basis for further research into productivity differences between regions.

Index of Names

Index of Subjects